FrontPage® 2002:
A Beginner's Guide

FrontPage® 2002:
A Beginner's Guide

Kirupa Chinnathambi

Osborne/**McGraw-Hill**

New York Chicago San Francisco
Lisbon London Madrid Mexico City
Milan New Delhi San Juan
Seoul Singapore Sydney Toronto

Osborne/**McGraw-Hill**
2600 Tenth Street
Berkeley, California 94710
U.S.A.

To arrange bulk purchase discounts for sales promotions, premiums, or fund-raisers, please contact Osborne/**McGraw-Hill** at the above address. For information on translations or book distributors outside the U.S.A., please see the International Contact Information page immediately following the index of this book.

FrontPage® 2002: A Beginner's Guide

1234567890 FGR FGR 01987654321

ISBN 0-07-213491-7

Publisher   Brandon A. Nordin
Vice President and Associate Publisher   Scott Rogers
Acqusitions Editor   Jim Schachterle
Project Editor   Jenn Tust
Acquisitions Coordinator   Tim Madrid
Tech Editor   Chris Dimaano
Copy Editor   Karyn DiCastri
Proofreader   Paul Medoff
Indexer   Valerie Robbins
Computer Designers   Tara A. Davis, John Patrus, Kelly Stanton-Scott
Illustrators   Alex Putney, Beth E. Young
Series Design   Gary Corrigan
Cover Design   Greg Scott
Cover Illustration   Kevin Curry

This book was composed with Corel VENTURA™ Publisher.

To my parents,
Guna and Karuppa Chinnathambi

About the Author

Kirupa Chinnathambi is the founder and sole employee of kirupa.com, a company that specializes in Web design and education about Web technologies. He is currently a junior at Hoover High School in Hoover, Alabama.

Kirupa's interests vary from computer programming to listening to the Bee Gees. He spends most of his time doing homework, experimenting with computer animation by using Macromedia Flash, and helping other people with their computer problems. When Kirupa is not working in front of the computer, he is rumored to be seen socializing with other people without relying on instant messaging software and e-mail.

Contents

PART III
Making Your Site Interactive

PART V
Appendixes

Acknowledgments

My parents, family, friends, and all the people at Osborne/McGraw-Hill who made this book you are holding a reality: Jim Schachterle, Tim Madrid, Christopher Dimaano (**frontpageguru.com**), Jenn Tust, Karyn DiCastri, Paul Medoff, Valerie Robbins, the Osborne production and illustration departments, and others who worked behind the scenes. Thank You!

Introduction

With each release of Microsoft FrontPage and its new features, people often become overwhelmed and don't use the new features to their maximum potential. In writing this book, my goal was to not only explain the majority of FrontPage 2002's features, but to explain them in such a way that you would be comfortable using the features in your Web sites.

FrontPage 2002: A Beginner's Guide helps you learn FrontPage by teaching you basic skills, such as learning the interface, to complex skills, such as saving form data to a database. All of the major features of FrontPage are covered in detail, and best of all, this book gives you the opportunity to apply your knowledge to Web pages by following easy to understand, step-by-step instructions.

Who Should Read This Book

Even though this book covers FrontPage's features at a fast pace, as long as you can answer "Yes" to the prerequisites below, you can read this book in its entirety:

- **Windows** Do you know how to copy and paste? Are you familiar with the Windows interface and how to minimize/maximize and switch between applications?

- **The Internet** Are you familiar with the Internet? Can you use a Web browser to navigate through Web sites?

What This Book Covers

To help you use FrontPage without overwhelming you with all of the program's features at once, the book is separated into five parts: "Planning and Creating a Site," "Designing and Publishing Web Pages," "Making Your Site Interactive," "Doing More with FrontPage," and "Appendixes."

Part I: Planning and Creating a Site

Part I introduces FrontPage and helps you to understand how FrontPage will help you in creating and maintaining Web pages. You will learn about Web design and how to use FrontPage to plan and create a site.

Module 1, "The FrontPage Interface," introduces the various menus, toolbars, and icons that you will use. In addition, you will also learn how to customize FrontPage's interface and how to use FrontPage's help feature.

Module 2, "Planning and Organizing Your Web Site," discusses how you should plan a Web site and use design in your pages. You will find tips ranging from targeting visitors to using color. Additionally, you will be introduced to an important facet of Web site development using FrontPage: the FrontPage Web.

Module 3, "Creating a Web Site," teaches you how to create a basic Web site using text and hyperlinks. You will learn how to incorporate and format text into your documents, and you will also learn to navigate by adding hyperlinks. Hyperlinks are an integral part of navigation, and various methods of hyperlinking are discussed.

Part II: Designing and Publishing Web Pages

Part II moves into the core of Web development: designing and publishing pages. After you learn how to design a page using various elements such as tables, images, and frames, you will learn to publish your Web site to a Web server.

Module 4, "Using Images in Your Web Pages," discusses how to insert and format images in FrontPage. This module also explains how to use FrontPage's built-in tools for inserting and searching for clip-art images.

Module 5, "Drawing and Using Multimedia," discusses the multimedia features of FrontPage. You will learn how to draw lines, shapes, 3-D objects, and more using FrontPage's intuitive drawing tools. This module also explains how to incorporate and modify video and sound.

Module 6, "Using Tables," details an important Web design element: tables. This module discusses everything from formatting tables to nesting tables to adjusting cells.

Module 7, "Using Frames," teaches you how to use frames. Besides explaining how to create and format frames, this module discusses the nuts and bolts of using FrontPage to create and format inline frames.

Module 8, "Creating Lists," teaches you how to organize information on a Web page using lists. This module discusses all aspects of lists from changing list styles to making lists interactive using animation.

Module 9, "Modifying and Publishing Your Site Online," concludes Part II by teaching you the various methods of publishing your Web site to the Internet. You will also learn how to modify page properties, analyze Web site reports, and more.

Part III: Making Your Site Interactive

Part III helps you make the most out of FrontPage by teaching you how to use the numerous tools to help enhance your Web site and make it interactive. You will learn how to create forms that receive data from visitors, how to animate objects such as text and images, how to create a navigation structure for your visitors, and more.

Module 10, "Using Forms," teaches you how to use FrontPage to enable your Web site's visitors to transmit information via a Web page. This module also teaches you how to save your visitor's input to a database and how to display the results from the database in your Web browser.

Module 11, "Animating Your Site," teaches you how to animate objects such as text and images. You will also learn how to create image rollovers, page transitions, and more.

Module 12, "Using FrontPage Web Components," explains how to use the FrontPage components, such as a search box, the banner ad manager, automatic Web content, and link bars, that you can use to save time in FrontPage.

Module 13, "Using Themes and Templates," teaches you about themes and how you can use them to enhance color, text style, and more in your Web pages. This module also tells you how you can use templates to create complicated pages easily.

Module 14, "Plug-Ins, ActiveX Controls, and Java Applets," covers how you can use FrontPage to insert and customize plug-ins, ActiveX controls, and Java applets.

Part IV: Doing More with FrontPage

Part IV extends what you have already learned about FrontPage to include programming and Microsoft Office XP. You will learn how to view and insert code, such as Hypertext Markup Language (HTML), and Cascading Style Sheets

(CSS). Because FrontPage is part of the Microsoft Office suite of applications, you will learn how to shuffle information among FrontPage and other applications, such as Word and Excel.

Module 15, "Web Programming Languages," helps you to understand how FrontPage handles various Web programming languages. You will learn how to view and incorporate HTML code, and how to create and modify your own CSS styles.

Module 16, "Integrating Microsoft Office into Your Site," discusses how you can use FrontPage to incorporate content from various applications into your Web sites.

Part V: Appendixes

The appendixes provide information that can be referenced quickly to help you better use FrontPage:

Appendix A, "Answers to Mastery Checks," provides answers to the questions at the end of each module.

Appendix B, "Resources," lists a few Web sites that you can visit to learn new tips and techniques about FrontPage and Web development in general.

How This Book Should Be Read

The content in the book is organized so that you can read any module and understand the topics covered in that module. Because the modules often build upon each other, I recommend that you read the entire book from beginning to end to have a complete understanding of FrontPage.

In most modules, you will follow step-by-step instructions and use your knowledge of the topics covered to work on a Web site. All of the files needed for your projects and examples are provided for you to download from **http://www.kirupa.com/frontpage** or **http://www.Osborne.com**.

Special Features

All the concepts and major features of FrontPage are divided into modules to make it easier for you to read the book. In each module, Tips and Notes are interspersed to provide more detail or information whenever needed. Each module begins with several goals that outline what you will acquire from reading that module. To help answer common questions that you may have during certain procedures, you will find question/answer sections called "Ask the Expert" in each module. To apply what you learn after reading each module to Web development, you will follow a project with step-by-step instructions.

FrontPage 2002: A Beginner's Guide goes beyond simply explaining how to use the various features of FrontPage. Instead, it provides easy-to-understand, step-by-step instructions to learn and apply the features of FrontPage into your Web sites. It also offers code that describes particular functions.

There are various checkpoints, called "1-Minute Drills," in each module that provide questions for you to answer to check your understanding of the topics covered. After completing a module, you will be further tested on your knowledge with questions in the "Mastery Check." The questions in the "Mastery Check" require a more complete understanding of the topics covered in the module, and the answers are in various formats such as multiple choice.

Getting Help

While I made sure that you were adequately prepared to complete the projects at the end of each module, mistakes and confusion may happen. If you have any questions or comments, please post on the book's message board. To access the *FrontPage 2002: A Beginner's Guide* message board, visit **http://www.kirupa.com/ frontpage/help.asp**. I, or other knowledgeable users, will answer any questions you have.

Part I

Planning and Creating a Site

Module 1

The FrontPage Interface

The Goals of This Module

- Discover the intricacies of the FrontPage interface
- Explore FrontPage's menus and toolbars
- Customize existing toolbars and create custom toolbars
- Learn to customize on-screen elements
- Utilize FrontPage Quick Help and FrontPage Help

As the number of people using the Internet grew dramatically worldwide, many people and organizations wanted to create Web sites to reach global audiences. Organizations and individuals that did not know how to create a Web site often hired expensive outside developers to create Web sites for them. Hypertext Markup Language (HTML) was created in 1989. The HTML language is popular because anyone with knowledge of the HTML programming language could create HTML-based Web pages using tools such as text editors that were already available for the computer, but the task of creating a Web page using HTML took a lot of time to complete.

As more Web sites were created, people wanted features that the traditional HTML could not support. While HTML has not changed much, new technologies such as Dynamic HTML (DHTML), Cascading Style Sheets (CSS), Extensible Markup Language (XML), JavaScript, and other programming languages have been introduced to offset the limitations posed by the HTML language. As more and more people want to create Web sites easily, tools such as Microsoft FrontPage prove to be invaluable. FrontPage enables you create, edit, and publish files without having to learn HTML or other programming languages. FrontPage enables you to concentrate on the creation of the site while it does the HTML programming for you.

As FrontPage has evolved to support more Web technologies, the program has also become much easier to use. FrontPage 2002 is no exception, and the following is a list of some of the features that FrontPage provides.

- **Ease of Use** An improved interface combined with the ability to enter help questions directly from the main program window makes using FrontPage easier than ever. Wizards also help you to get your work done quickly and easily.

- **Improved Tools** Features such as the Top 10 List help you to make important decisions regarding the organization of your site. Using the FrontPage components, you can easily add a search box, message board, photo gallery, or other feature. FrontPage now includes new components that automatically update information from the sites of MSN, MSNBC, bCentral, and others.

- **Site Management**   FrontPage has a very easy method in which you can configure and modify all your files in little time. Using the FrontPage Web, all of your site's management tools, files, settings, and more are placed in one easy-to-use location.

- **Database Integration**   FrontPage makes it easy for you to view and send information to a database. If you do not have a database, FrontPage automatically creates a database for you.

- **Themes**   The themes feature provides an easy way for you to customize the style of your site, and it enables you to have command over your site's page properties such as colors, fonts, graphics, bullets, and more.

- **Interactive Content**   In a matter of a few mouse clicks, you can insert images, sounds, and videos into your site. FrontPage includes built-in support for animation technologies such as DHTML to enable you to easily create simple animations for your pages.

- **Source HTML Editing**   FrontPage is enabled for direct HTML code editing. You can edit existing HTML scripts and paste code from various locations. FrontPage's HTML editing features enable the editing of other Web technologies, such as Active Server Pages (ASP) files, CSS files, and more, from one central location.

Program Interface

When you look at FrontPage 2002, one of the most striking features is that it has a more refined interface than the previous versions. The new look of FrontPage makes it easier for beginners to get a feel for the program, while simply making the program more aesthetically pleasing. Figure 1-1 shows the various interface elements that you will use in your journey through FrontPage.

Menu bar   Toolbar

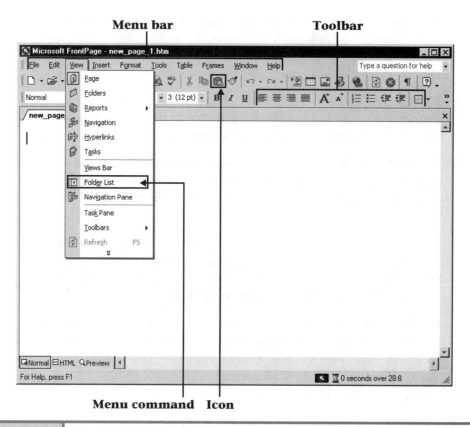

Menu command   Icon

Figure 1-1   The FrontPage interface

FrontPage Menus

Menus are lists that contain a group of options. Menus are located within a menu bar, and, usually, the menu bar is located at the top of the window. To start off in FrontPage, click View on the menu bar. When you click View, a pull-down menu will appear, giving you a set of options. There are more options

1

available besides the ones that are immediately displayed: scroll to the two small down arrows at the bottom of the View pull-down menu, and you will see an expanded list. These extra options will become part of the default view once they are used at least once.

Another feature of menus is that they contain submenus. Click the View menu again and place the mouse pointer over the Reports option. Because the Reports option has a submenu (indicated by the right-pointing arrow to the right of the word), placing the mouse pointer over the Reports option will expand a submenu that shows even more options. Since some submenus have more submenus, you can expand a menu until there are no more submenus left. See Figure 1-2 for an example of a menu with submenus.

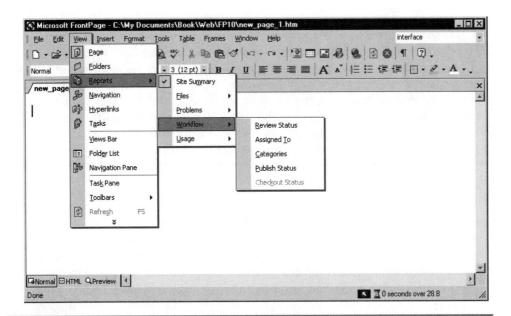

Figure 1-2   A menu with submenus

FrontPage Toolbars

When creating files in FrontPage, toolbars are used extensively. Toolbars contain icons and menus, while menu bars contain only the names of the menus. The default Standard and Formatting toolbars found at the top of the FrontPage window are shown here:

Standard toolbar

Formatting toolbar

Hint

Whenever you see a single small arrow to the right of a menu or toolbar, it means that the toolbar or menu can be expanded to show more commands. Hovering the mouse pointer over the single small arrow in a menu will expand the menu to show more commands. You will need to click the single small arrow in toolbars to expand the toolbar to display more commands. The single small arrow on a floating toolbar is located in the upper-right corner. Floating toolbars will be discussed in the "Viewing Toolbars" section.

Viewing Toolbars

You can add or remove the existing toolbars easily. To add a toolbar, click View from the menu bar and select the Toolbars command. From the submenu that pops up, you can select or deselect any toolbar. For example, when you select the option for Pictures, the Pictures toolbar will appear in the main window. To remove the Pictures toolbar, you can either go back to View | Toolbars and deselect the Pictures toolbar or you can simply click the small *x* in the upper-right corner of the Pictures toolbar.

One of the great things about toolbars is that they can be moved from their default locations and floated anywhere on the screen. To float a toolbar, simply click one of the toolbar's darkened left edges and drag it anywhere on the screen. To move the toolbar back to its usual location above the work area, simply drag the toolbar toward its original location in the FrontPage interface. As you drag the toolbar toward its original location, the toolbar will automatically snap to that location.

Hint
When you drag a toolbar toward the left, right, top, or bottom in the FrontPage window, the toolbar will snap to that place.

You can resize a toolbar by dragging one of the edges after the toolbar has been docked, and you can have multiple toolbars in the work area at the same time. A docked toolbar is a toolbar that is floating. See Figure 1-3 for an example of the Formatting toolbar that has been docked out of its usual position above the work area and resized.

Adding More Toolbars

The simplest method of adding toolbars is to right click any existing toolbar on the screen. When you right click an existing toolbar, a menu with all the toolbars will appear. Select a toolbar from the menu, and it will instantly appear on the program window. To remove a toolbar, simply right click any toolbar again and uncheck the toolbar that you want removed.

To have more control over adding and removing toolbars, you can go to the Customize window by navigating to View | Toolbars | Customize from the

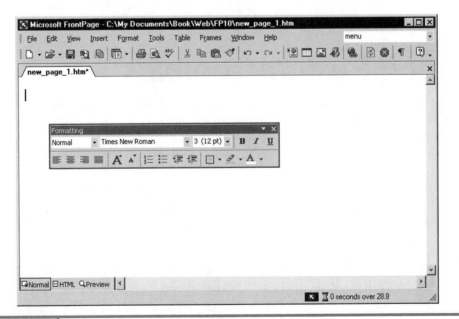

Figure 1-3   A floating Formatting toolbar

menu bar. The Customize window has three tabs: the Toolbars, Commands, and Options tabs. As you can see in the next illustration, the Toolbars tab enables you to add or remove toolbars from a single location: by simply checking a box, the corresponding toolbar appears on the screen; by unchecking a box, the corresponding toolbar disappears from the screen.

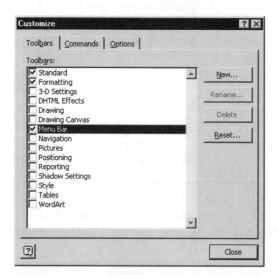

Creating Custom Toolbars

In the Customize window, shown in the previous illustration, there is a New button. Clicking the New button will enable you to create a custom toolbar with the icons you select.

The following are the instructions for creating a custom toolbar:

1. If it is not already open, go to the Customize window by navigating to View | Toolbars | Customize from the menu bar. Click the New button in the Customize window, and the New Toolbar window will appear. Name your toolbar.

2. After you have named your toolbar, click OK. You will now see the gray border of the toolbar in your work area. If you do not see an empty toolbar in your work area, move the Customize window until you do see it.

1

3. Going back to the Customize window, click the Commands tab. You will see various icons and commands in the Customize window. The Customize window will display the Categories column and the Commands column. The Categories column on the left displays commands you will use, and the column on the right displays the icons for the command selected on the left.

4. Drag the icons that you would like to use onto your new toolbar. As you drag an icon onto the new toolbar, a bracket will be appear on the toolbar to help you place the icon. An example of a custom toolbar is shown here:

A custom toolbar can contain any kind of interface element such as an icon or menu supported by FrontPage. You can combine icons, menus, and commands easily with the drag-and-drop technique. The new custom toolbar can be treated just like a regular toolbar: it can be docked, floated, resized, customized, and so on.

Description of Toolbars

In this section, you will find descriptions of the major toolbars in FrontPage. All of the major toolbars can be accessed by selecting the View menu and choosing the toolbar from the Toolbars command.

Note

It is not expected that you know how to use the toolbars listed next. This is just an introduction to the commonly used toolbars. Toolbars not listed will be covered in more detail in subsequent chapters.

Standard Toolbar

The Standard toolbar contains some of the most-used functions of FrontPage. Table 1-1 shows each icon found in the Standard toolbar and gives its name and function.

Icon	Name	Function
	New	Creates a new file
	Open	Opens a file
	Save	Saves current document
	Search	Searches your computer for files
	Publish	Publishes your FrontPage Web to a server or hard drive
	Toggle Pane	Toggles between several views
	Print	Prints existing page
	Preview	Previews current document in your browser
	Spelling	Checks the current document for spelling mistakes
	Cut	Cuts a document element (for example, text or image) to be moved elsewhere
	Copy	Copies a document element so that it can be pasted elsewhere

Table 1-1   The Standard Toolbar Icons and Menus

Icon	Name	Function
	Paste	Pastes a document element (that has previously been copied) to a location you specify
	Format Painter	Copies a style and applies it to another object
	Web Component	Inserts elements that enhance and speed up common Web-page tasks
	Table	Inserts a table in your document
	Picture	Inserts a picture from the Web or your hard drive
	Word Art	Formats your text with special 3-D effects that you can customize
	Hyperlink	Add links that connect to other pages
	Refresh	Reloads the current document to a previous state
	Show	Toggles to show or hide document-formatting marks
	Help	Launches Help

Table 1-1   The Standard Toolbar Icons and Menus (*continued*)

Formatting Toolbar

The Formatting toolbar is toolbar that is used to modify text and other elements. Table 1-2 shows each icon found in the Formatting toolbar and gives its name and function.

Note

You can format your styles either before you type or after you have typed.

Icon	Name	Function
Normal	Style	Changes the style of text, tables, or anything else that you select
Times New Roman	Font	Changes the font
3 (12 pt)	Font Size	Changes the size of the text
B	Bold	Adds emphasis to text
I	Italic	Slants the text slightly to the right
U	Underline	Draws a line under the text
≡	Text Alignment	Customizes how text is aligned in your document
A A	Change Font Size	Increases or decreases font size
≣	Numbered List	Adds a list that numbers sequentially
≣	Bulleted List	Adds a bulleted list
⇥ ⇤	Indent	Moves text or other elements left or right by a set amount
⊞	Table	Adds a table
✎	Highlight	Chooses a custom highlight or background color for text, tables, and more
A	Font Color	Changes the font color

Table 1-2   The Formatting Toolbar Icons and Menus

DHTML Effects Toolbar

The DHTML Effects toolbar covers the animation available in FrontPage. You can animate text, graphics, or table elements to respond to various user commands:

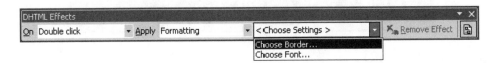

Drawing Toolbar

The Drawing toolbar docks itself to the bottom of the screen when selected. This toolbar is useful for drawing simple shapes such as circles and polygons, for inserting pictures and clip art, for inserting 3-D text, for using custom formatted shapes such as arrows, for adding 3-D to objects, for changing a polygon's fill color, and for adding line color and more:

Navigation Toolbar

The Navigation toolbar aids in the navigation of the site. You can easily zoom in on your navigation structure (how your pages are organized from the main page), modify page properties, add extra pages, and customize the viewing options. This toolbar is used primarily in circumstances that require a layout of the entire site:

Pictures Toolbar

The Pictures toolbar enables you to modify images. From this toolbar, you can modify many attributes of images including the contrast, the brightness, the rotation, and more:

Positioning Toolbar

The Positioning toolbar enables you to customize, with pixel precise placement, where your text, images, and other objects will be placed:

Reporting Toolbar

The Reporting toolbar is used to generate a snapshot of your entire site. From this snapshot, you can find information ranging from how much space your site takes to how many broken links are in your site:

Style Toolbar

 The Style toolbar is used to customize the document styles. Document styles can vary from the color of text to the width of a table.

Tables Toolbar

The Tables toolbar enables you to add or modify tables. From this toolbar, you can merge cells, add and change table background colors, and more:

Task Pane Toolbar

The Task pane toolbar provides a single location from which common tasks can easily be accomplished. The Task pane toolbar appears on the right side of the FrontPage window:

WordArt Toolbar

The WordArt toolbar enables you to add and modify WordArt. WordArt is a feature that allows you to add custom effects to text:

1-Minute Drill

● Can toolbars float?

● How do you access the Toolbars menu?

Adding and Removing Icons

The following are the instructions to add or remove icons:

1. Click the down arrow to the right of the toolbar.

2. From the drop-down menu, select the Add or Remove Buttons command. A submenu will appear with the name of the toolbar you are modifying. Place your mouse pointer over the submenu with the toolbar name. Another submenu will appear containing all the icons that are in the toolbar.

3. From the submenu containing the icons, you can check or uncheck the icons that you wish to appear or not appear on the toolbar. See Figure 1-4 for an example of how the icon submenu for the Drawing Canvas toolbar after the Scale Drawing icon has been unchecked:

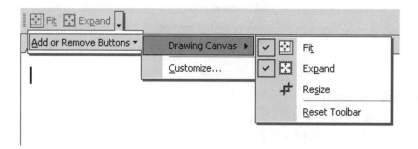

Figure 1-4   The icon submenu for the Drawing Canvas toolbar

● Yes. To float a toolbar, simply drag the darkened left edge of the toolbar to any location on screen.

● Go to View | Toolbars.

When toolbars are docked against each other, you can show all the icons in one single line. You will notice that the Formatting toolbar is docked to the Standard toolbar. To show the icons of both the toolbars docked to each other in one line, click the down arrow to the right of the Standard toolbar or the arrow to the right of the Formatting toolbar, and you will see a submenu. From that submenu select the Show Buttons on One Row command. Selecting that command will move all the icons to one row.

To show the icons in the Standard and Formatting toolbars on two rows again, just click the arrow to the right of the toolbar and select the Show Buttons on Two Rows option:

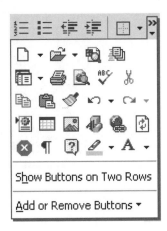

Using Panes

A new feature of FrontPage is panes. Panes in FrontPage simplify common tasks to a few clicks. The two panes available are the Navigation pane and Task pane. You can see these panes by selecting View | Task Pane or View | Navigation Pane. You can easily float a pane by dragging the top border onto the screen. Figure 1-5 shows an example of the Task pane.

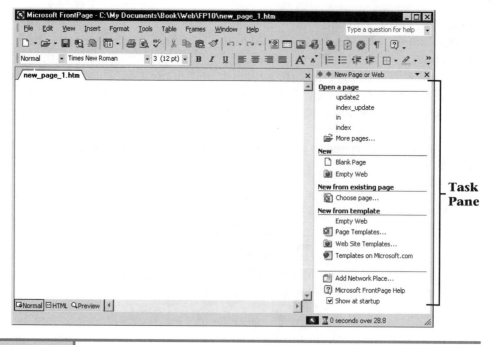

Customizing On-Screen Elements

FrontPage includes a lot of bells and whistles to enhance the look of your Web page. To customize the elements you wish to use or not use, go to the Customize window by navigating to View | Toolbars | Customize from the menu bar. From the Customize window, click the Options tab:

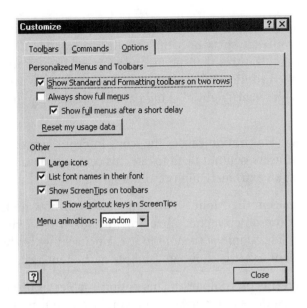

In the Customize window's Options tab, you can see that there are a lot of options that can be tweaked to your choosing. The following is a list and brief explanation of each of these options:

- **Show Standard and Formatting toolbars on two rows**   This check box places the Standard and Formatting toolbars on two rows.

- **Always show full menus**   Since FrontPage personalizes the menus according to how many times you use each command, you will not be able to see all the commands unless you click the expand arrow at the base of each menu. Checking this box will display all the commands at the same time.

- **Show full menus after a short delay**   This option can only be used if the menus are not set to show all of the commands at the same time. If that is so, checking this box will display the full menu when the mouse stays over the partial menu for a few seconds.

● **Reset my usage data** When you click the Reset my usage option, the menus in FrontPage show only the default commands. All of the various personalization features that the menus acquired from your daily use will be reset to the FrontPage default menus. As you use the menus again, FrontPage will relearn your clicking pattern and display the menus accordingly.

● **Large icons** This option causes the icons in FrontPage to be increased in size. Most users will not need to use this option unless they have their display set at an extremely high resolution.

● **List font names in their font** This option controls how fonts are displayed in the Font drop-down menu. Checking this box will provide the name of the font and an example of the font in use. Unchecking this box will simply display the font name without an example of the font's characteristics.

● **Show ScreenTips on toolbars** This option enables or disables the helpful text captions that appear when you hover your mouse pointer over a FrontPage element (for example, a button or a menu).

● **Show shortcut keys in ScreenTips** This option enables the ScreenTips to include the keyboard shortcut for an option or feature that you hover your mouse pointer over.

● **Menu animations** This option enables you to choose how the menus appear when you click them. Choosing None will simply display the menus with no small animation.

Ask the Expert

Question: Why do many people turn off the menu animations and the option for showing a preview of the font?

Answer: The FrontPage interface animations and extra features can be quite taxing on a computer's resources. For older computers, it is best to disable some of the processor and graphic intensive tasks such as menu animations and displaying font styles in the font selection menu. Menu animations and drawing and displaying an example of each font under the Font menu reduce the available system memory.

FrontPage Quick Help

FrontPage comes with a great time-saving feature to help answer your questions: FrontPage Quick Help. FrontPage Quick Help allows you to find the answer to your question without having to use the more advanced interface of FrontPage Help. In the upper-right corner of the FrontPage window, you will see a search box. When you type a question in the box, FrontPage Quick Help provides you with a list of possible solutions to your problem. See Figure 1-6 for an example of the search box with results displayed.

Clicking a search result will launch the FrontPage Help interface with a more detailed explanation of how to go about solving your problem. If you cannot find the solution from one of the choices listed, you also have the option of clicking the appropriate link and going to the Internet to search for the answer.

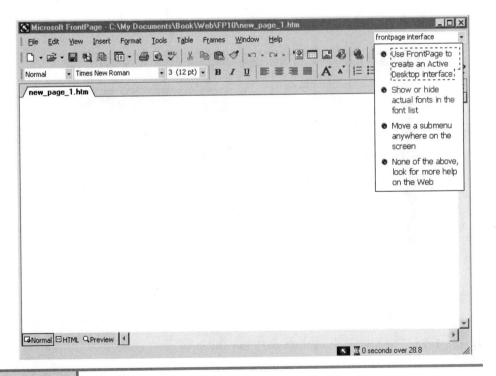

Figure 1-6 An example of the FrontPage search box

If you have multiple questions or would like to browse through the FrontPage Help categories, you can access the FrontPage Help by pressing F1 or by selecting the Microsoft FrontPage Help command from the Help menu. Figure 1-7 shows the Microsoft FrontPage Help window.

The following is a description of each of the tabs available in FrontPage Help:

- **Contents**   You can browse through the Help pages by simply double-clicking a topic in the Contents tab.

- **Answer Wizard**   You can type your problem in question format, and the Answer Wizard will try to find the best solution for your problem.

- **Index**   You can enter a word, and the Index will show information regarding that topic; sometimes, in the right-hand pane, it even displays the most common questions regarding your topic.

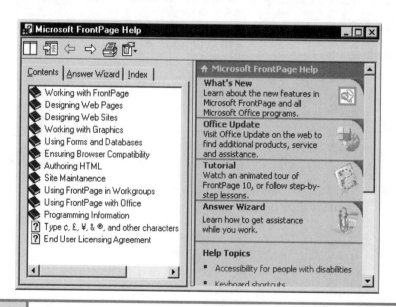

Figure 1-7   The Microsoft FrontPage Help window

Summary

The FrontPage interface makes it easier for you to use the application and find help. Toolbars, menus, buttons, icons, and other tools help you find your way around the application. As you become more experienced with FrontPage, you can customize the various menus and toolbars to your liking. If you have ever used Office applications, such as Word or Excel, you will already be familiar with the interface because FrontPage's interface resembles that of other Microsoft Office applications.

☑ *Mastery Check*

1. How can you tell if a menu has submenus?

_____

_____

2. What would be the easiest way to get help on a given topic?

_____

_____

3. What steps are necessary to create a custom toolbar?

_____

_____

4. Why is the Task pane useful?

_____

_____

5. How do you place the Standard and Formatting toolbars on one row?

_____

_____

Module 2

Planning and Organizing Your Web Site

The Goals of This Module

- Plan your FrontPage Web site
- Explore the design issues associated with your site
- Create a FrontPage Web
- Learn to employ and customize the FrontPage Web
- Practice using predefined templates in FrontPage

It used to take hours to create a Web page, and the developer had to have a broad knowledge of various Web languages beyond Hypertext Markup Language (HTML) in order to create a successful site. Using FrontPage, you can create a simple site or a complex site with very little effort, and you don't need to have any prior knowledge of HTML or any other Web language to use FrontPage; while you create the site and maintain it, FrontPage does all the tedious HTML coding for you.

Proper planning and organization are critical when you create a Web site. While FrontPage makes it easy to organize a site, there is still a great deal of preparation that goes into making a Web site successful. This module will help you create a well-planned Web site using FrontPage's management tools.

Planning a Web Site

When you create a Web site, you are creating it for a purpose. The purposes of Web sites vary greatly: to inform, entertain, sell products, promote brands, and more. Often times, the purpose of a site is expressed through its design and content.

For you to understand better how a site's purpose affects the layout and content, we will compare the differences between two Web sites. Notice the differences between their design and content. Figure 2-1 shows the home page of Jakob Nielsen's useit.com Web site. Jakob Nielsen has long been one of the leaders in promoting usability on the World Wide Web. The purpose of his site is to share information about himself, his work, and World Wide Web usability.

Figure 2-2 reveals the home page of shockwave.com. Notice the stark contrast between the home pages in Figures 2-1 and 2-2. You can see that the shockwave.com site is mainly for interactive entertainment. This site features cartoons, shows, games, music, and more. In contrast to useit.com's simple colors and layout, shockwave.com uses more colors and images to promote their shows, games, and more. The navigation of the two sites varies also. useit.com has a simple navigation system that comprises of text links, while shockwave.com's navigation uses images and text to aid in navigation. Notice that the links for the main portions of the shockwave.com site are placed on the top of the page.

Before creating your site, it is important to know who your target audience is. You should know who it is that will be inclined to visit your site, and you should always keep them in mind while developing your site. The following are examples of potential audiences:

2

- People who might be interested in a product you sell

- People who want to know more about a particular topic

- Users of a specific product

The mission of your site and the audience your site will target plays a key role in the developmental stages of a Web site. Once you understand your audience, you need to create a design that will keep them interested in your site.

Though FrontPage makes it easy to create a site, you need to do some planning before you start, or you may waste a lot of time. Consider issues such as the number of pages, the basic site structure, and the page content. A lot of people plan a Web site exactly right, but continue to add things after the initial design is set.

Figure 2-1 The purpose of Jakob Nielsen's Useit.com is to share information.

shockwave.com's interactive entertainment home page

This results in *scope creep:* creating and re-creating a site before it's finished because of a new idea or design. Because the Internet gives you the ability to update regularly, it is best to complete your Web site and update it gradually as feedback and opinions from people pour in. Most sites are updated frequently to keep the content fresh and engaging to visitors, and any minor design modifications can be made then. Sites that get updated often attract not only new visitors, but also existing visitors who will visit the site often to see what is new.

A great way to find out about the appeal and functionality of your site is to ask people you know to take a look at it and give you their feedback. Often, the comments provided by them will give you valuable insight into what you are doing correctly and incorrectly. While it may take some time to gather the opinions and incorporate the modifications, it is well worth the time and effort.

Understanding Design

One of the most difficult skills to acquire is design. While it is not imperative that you have extensive knowledge in design, a bit of knowledge can help you in creating your site and attracting visitors. There is always a balance between information on the site and the site's overall design. A good site should feature a complimentary combination of design and information. With experience, it is possible to create a site that combines great design with great information. This section will briefly introduce you to some key design elements and give you tips on using good design techniques in your site.

Typography

Typography is the text and style of text that you present to your visitors. The style of text you use throughout your site sets the atmosphere of what your site is about. Make sure that the type of font, font colors, and font size suit your site's purpose. Many users do not read a lot of text while visiting a Web site, but they do scan for things they might find useful, so make key phrases or words stand out.

The following tips will help you to use typography to your benefit in your Web site:

- Do not overwhelm your visitors with large chunks of text. Instead, break large pieces of text into smaller paragraphs.

- Do not use extremely large fonts in your site's body text; likewise, do not use fonts that are too small. Fonts that are too large or too small make it hard for the reader to follow the text on the page.

- Try to use fonts that are suited for reading. Some of the more artistic fonts are distracting and make reading very difficult. While there are thousands of fonts available, most of them fall into a few categories. The two more common categories are serif and sans serif. Times New Roman and Garamond are examples of serif fonts, and Helvetica and Avant Garde are examples of a sans serif fonts. Note the extra design elements on the ends of the letters in the Times New Roman and Garamond fonts. These extra design elements are called "serifs"; therefore, because Helvetica and Avant Garde do not have these extra design elements, they are "sans serif" (*sans* means "without" in French). When you have a large block of text, it is commonly recognized that serif fonts are easier to read than sans serif fonts.

- Make the text contrast with the background. It is much easier for the eye to follow text that contrasts with the background.

The following are good resources for information on typography:

- **Yale Style Guide** http://info.med.yale.edu/caim/manual/pages/typography.html

- **Microsoft Typography** http://www.microsoft.com/typography/default.asp

- **Adobe Type Topics** http://www.adobe.com/type/topics/main.html

Color

One of the most important aspects of planning a site is determining what type of a color scheme to use. While FrontPage comes with several predefined themes that offer a wide assortment of great color schemes, you may want to choose your own color combination that will suit your site. The colors of a site can reflect the nature of the site: flashy colors can be used for the promotion of products, while more subtle colors can be used for a site that is informative.

Here are some tips that can help you to use color effectively on your site:

- Use color to enhance your message, but try not to use color in a way that takes away from the message.

- If you are adding color to the text or a text background, make sure that the text is still legible. The lack of contrast between colors can make text hard to read.

- Try not to use colors that are too bright or hard on the eyes. Neon text usually annoys visitors.

- As an alternative to colored text and backgrounds, many people use images in their place. Instead of having a text link, you could use an image. Instead of using a single background color, you can create a repeating background pattern. For more information regarding images, please refer to Module 4.

Tip

A great way to learn about color is to check out other Web sites that use color well. A Web site that has numerous links to sites that use color and design well is http://www.coolhomepages.com/.

Layout

Another important area of your site is the layout. Layout is how information and other elements on your site are organized. The following guidelines will help you with layout:

- Try not to have your site be cluttered with information. Use space to your benefit. Having too much information on one page can actually dissuade people from reading the site.

- Test to see how your site looks on smaller monitors. Different-sized monitors provide different results.

- Try to keep the site's layout effective at all monitor resolutions. The most popular resolutions are 640 × 480 pixels, 800 × 600 pixels, and 1024 × 768 pixels.

- Because your home page is the primary entry to your site, the home page should give your visitors a sense of what your site is about without them having to scroll excessively. Key topics and features should immediately stand out once the page has been loaded.

Caution

If a page fills the whole screen of a browser that is running at a 1024 × 768-pixel monitor resolution, more than likely, users who have monitor resolutions of 640 × 480 pixels and 800 × 600 pixels will have to scroll horizontally.

Figures 2-3 and 2-4 show the same Web site at a 640 × 480-pixel resolution and an 800 × 600-pixel resolution. Notice how the page conforms to the size of the browser and that there are no horizontal scrollbars.

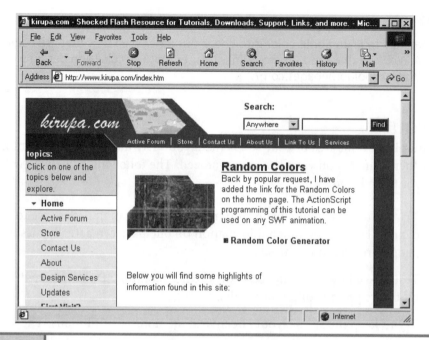

Figure 2-3 Web site at a 640 × 480 pixel resolution

Ask the Expert

Question: With so many different browsers in use today on the World Wide Web, should I try to make my site be compatible with all those browsers?

Answer: While you should try to make your site look acceptable on most browsers, it can be very difficult to make it compatible with all browsers. Many browsers have their own method of interpreting HTML, some browsers do not support the use of images, and some browsers do not support the use of certain Web languages that FrontPage uses. There is no way of determining how your site will look unless you test it in several browsers. The most popular browsers available today are Internet Explorer and Netscape Navigator. If your site looks acceptable on both browsers, over 90 percent of your site's visitors will be able to see your site correctly.

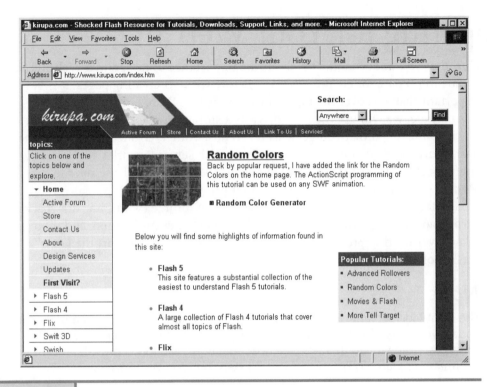

Figure 2-4   Web site at an 800 × 600 pixel resolution

The Structure of a Web Site

All Web sites contain a home page, which is the first page that your visitors will see when they enter your site. Below the home page, there will be several subpages, and those subpages may have their own subpages. Figure 2-5 shows an example of how a Web site is organized (*index.htm* is the home page).

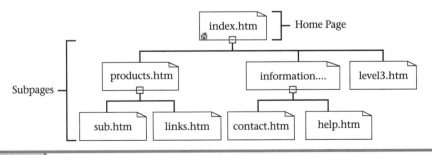

Figure 2-5   A Web site's organizational structure

Preparing for Your Web Site

Now that you understand a bit about the importance of design in a Web site, it is time to prepare for creating the site. Before we start creating pages, it is very important that we cover the topic of the FrontPage Web. For the exercises in this module, we will use the hard drive as a storage area for the Web site. But it is recommended that you get a server to host your Web site sometime in the near future, because you will need to have a Web server to work with FrontPage components. To learn more about choosing a Web server, please refer to Module 9. There are many companies that provide hosting for a relatively modest fee, and some companies provide hosting for free (with some drawbacks such as advertising, slow access speeds, less tools for customization, and more). Whichever hosting provider you choose, make sure they support the latest version of FrontPage Server Extensions.

Note

The FrontPage Server Extensions is a set of tools designed to help you modify and update your site. The tools integrate themselves with the Web server to enable you to use some of FrontPage's advanced functions. Module 9 provides more information regarding FrontPage Server Extensions and Web servers.

FrontPage Webs

One of the important features of FrontPage is the FrontPage Web. The FrontPage Web is the directory in which your entire site will be located. Inside the FrontPage Web, you can add files, create folders, move files around, and perform other basic tasks.

Creating a FrontPage Web

To begin, we will create a FrontPage Web on your hard drive. A FrontPage Web stored locally on your computer is an easy way to explore and try some of the basic features of FrontPage. We will eventually use a Web server dedicated to hosting sites for some of FrontPage's advanced tools.

The following steps tell you how to create a FrontPage Web on your hard drive:

1. From the menu bar, click File | New | Page or Web. Once you have clicked that option, the Task pane will appear on the right side of the FrontPage window. In the New section of the Task pane, select Empty Web:

2

2. After you click the Empty Web command, the Web Site Templates window, shown in Figure 2-6, will appear with various FrontPage Web options. On the right side of the Web Site Templates window, in the Specify the location of the new web field, select the location where you want to store your Web by either typing it in or browsing for it using the Browse button. Once you have selected the location of your Web, double click the icon for Empty Web on the left. As an alternative, you may also select it and click the OK button:

3. After you have selected the Empty Web option, the Web Site Template window will close, and FrontPage will take a few seconds to create the necessary folders and files. Once the Web has been created, your screen should look similar to Figure 2-7. If you only see the gray FrontPage background, click View | Folders. That will put you in FrontPage's Folder view, and you will be able to see all the files and folders stored in your FrontPage Web:

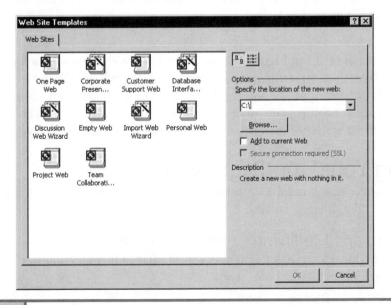

Figure 2-6   Various FrontPage Web options are shown in the Web Site Templates window.

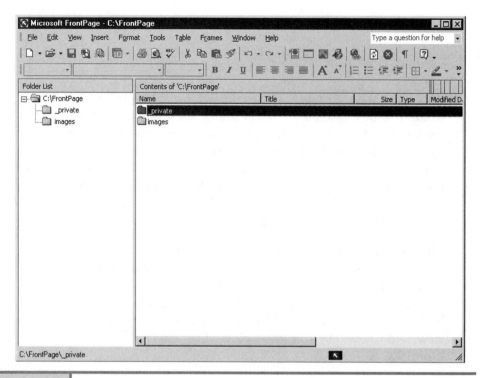

Figure 2-7   A FrontPage Web

As you can see from Figure 2-4, the FrontPage Web does not look much different than the file management system used by Windows. On the left side of the window, you see all the folders that are currently in the Web. On the right side, you see the folders and any files that may be available there. The right side is where the majority of the options and properties can be customized.

Using Your FrontPage Web

Now that you have created a FrontPage Web, it is time to start using it and filling it with our files, images, and more.

Creating and Modifying Pages

FrontPage's file management system is very similar to that of Windows. To create a new blank page, follow these directions:

1. Right click anywhere in the Folders View that is not a file or folder. Once you right click, a menu will appear at your mouse pointer. From the menu, select New | Page:

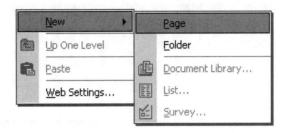

2. After you have selected the Page command, a new page will be created in your FrontPage Web. Because the page you just created is the first page in your Web, FrontPage will assign it the name *index.htm* (*index.htm* is always the default page for all your folders):

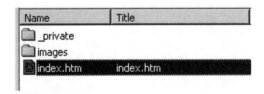

Note

You can assign any name you want to your new page, but you must make sure that the file extension ends in *.htm* or another Web-specific filename. The file extensions that FrontPage recognizes include *.html*, *.asp*, *.shtml*, and a few others. FrontPage may give you a warning stating that these files may lose their ability to work if the extension is changed, because FrontPage cannot open and edit files that have extensions that are not supported by it.

3. When you right-click on the *index.htm* file in the FrontPage Web, a menu will appear with many options, as shown in Figure 2-8.

The following is a list of each of the commands with a brief description:

● **Open**   Opens the file in FrontPage. You may also double-click the file itself to open it in FrontPage.

● **Open With**   Opens two things: a file that is not a FrontPage-supported file, and a file that you wish to edit in another program. Even though you will be using FrontPage for all your Web design needs, only Web pages can be edited by FrontPage. For example, if you need to open or edit an

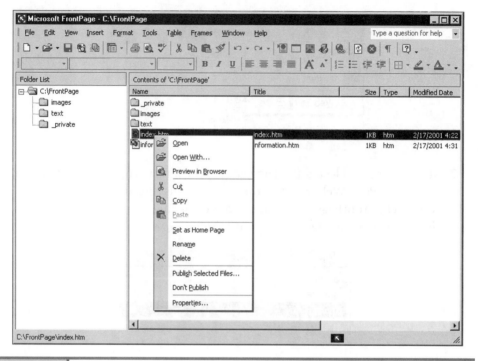

Figure 2-8 FrontPage file commands are used to simplify common tasks such as copy, paste, and publish.

image file, you can use the Open With command to see if any applications are configured for editing images. If there are applications configured for editing images, you can open that image file in the image application displayed by the Open With command.

- **Preview in Browser** Allows you to preview the selected file in your Web browser.

- **Cut** Enables you to cut a page or folder so that you can place it somewhere else, such as in another FrontPage Web or a different folder.

- **Copy** Copy is similar to Cut, except the original files or folders remain in their position. This option is used to place another copy of a file or folder in another folder.

- **Paste** Used in conjunction with Cut and Copy. Once you have cut or copied a file or folder, you can use the Paste option to place it in a different location.

2

- **Set as Home Page**   Enables FrontPage to select the home page for your site. Right now, the *index.htm* file in your Web is the home page. Selecting the Set as Home Page command for another file will make that file the home page. The selected file will be renamed to *index.htm*, and the previous home page will be named *index-old.htm*.

- **Rename**   Renames the file or folder to another name you specify.

- **Delete**   Deletes the entire file or folder from your FrontPage Web.

- **Publish Selected Files**   Used to send files to the server. Since our Web, for now, is going to be stored on the hard drive, we don't need to worry about this feature at this time. You will learn more about publishing your Web in Module 9.

- **Don't Publish**   Specifies the files or folders you do not want published.

- **Properties**   Enables you to perform page-sensitive modifications such as assigning categories, changing the title, and more.

Creating and Modifying Folders

To create a new folder, follow these directions:

1. Right-click any empty location on the Web view and choose New | Folder:

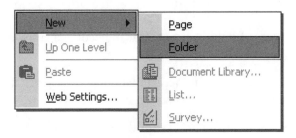

2. After you select Folder, a new folder will be created and FrontPage will highlight the folder and ask you to specify a name for the folder. You may give the folder any name you wish, but it is best to keep folder names short.

3. Now we will modify the folder. Right-click the folder you just created, and a menu will appear with many options, as shown in Figure 2-9.

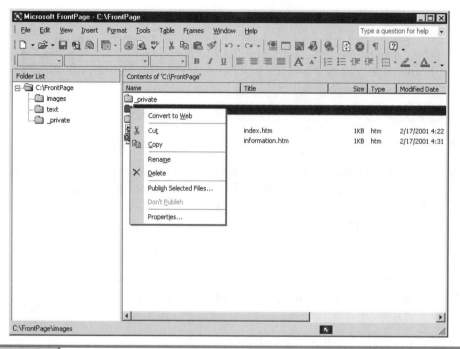

Figure 2-9   Options for modifying a folder

The following is a list of the commands with a brief description of each:

● **Convert to Web**   Enables your folder to become a subweb inside the FrontPage Web.

● **Cut**   Enables you to cut a folder so that you can be place it in another location. The location you choose can be in your Web or outside your Web.

● **Copy**   Is very similar to cut, except the file being copied will stay in its original location, and a copy of the file will be placed in the location of your choice.

● **Rename**   Enables you to change the name of your folder.

- **Delete**   Deletes your folder from the FrontPage Web.

- **Publish Selected Files**   This is used if you want to publish the folder and files inside it to a Web server. Since we are keeping our Web is on the hard drive at this time, there is no need to worry about this option now. You will learn more about publishing files and folders in Module 9.

- **Don't Publish**   Specifies the folders you do not want published.

- **Properties**   When you select the command for Properties, you will see several options related to the current folder. You can use these options to modify the current folder by allow programs or scripts to be run, allow users to upload files to this folder, and allow for the overwriting of files when they are uploaded to this folder. These options work only when folders are located on a Web server. Because you have your Web stored on your hard drive, you will have these options grayed out.

1-Minute Drill

- Can files and folders in a FrontPage Web be modified just like any file or folder in Windows?

- When you copy files or folders from one location to another, do files get moved from one location to another, duplicated to a folder you specify, or permanently removed from your FrontPage Web?

Importing Files, Folders, and Webs into Your Web

Now that you know how to create and modifying files and folders, let's learn how to import files into your FrontPage Web. More than likely, you would like to add your own files and folders to your Web site. Files such as images, sounds, videos, documents, and others have to be imported into FrontPage.

- Yes. Files and folders in the FrontPage Web can be moved, renamed, deleted, copied, cut, pasted, and more, just like in Windows.
- Duplicated to a folder you specify. The original file stays in its same location, while another copy of the same file is placed in another location that you specify.

To import files and folders, follow these steps:

1. Select File | Import. The Import window will appear:

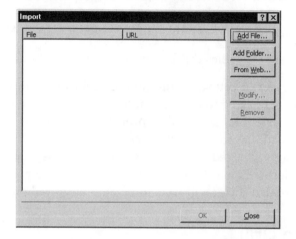

2. To add a file, click the Add File button on the right side of the Import window. After you click the Add File button, the Add File to Import List window, where you can browse and select a file you want, will appear.

3. Does anything happen to let us know that it's been double-clicked?

4. After you have found the file you want to add, double-click it. Then click the OK button to close the Add File to Import List window, and your file will be listed in the Import window.

5. To add a folder to your FrontPage Web, click the Add Folder button on the right. After you click the Add Folder button, the Add Folder to Import List window, where you can browse and select the folder you want, will appear. Selecting a folder will import the folder as well as any files inside it.

6. After you have found the folder you want to add, double-click it, and click the OK button to close the Add Folder to Import List button window.

7. Sometimes you may want to import files and folders from another FrontPage Web into your current FrontPage Web. The most effective method of importing files and folders from another Web is to import the entire FrontPage Web into your current FrontPage Web. To do that, click the From Web button in the Import window, and the Import Web Wizard will appear.

8. In the Import Web Wizard window, use the Browse button to browse your hard drive for the Web you want to import. (At this time, because we are not yet using a server, our only option is to import from our hard drive. When we have a server, we will be able to import from the World Wide Web as well. You will learn how to import from the World Wide Web in Module 9.) After you have selected the Web, it's path will appear in the Location field.

9. After you have selected the Web and placed its path in the Location field, click the Next button, and you will see all the files and folders that will be imported into your current Web.

10. Click the Next button again and the Import Web Wizard will confirm that the Web and its files and folders have been imported. The Import Web Wizard window will be closed automatically, and a confirmation window will be displayed after all the files, folders, or Webs have been imported.

11. Click the Finish button to close the confirmation window, and you will be taken back to your Web, which contains the importing items such as files, folders, or Webs.

Using Web Templates

FrontPage includes several predefined templates for you to modify and use. The FrontPage Web templates allow you to create custom-formatted Webs and several Web Site Templates with files and images already customized for your site. Most of the templates create a new Web, and some of the templates have a wizard that guides you through creating a Web.

The following steps show you how to create a Web using a template:

1. Select File | New | Page or Web. The Task pane will appear on the right side of the FrontPage window.

2. In the Task pane, click Web Site Templates. The Web Site Templates window will appear with ten template options to choose from, as shown in Figure 2-10.

3. Select one of the options in the Web Site Templates window, and a custom Web will be created for you on your hard drive.

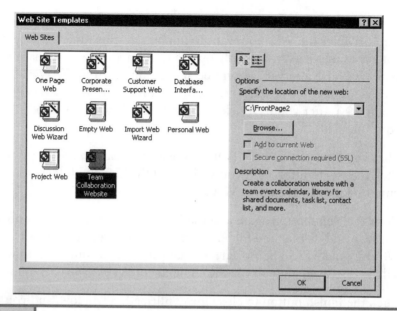

Figure 2-10 There are ten templates to choose from when using the Web Site Template window.

Table 2-1 lists the options available in the Web Site Templates window and gives a brief description of what each option does.

Web Site Template	Description
One Page Web	Creates a Web with a single blank page in it
Corporate Presence Wizard	Uses a wizard that guides you through various steps and procedures to create a custom set of pages tailored to your company
Customer Support Web	Creates a set of pages with a custom theme to help you create a support site for the Internet
Database Interface	Guides you to create a site that connects to either an existing database or a new database created by FrontPage
Discussion Web Wizard	Creates a discussion group: a scaled-down version of an online message board

Table 2-1 Web Site Template Options and Descriptions

Web Site Template	Description
Empty Web	Creates the basic structure of a Web and enables you to handle everything pertaining to it (this is the Web template you used in creating the FrontPage Web earlier in this module)
Import Web Wizard	Guides you through importing a Web from either an online Web site or another Web stored on your hard drive
Personal Web	Creates a personal Web that enables you to post information, a picture gallery, or other information found on a personal site
Project Web	Creates a Web that enables you to collaborate with other people, display a list of members, configure a schedule, or other information found on a project site
Team Collaboration Website	Used by people in other locations to share calendars, documents, view member-created lists, and more. The advanced features of this Web enable it to only be used on a Web server. You cannot store this Web locally on your hard drive.

Table 2-1   Web Site Template Options and Descriptions (*continued*)

All of the Webs created with Web site templates can be worked with as the Webs you created at the beginning of this module can: their files and folders can be modified, files can be imported into them, and more.

Using Page Templates

Page templates are basically the same as Web site templates, except they are templates that create pages instead of Webs. Page templates are used extensively to simplify repetitive tasks by allowing you to focus on the content while the template takes care of the layout and any programming necessary. While using page templates is not necessary, it is easier to modify a photo gallery template, for example, than create a photo gallery manually.

The following instructions teach you how to incorporate a page template into your FrontPage Web:

1. Select to File | New | Page or Web. The Task pane will appear on the right of the screen.

2. In the Task pane, click the Page Templates option. The Page Templates will appear.

   Table 2-2 lists the options available in the Page Templates window and gives a brief description of what each option does.

Page Template	Description
Normal	Creates a blank page with no information in it
Bibliography	Creates a set of references
Confirmation Form	Displays a page that acknowledges that information has been received when a user submits a form, discussion, or registration page
Feedback Form	Creates a page where visitors can input feedback
Form Page Wizard	Guides you through a series of steps and creates a custom form based on your selections
Guest Book	Receives comments from visitors and lets other visitors see and read those comments
Photo Gallery	Enables you to add photos
Search Page	Creates a page in which the visitor can search your site by typing keywords into an input box
User Registration	Creates a page in which visitors can register to gain access to certain areas of your Web site

Table 2-2 Page Template Options and Descriptions

3. In the Page Templates window, click the One-column Body with Contents on Left icon. Click the OK button to close the Page Templates window.

4. After you click OK, FrontPage will display the template you selected with text and helpful hints to help you create the page. You can delete the hints FrontPage provides. Your template page should look like Figure 2-11.

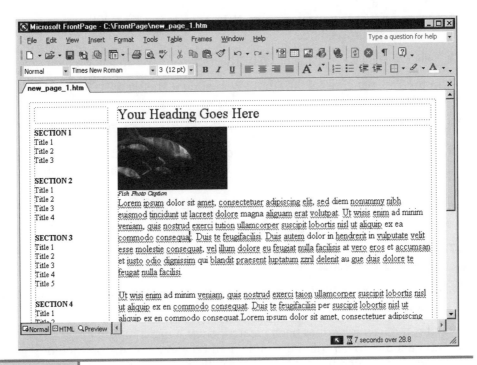

Figure 2-11   This page was created using the FrontPage template.

Project 2-1: Using a FrontPage Web

The following are the goals of this project:

● Create a FrontPage Web

● Add files and folders to a Web

● Import files into a Web

Step-by-Step

1. Make sure that there are no other Webs open at this time. If there are, close them before proceeding.

2. Select to File | New | Page or Web. The Task pane will appear on the right.

3. In the Task pane, select the Empty Web option. The Web Site Templates window will appear.

4. In the Specify the location of the new web field, type **C:\FrontPage.**

5. Once you have specified your Web's location, click OK to close the Web Site Templates window. You will now see an empty FrontPage Web with two folders.

6. Right click an empty spot below the folders and select New | Page. Since this is your first page, FrontPage will give it the name *index.htm*.

7. Add two more pages by repeating Step 5 two times; give each file a different name. Make sure that the filenames end with *.htm*.

8. Add a folder by right clicking an empty spot below the *index.htm* file and selecting New | Folder.

9. After the new folder has been created, enter a name for the folder. Add another folder using the same method and name it. You should now have created two folders. Along with the two folders FrontPage automatically created, you should have four folders displayed in your Web.

10. Import a file into your Web by clicking File | Import. Import any file that you wish. A Word document would be a good thing to import here.

Your FrontPage Web should look similar to Figure 2-12. Your Web will have some minor differences, but you should have four folders, three pages, and an imported file. The imported file in Figure 2-12 is a blank word document (*blank.doc*).

Summary

It is important to plan properly before creating your site to know what the purpose of your site is and who your audience is. It is also helpful to know a little about typography, layout, and color before starting your site. The FrontPage Web will help you tremendously to creating your site. It is used to create pages and folders, import files, and more, and it provides a central location where you can control your entire site.

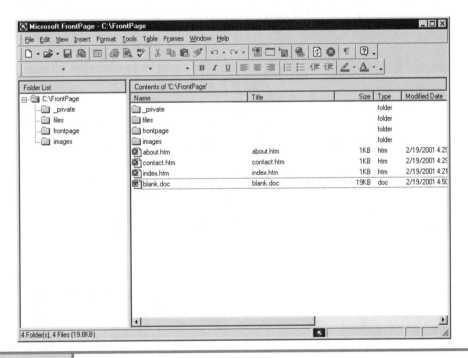

Figure 2-12   This FrontPage Web shows an imported file.

✓ Mastery Check

1. What is typography?

_____

_____

2. What are some benefits to updating a Web site often?

_____

_____

3. Briefly, what is layout?

_____

_____

4. What is a FrontPage Web?

_____

_____

5. How can templates help you?

_____

_____

6. How can you change the default location for a FrontPage Web?

_____

_____

7. How do you create files or folders in the FrontPage Web?

_____

_____

8. What are the steps necessary to import files into a FrontPage Web?

_____

_____

Module 3

Creating a Web Site

The Goals of This Module

- Learn the basics of the HTML language
- Add and format text in your Web pages
- Create hyperlinks

In this module, you will learn how to add and format text and how to create hyperlinks. Before we delve into these two topics, it is necessary for you to know a bit about Hypertext Markup Language (HTML) and how it works in FrontPage.

HTML Basics

HTML was created in 1989 to provide a language for generating text-formatted documents for the World Wide Web. Since then, HTML has had many revisions. Today HTML has the capability to support images, sounds, styles, and more. When you create something in FrontPage, you can view the HTML code by clicking the HTML button in the lower-left corner of the program window. Figure 3-1 shows an example of HTML created by FrontPage:

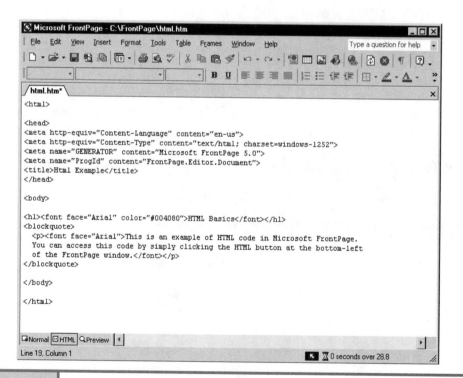

Figure 3-1 HTML code created by FrontPage

3

Note

FrontPage creates HTML files with the extension *.htm*, while other programs and HTML pages created by individuals are often saved in the *.html* file format. There is no difference between files with the *.html* extension and the *.htm* extension, as browsers recognize them both as HTML documents.

You don't need to know how to write HTML to use FrontPage, but so you will be familiar with how HTML looks and works, I will show snippets of the HTML code FrontPage creates for some of the exercises we'll complete in this book.

HTML Tags

In HTML, tags are used to denote sections of code. Tags always work in pairs: there is an opening tag and a closing tag. For example, to add an italicize tag (which italicizes the text), you would open the tag by using the opening tag `<i>`. Now, you would need to add a closing tag, or the entire series of text following that tag will be italicized. You signify a closing tag by using a forward slash / preceding the same tag you used to open. So, the closing tag for the italic tag would be `</i>`. The following is an example of the italic tag used in FrontPage:

```
<p><i>Italic</i></p>
```

HTML Attributes

The attributes of HTML are simply characteristics of an HTML object you can customize. The attributes always fall in between the opening and closing tags of the code:

```
<font color="#800000" face="Arial">frontpage</font>
```

In the previous code, the attributes are color and face. Notice how both of them fall in between the opening and closing tags of font.

Since you will primarily be using FrontPage to create your site, you do not need to worry about any of these tags. FrontPage writes these tags and attributes as you create and edit a document. If you want to see how the document's HTML changes as you create and modify a document, click the HTML tab in the lower-left corner of the FrontPage window as you work.

Adding Text in FrontPage

In Module 2, you learned how to create a FrontPage Web. In this module we will extend on that knowledge to actually create and modify a Web page. Since text is an integral part of a Web site, let's start by learning how to enter and format text in a Web page.

Follow these directions to enter and format text:

1. Open your FrontPage Web. You can open your FrontPage Web by going to the menu bar and choosing File | Recent Webs. From the Recent Webs submenu, choose the FrontPage Web that you created in Module 2. If you don't have a FrontPage Web, please go back to Module 2 and create one there.

2. To create a new page in your Web, select View | Folders from the menu bar. You will be in FrontPage's Folders View.

3. Create a new page in your FrontPage Web. To create a new page, right-click an empty part of your Web and choose New | Page from the menu that appears. Name the new page *text.htm*.

4. Double-click the *text.htm* page. You will now see a blank document in your FrontPage window. Let's add some text!

5. To add text, click in the document and type **Text**. You can add text, delete text, and more just as you would in any word-processing application.

Keep the document *text.htm* open, as we will be using it in the next section.

Formatting Text

Now that you know how to add text to your document, let's learn how to format the text. Before we start, you must understand the definitions of two terms, *font* and *text*, and how they are different from one another:

3. If you still don't see the color you want, you may click Custom in the More Colors window. You will then see the Custom Color window, and you can choose any color you wish by clicking in the colored box.

The following is the HTML code FrontPage outputs for changing the font color:

```
<font color="#800000">color</font>
```

Modifying Text

Just like font styles, text can be modified. To modify text, you can change the text alignment, indent text, and add line breaks. The following sections will help you to modify text.

Changing Text Alignment

Text alignment is how text is horizontally positioned on screen. The options for alignment are align left, center, align right, and justify. By default, all your text will start on the left side of the document. You can easily change the alignment of text in FrontPage by using the four alignment icons in the Formatting toolbar:

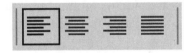

Follow these steps to align text:

1. Create a new document in FrontPage. Type Highlight the words that you would like to change the alignment of.

2. Click the appropriate icon on the Formatting toolbar:

- **Align Left**   Aligns the text to the left side of the page.
- **Center**   Aligns the text to the center of the page.
- **Align Right**   Aligns the text to the right of the page.
- **Justify**   Aligns the text so that the lines are even at both margins (the right margin is not jagged).

The following image shows separate lines of text with each alignment applied to it:

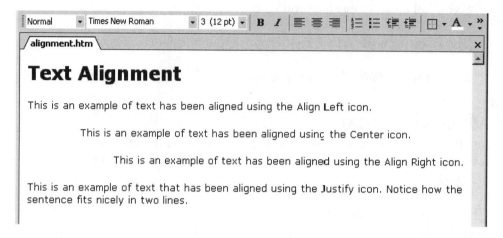

Indenting Text

Sometimes, you may wish to move a word or words of text away from the margin. You may want to do this at the beginning of a paragraph or to emphasize a word, a group of words, or an entire sentence. FrontPage provides two icons for indenting text: the Decrease Indent and Increase Indent icons decrease and increase the level of indentation that is applied to text, respectively:

The following is the HTML code FrontPage outputs to increase the indent (the HTML tag for indenting is **<blockquote>**):

```
<blockquote>
    <p>Building</p>
</blockquote>
```

Creating Line Breaks

At some point, you will probably want to separate lines of text by inserting line breaks. In FrontPage, pressing ENTER twice enables you to type again after the skipped line (you end up with a line of text, a skipped line, and another line of text); this is known as a *hard return*. In contrast, you may want to add a line break that breaks off one line and starts on the very next line (no space in between the lines of text); this is known as a *soft return,* and for that, you need to use the combination of SHIFT-ENTER. The following image shows you an example of both the hard return and the soft return:

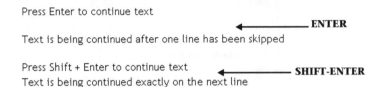

The following is the HTML code FrontPage outputs for a hard return and a soft return, respectively:

```
<p>Press Enter to continue text</p>
<p>Text is being continued after one line has been skipped</p>
<p>Press Shift + Enter to continue text<br>
    Text is being continued exactly on the next line</p>
```

The Font Window

The Font window contains more advanced options for customizing fonts. It contains the Font tab, which enables you to adjust the font, and the Character Spacing tab, which enables you to adjust the spacing between characters and the alignment of the text.

Font Tab

The following instructions will show you how to use the options found in the Font tab:

1. Create a new page in FrontPage. In the page, type a few words. Highlight the words with the cursor, and with the words highlighted, right-click and select the command for Font. The Font window will appear.

2. In the Font window, if it is not already selected, select the Font tab. The Font tab contains the Font, Font style, Size, Color, and Effects sections and all options available in each. At the bottom of the Font window is the Preview window, which shows the results of each selection on your text. Figure 3-3 shows the Font window with the Font tab selected, and Table 3-1 describes its options.

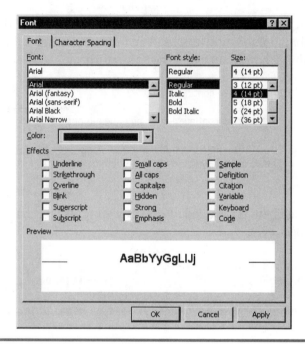

Figure 3-3 The Font tab in the Font window

Note

Some of these effects may not work in browsers that do not support the Cascading Style Sheets (CSS) formatting standard. Newer browsers with CSS support will be able to display the text effects.

Font Effect	Description
Underline	Underlines selected text
Strikethrough	Draws a horizontal line through the text
Overline	Creates a line over the text
Blink	Makes text blink only in Netscape Navigator
Superscript	Raises the text above the base line
Subscript	Lowers the text below the base line

Table 3-1 Font Effects and Descriptions

Font Effect	Description
Small caps	Changes lowercase letters to small caps, which are capital letters on a smaller scale than regular capital letters
All caps	Capitalizes all the letters
Capitalize	Capitalizes the first letter of each word
Hidden	Hides the text from being seen in a browser
Strong	Makes the text bold
Emphasis	Italicizes the text
Sample	Formats the text in a fixed-width font such as Courier
Definition	Makes the text italic
Citation	Makes the text italic
Variable	Makes the text italic
Keyboard	Formats the text using a fixed-width font such as Courier
Code	Uses a fixed-width font to display the text, similar to the Sample font effect.

Table 3-1   Font Effects and Descriptions (*continued*)

Note

A fixed-width font is simply a font that has even spacing between the letters. Most fonts usually have varying spaces in between each letter, while fixed-width fonts have a specific spacing.

The following is the HTML code FrontPage outputs for applying effects:

```
<span style="text-decoration: overline">font style</span>
```

Character Spacing Tab

The following instructions will guide you to expand, condense, and adjust the position of text:

1. Create a new page in FrontPage. In the page, type a few words. Highlight the words with the cursor, and with the words highlighted, right-click and select the command for Font. The Font window will appear.

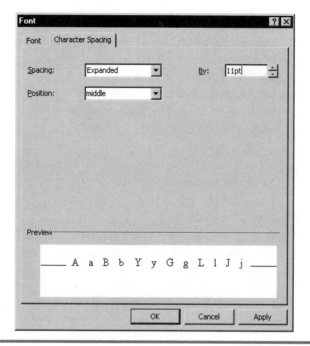

Figure 3-4 The Character Spacing tab in the Font window

2. In the Font window, select the Character Spacing tab. Figure 3-4 shows the Font window with the Character Spacing tab selected.

3. In the Character Spacing tab, click the arrow for the spacing menu and select the Expanded command.

4. In the By field, enter **3**. You may use the arrows to the right of the By field to select the number. Look in the Preview window to see the results of your selection.

Note

Entering a negative value into the By field while the Expanded command is selected will condense the text. The exact opposite is true when you enter a negative value when the Condensed command is selected—entering a negative value into the By field while the Condensed command is selected will expand the text.

5. To decrease the spacing between letters, click the Spacing menu and select the Condensed command. Again, enter **2** in the By field. This time, the value you enter in the By field will determine how condensed the letters are. The Preview area will show you an example of how your spacing selection will look when applied to a word.

6. To adjust the vertical position of letters in a word, click the Position menu. From the list of commands, select the *text-top* position.

7. Press OK to close the Font window.

1-Minute Drill

● Is the Formatting toolbar the only method in which you can modify font color and font size?

● What command would you click to access the HTML view in FrontPage?

Hyperlinks

Hyperlinks are the links that you use to go from page to page and site to site. If there were no hyperlinks, we would have to type in the Uniform Resource Locator (URL) of each page and site manually.

When you click a hyperlink, the hyperlink transmits a message to the Web server and requests it to send the page and additional files to your browser.

Most people associate hyperlinks with text, but hyperlinks can be applied to various other elements such as videos, images, tables, and more. In this module, you will learn the following hyperlinking techniques:

● How to link to other pages

● How to hyperlink to a new window

● How to hyperlink to an e-mail address

● How to hyperlink to a bookmarks

For the exercises in this module, you need to download the source files for Module 3 from http://www.Osborne.com or http://www.kirupa.com/frontpage. After you have downloaded the files, you need to extract them to a directory on your computer by using a program such as Win-Zip.

● No. You can use the Font window by right-clicking on text and choosing Font.
● The HTML command found at the bottom of the FrontPage window.

Note

If you don't know how to import files, please refer to Module 2.

Hyperlinking to Other Pages

The hyperlink you will use most often is the one that will take the visitor to another page.

To create a hyperlink to another page, follow these steps:

1. While in your FrontPage Web, open the *hyperlink.htm* file. (That file is included with the source files you should download for this module from http://www.Osborne.com or http://www.kirupa.com/frontpage.) You will see the page shown in Figure 3-5.

2. Highlight all the words in the first bullet: "Hyperlink to another page."

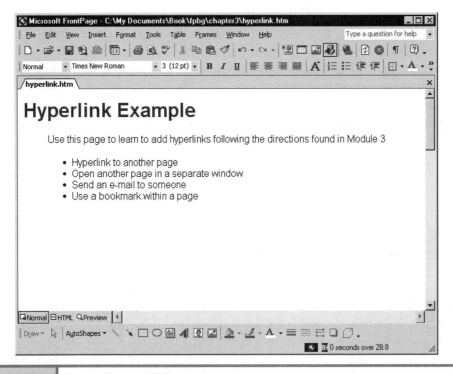

Figure 3-5   Using the Hyperlink page

3. After you have highlighted all the words, launch the Insert Hyperlink
window by doing one of two things:

● Right-click the highlighted words and choose the Hyperlink command:

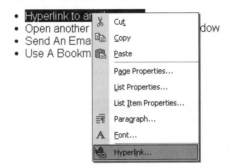

● Click the Insert Hyperlink icon on the Standard toolbar:

Whichever way you choose, the Insert Hyperlink window will appear, as shown
in Figure 3-6.

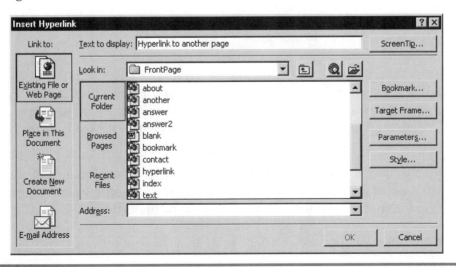

Figure 3-6   Use the Insert Hyperlink window to insert a hyperlink into your Web page.

4. In the Insert Hyperlink window, select the *another* file in the main menu box or type *another.htm* into the Address field at the bottom of the window:

5. After you have selected the file *another.htm*, click OK to close the Insert Hyperlink window.

6. In your page, you will see that the first bulleted item is underlined in blue; this indicates that the text is an active link and that it can be clicked.

7. So, to see if your hyperlink works, preview the *hyperlink.htm* page by clicking the Preview command at the bottom of your FrontPage window:

8. When you click Preview, you will see the *hyperlink.htm* page in FrontPage again, but you will not be able to modify or add information to the page. Click the hyperlink you just created, and if you hyperlinked it correctly, the *another.htm* page will load in FrontPage.

9. To go back to FrontPage's default view, click the Normal command at the bottom of the page. Clicking that will display the *hyperlink.htm* file again, and from there you will be able to modify the file as usual.

Keep this page open, as we will be using it in the next section.

Hyperlinking to a New Window

A link that opens a new browser window is useful for keeping visitors on your site while they simultaneously explore another site.

The following are the instructions for creating a hyperlink that loads a page in a new browser window:

1. Using the file from the last section, highlight all the text in the second bullet: Open another page in a separate window.

2. After you have highlighted all the words, launch the Insert Hyperlink window by either right-clicking and choosing Hyperlink from the menu that appears or by clicking the Insert Hyperlink icon on the Standard toolbar.

3. In the Insert Hyperlink window, type the name or browse for the file *window.htm*. Before you click OK, there is one more step in order to open the page in a new window.

4. With the file *window.htm* shown in the Address field of the Insert Hyperlink window, click the Target Frame button on the right of the Insert Hyperlink window. The Target Frame window will open.

5. In the Target Frame window, you will see various options under Common targets. In the Common targets menu box, choose the option for New Window:

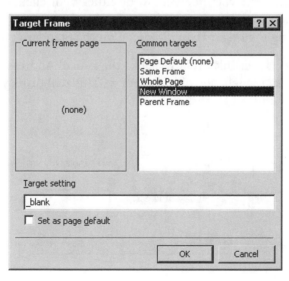

6. Click OK to close the Target Frame window. Click OK to close the Insert Hyperlink window. You will be taken back to your main page in FrontPage. You will notice that the second bullet is now underlined and in a different color.

7. To test the hyperlink you created, preview the *hyperlink.htm* page. To preview the page, click the Preview button at the bottom of your window. After you click the Preview button, the page will be displayed in FrontPage. Click the hyperlink you just created, and if you hyperlinked correctly, the *window.htm* page will open in a new browser window.

Keep this page open as we will be using it in the next section.

Hyperlinking to an E-mail Address

In this exercise, you will learn how to create a hyperlink that launches an e-mail program from a Web page:

1. Open the *hyperlink.htm* file.

2. From the *hyperlink.htm* file, highlight the words in the second bullet "Send an e-mail to someone."

3. Launch the Insert Hyperlink window by either right-clicking the highlighted text and selecting the command for Hyperlink from the menu that appears or by clicking the Insert Hyperlink icon on the Standard toolbar.

4. In the Insert Hyperlink window, select the E-mail Address option from the Link to list on the left side of the window. This will display the E-mail options in the Insert Hyperlink window:

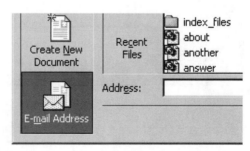

5. In the Insert Hyperlink window, in the E-mail address field, enter your
e-mail address. In the Subject field, you can enter a subject, if you wish to:

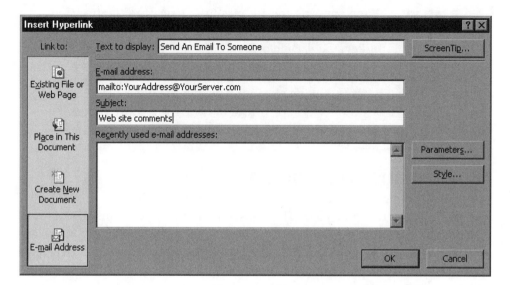

—┼**Note** —————————————————————————————————

When you type in an e-mail address, *mailto:* will automatically be added.

6. After you enter the information, click OK to close the Insert Hyperlink
window. After you click OK, you will be taken back to your main page
in FrontPage.

7. To test the hyperlink you created, click the Preview button at the bottom
of your window. After you click Preview, your page will be displayed in
FrontPage. Click the hyperlink you just created, and if you hyperlinked
correctly, your e-mail program will launch with the address field filled in.

Keep this file open because we will be using it in the next section.

Ask the Expert

Question: When entering the address for a page into the Insert Hyperlink window, is there a shorter method than typing out, for example *C:\FrontPage\Folder\index.htm*?

Answer: Yes. If the page you are linking from is in the same folder as the page you will be linking to, simply type in the name of the file in the address box. For example, instead of typing the entire address **C:\FrontPage\Folder\index.htm**, you would simply type **index.htm**.

Hyperlinking to a Bookmark

You may want to create a link that takes the visitor to another place, called a *bookmark*, within the same page. This is useful for allowing visitors to skip over material they are not interested in and get right to the part that they are interested in. Hyperlinking to a bookmark has two parts to it: creating the bookmark, and then creating the link that goes to the bookmark. The instructions in this section will cover both the bookmark and the link separately.

The following are the instructions for creating a bookmark:

1. Open the *hyperlink.htm* page.

2. Scroll down to the very bottom of the *hyperlink.htm* page, and stop when you see the text "This is an example of the bookmark feature."

3. Click anywhere on the text, and select Insert | Bookmark from the menu bar. The Bookmark window will appear:

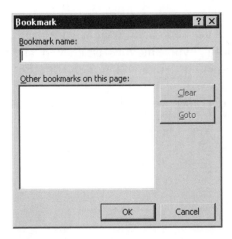

4. Enter the word *guide* into the Bookmark name field, and click OK to close the Bookmark window.

5. After you close the Bookmark window, you will see a flag icon in your text that represents the bookmark. Don't worry if the bookmark is in the middle of the sentence. When your Web site is previewed, you will not see the bookmark at all:

3

Bookmark. Add the

Now that you have created the bookmark, it's time to hyperlink to the bookmark. The following instructions are for hyperlinking to the bookmark:

1. Go back to the bulleted list at the top of the *hyperlink.htm* page.

2. Highlight all of the text contained in the fourth bullet: "Use a bookmark within a page."

3. Once the text has been highlighted, launch the Insert Hyperlink window by right-clicking the highlighted text and choosing the Hyperlink command.

4. In the Insert Hyperlink window, select the Place in This Document option from the Link to list on the left side of the window.

5. After you have clicked the Place in This Document option, in the Select a place in this document box, you will see the following:

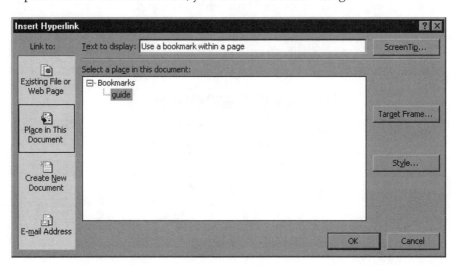

6. Select the guide bookmark and click OK to close the Insert Hyperlink window.

7. To test the hyperlink you created, click the Preview button at the bottom of your window. After you click Preview, your page will be displayed in FrontPage. Click the last bulleted item, and if you hyperlinked correctly, you will be taken to the bottom of the page, where your bookmark is.

Customizing Hyperlinks

Now that you know how to create hyperlinks, let's explore and customize some of the hyperlink properties.

ScreenTips

Oftentimes, when you hover your mouse pointer over a hyperlink, a small rectangular box will appear with additional information regarding the hyperlink you are hovering over. That small window and its contents is called a *ScreenTip*:

- Send an e-mail to someone
- Use a bookmark within a page

Click on this link to be taken to the bookmark in this page

The following are the instructions for creating a ScreenTip:

1. Open the *hyperlink.htm* page. Right-click the fourth bullet, "Use a bookmark within a page," and select the Hyperlink command.

2. In the Insert Hyperlink window, click the ScreenTip button in the upper-right corner. The Set Hyperlink ScreenTip window will appear. In the ScreenTip text field of the Set Hyperlink ScreenTip window, type **Link**:

3. Click OK to close the Set Hyperlink ScreenTip window. Press OK to close the Insert Hyperlink window.

4. To preview the page *hyperlink.htm* click the Preview command from the bottom left of the FrontPage window. When you preview the *hyperlink.htm* page, move the mouse pointer over the *Use a bookmark within a page* link. After about a second, the text that you entered into the ScreenTip text field (*Link*) will appear as a ScreenTip.

Keep this file open because we will be using it in the next section.

3

Creating New Documents

Oftentimes, while you are creating a site, you may need to link to a page that you haven't yet created. When this occurs, you can use FrontPage's Create New Document command to create a new page to hyperlink to.

—┤*Note* ———————————————————————————

The Create New Document command will create new documents located within your FrontPage Web.

To create a new page to hyperlink to, follows these directions:

1. Open the *hyperlink.htm* page. Right-click any bullet in the *hyperlink.htm* page, and select the Hyperlink command. From the Insert Hyperlink window, click the Create New Document option.

2. In the Name of new document field of the Insert Hyperlink window, enter *create.htm* (remember that the page that you want to link to does not exist yet, so you can give it any name you would like):

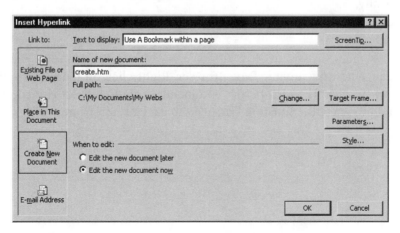

3. After you have entered the name of the new document, you have to make one of two choices: you need to decide whether you want to work on the new document immediately and therefore have the document open as soon as it is created, or whether you want to open it and work on it later:

● To open the new document later, select the Edit the new document later option.

● To open the document immediately after creation so you can edit it now, select the Edit the new document now option.

4. After you have chosen one of the two edit options, click OK to close the Insert Hyperlink window. After you close the window, FrontPage will automatically link the bullet you chose to the new page *create.htm*, and will open the page immediately or not, depending on the edit option you selected.

Save this file and preview it in your browser. Click on the links to see how each hyperlink works.

Hyperlinking to Other Web Pages from Your Browser

Sometimes, you may want to link to external pages on the World Wide Web that are not in your current FrontPage Web. While many users simply copy the Web site address from the Web browser into the Hyperlink field of the Insert Hyperlink window, FrontPage includes a simple function that does that automatically.

Follow these directions to hyperlink to another Web page on the World Wide Web:

1. Create a new document. Type **Browser**. Right-click on that word and select the Hyperlink Properties command. From the Insert Hyperlink window, select the Existing File or Web Page option from the Link to list

on the left side of the window. In the middle of the Insert Hyperlink window, you will find directories in which you can browse for files.

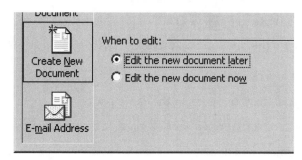

3

2. In the upper-right corner of the Insert Hyperlink window, click the Browse the Web icon:

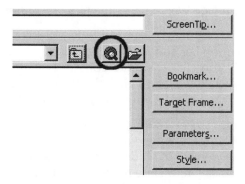

3. Clicking the Browse the Web icon will launch your browser. In your browser, go to a page that you want to link to. After the page you want is loaded in your browser, simply go back to FrontPage, and the address will be automatically filled in the Address field in the Insert Hyperlink window.

4. Click OK to close the Insert Hyperlink window. Save this file and preview it in your browser. When you click on the hyperlink, you are taken to the page that you linked to from the browser.

project.htm
same.htm
window.htm

Project 3-1: Hyperlinking and Formatting Text

The following are the goals of this project:

● Format text in a document

● Create a hyperlink that opens in the same page

● Create a hyperlink that opens a Web page in a separate browser window

● Create an e-mail hyperlink

● Create a bookmark hyperlink

Step-by-Step

1. Create a new FrontPage Web. Import the files *project.htm*, *same.htm*, and *window.htm*.

2. Open the *project.htm* file and scroll down to Format Text. Highlight the word "Bold", and click the Bold icon on the Formatting toolbar. Highlight the word "Italic," and click the Italic icon on the Formatting toolbar. Highlight the word "Underline," and click the Underline icon.

3. Highlight the word "Strikethrough," right-click, and select the Font command. In the Font Properties window, check the Strikethrough check box. Highlight the words "Colored Green," and select the color green from the Color menu. Click OK to close the Font Properties window. Your text should look similar to the following image:

Format Text:

Bold   *Italic*   <u>Underline</u>   ~~Strikethrough~~   Colored Green

4. Now that you finished formatting the text, let's start editing the hyperlinks. In the *project.htm* page, highlight the words "Existing Window," and right-click and choose Hyperlink. In the Insert Hyperlink window, select the Existing File or Web Page option on the left. Enter the path to the file *same.htm*. Close the Insert Hyperlink window by pressing the OK button.

5. Select the words "New Window" in the second bullet. In the Address field, type in *window.htm*. Click the Target Frame button, and in the Target Frame window, select the New Window option. Click OK to close the Target Frame window. Click OK to close the Insert Hyperlink window.

6. Highlight the words "E-mail" Link in the *project.htm* page, and go back to the Insert Hyperlink window by right clicking on the words and choosing Hyperlink. Click the E-Mail Address option on the left, and enter **YourAddress@YourServer.com** in the E-mail address field, and **Project Example** into the Subject field:

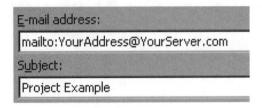

7. Click OK to close the Insert Hyperlink window.

8. To add a bookmark, scroll all the way down in *project.htm* page. Click on Bookmark. Add the bookmark anywhere, and select Insert | Bookmark. In the Bookmark window that appears, enter **bookmark** into the Bookmark name field. Click OK to close the Bookmark window.

9. Now, in the *project.htm* page, scroll up to the Bookmark bullet and highlight it. Open the Insert Hyperlink window. Select the Existing File or Web Page option on the left. Click the button for Bookmark, and in the Select a place in this document menu box, select bookmark from the list:

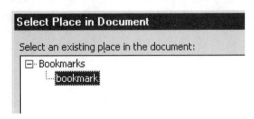

10. Click OK to close the Insert Hyperlink window.

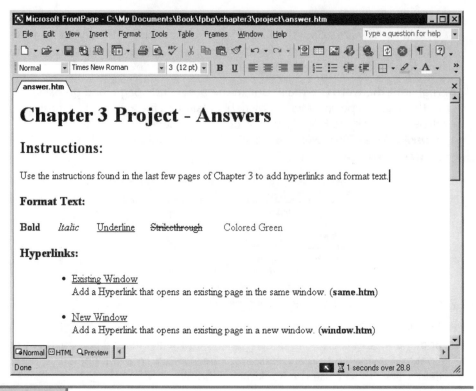

Your finished Project 3-1 should look similar to this screen shot

See Figure 3-7 for an example of what your finished project should look like. To see a working example of this project, open *answer.htm*.

Summary

Text and hyperlinks are found in almost all Web sites. By using text, you can communicate to your visitors. The style and formatting of text in a Web site helps the text to look appealing and readable at the same time. Hyperlinks provide a way for your visitors to navigate through your site's Web pages. Without hyperlinks, your visitors will have a difficult time navigating through your Web site. It is much easier to click on a link and be taken to that page than type the path of each page in your browser manually.

☑ *Mastery Check*

1. Why are hyperlinks used?

_____

_____

2. Why are bookmarks important?

_____

_____

3. What is the difference between the extensions *.html* and *.htm*?

_____

_____

4. When formatting text, should text be all bold?

_____

_____

5. When clicked, does an e-mail hyperlink launch an e-mail program?

_____

_____

6. How can you add font styles to text?

_____

_____

7. How are ScreenTips helpful?

_____

_____

3

Part II

Designing and Publishing Web Pages

Module 4

Using Images in Your Pages

The Goals of This Module

- Insert and format images
- Learn to position images
- Hyperlink images using hot spots
- Insert clip art

Since the first browser that supported graphics was introduced, the World Wide Web has not been the same. The transition from text-only Web sites to Web sites using images played a factor in helping make the internet appeal to numerous people. FrontPage supports not only the inclusion of images in your documents, but it also enables simple editing of those images. In Module 3, you learned about incorporating and formatting text in your Web documents. In this module, we will build upon that knowledge and show you how to use images to liven up your Web site.

Inserting and Modifying Images

In this section, you will learn how to insert images into a document and modify those images using FrontPage's wide assortment of simple image-editing tools. For the directions in this module, please download the various images and sample source files for Module 4 from http://www.kirupa.com/frontpage or http://www.Osborne.com.

Note

Most image file extensions are *.gif*, *.jpeg*, *.bmp*, and *.png*, but FrontPage automatically converts your images to either a Graphics Interchange Format (GIF, or *.gif*) or Joint Photographic Experts Group (JPEG, or *.jpg*) format when saving your page. The JPEG format is used for photos or images with many colors, while the GIF format is used for images with few colors: a JPEG is capable of 16,772, 216 colors per image, while a GIF is limited to only 256 colors.

Inserting Images

Follow these steps to insert an image into your document:

1. Open a new document in FrontPage and click the Insert Picture From File icon on the Standard toolbar:

2. After you have clicked the Insert Picture From File icon, the Picture window will appear. Select the *underwater.jpg*.

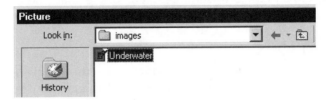

4

3. Once has been selected, click the Insert button on the Picture window.

4. After you have clicked the Insert button in the Picture window, the window will close, and the *underwater.jpg* image will be displayed in the FrontPage document you created:

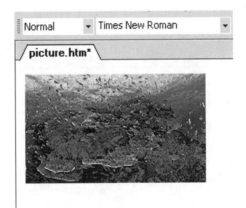

Note

There are many ways you can insert an image into FrontPage. You can drag and drop images, copy and paste images, use the Insert Picture From File Button, or drag images from one Web page to another.

The following is the Hypertext Markup Language (HTML) code FrontPage outputs to insert an image:

```
<img border="0" src="images/Fish.jpg" width="188" height="103">
```

Note

In HTML, image tags are introduced with the img tag and then followed by the src tag. The src tag tells the browser the location of the image file.

Editing Images

While FrontPage is not as powerful as major image-editing software packages, it does include some useful, easy-to-use tools. Now that you know how to insert an image into your document, let's learn how to edit the image.

To edit an image, you'll use the Pictures toolbar. There are two ways to get the toolbar to appear on your screen: If you already have an image in your document, you can select the image using your mouse pointer, and the Pictures toolbar should appear automatically. If it does not or if you don't yet have an image in your document, you can also go to View | Toolbars | Pictures to get the Pictures toolbar. This is what the Pictures toolbar looks like:

Table 4-1 shows each icon found in the Pictures toolbar and gives its name and function.

Icon	Name	Function
	Insert Picture From File	Inserts a picture from a location on your hard drive
A	Text	Adds formatted text over an image
	Auto Thumbnail	Replaces a larger image with that of a smaller one; hyperlinks the smaller image to display the larger image when clicked
	Position Absolutely	Enables for pixel-precise positioning and layering of an image
	Bring Forward	Moves the image one position forward in relation to other content

Table 4-1   Pictures Toolbar Icons

Icon	Name	Function
	Send Backward	Moves the image one position backward in relation to other content
	Rotate Left	Rotates an image 90 degrees to the left
	Rotate Right	Rotates an image 90 degrees to the right
	Flip Horizontal	Flips an image right to left
	Flip Vertical	Flips and image top to bottom.
	More Contrast	Increases the contrast in an image by darkening dark colors and lightening light colors
	Less Contrast	Decreases the contrast in an image by lightening dark colors and darkening light colors
	More Brightness	Brightens the image by adding white
	Less Brightness	Darkens the image by adding black
	Crop	Removes portions of the image
	Line Style	Modifies the thickness and type of line some elements use
	Format Picture	Formats elements, such as color, of your image
	Set Transparent Color	Sets a color as transparent
	Color	Changes the color of an image by making it either black and white, gray scale, or washed out
	Bevel	Creates 3-D edges around your image

Table 4-1   Pictures Toolbar Icons (*continued*)

Icon	Name	Function
	Resample	Cleans up an image after it has temporarily been scaled to a new size by removing jagged edges in the image
	Select	Selects elements such as images or hot spots
	Rectangular Hotspot	Creates a rectangular hot spot
	Circular Hotspot	Creates a circular hot spot
	Polygonal Hotspot	Creates a polygonal hot spot
	Highlight Hotspots	Displays hot spots on a white background
	Restore	Restores an image to its previously saved state

Table 4-1   Pictures Toolbar Icons *(continued)*

You can refer back to Table 4-1 and the Pictures toolbar icons while learning to format and edit images in this module.

Rotating and Flipping Images

Sometimes images need to be rotated or flipped to achieve a better look. In FrontPage, you can easily do that by using the Rotate Left, Rotate Right, Flip Vertical, and Flip Horizontal icons.

To rotate or flip an image, follow these steps:

1. Open a new document in FrontPage. Insert the image *tower.jpg* into your document. Select the image using your mouse pointer.

2. After you have selected the image, click either the Rotate Left or
Rotate Right icon. The image will rotate to your left or to your right,
depending on which icon you selected. The following is an example
of a rotated image:

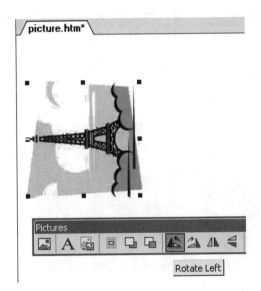

You can follow these same steps for flipping an image. The only difference is
that you will select the Flip Vertical and Flip Horizontal icons instead.

Creating Thumbnail Images

If you have large images on your page, it can increase the download time for your
visitors, which forces them to wait. To avoid long download times, you can use
FrontPage to thumbnail the large images. When an image is thumbnailed, a large
image file gets replaced with a smaller file, and the smaller image is hyperlinked
to the larger image. Then, when your visitors click the small image, the original
large image will display.

To use the Auto Thumbnail icon, follow these steps:

1. Open a new document in FrontPage. Insert *mountain.jpg* into your
   FrontPage document:

2. To make the image smaller so it will take less time to download, select
   the image with the mouse pointer. Once the image is selected, click the
   Auto Thumbnail icon on the Pictures toolbar. The image, which is now
   a thumbnail, will become much smaller:

3. Previewing the page by clicking the Preview icon in the bottom-left corner
   of your page. In preview, you will be able to click the small image. When
   you click the small image, the large image will display in a new page.

The following is the HTML code FrontPage outputs for thumbnailing an image:

```
<a href="images/mountain.jpg">
<img border="2" src="images/mountain_small.jpg"
xthumbnail-orig-image="images/mountain.jpg" width="100"
height="54"></a>
```

Adding Text to Images

FrontPage provides an easy method for adding text to GIF images. This feature is helpful, for example, when you need to point something out in a graphic.

Note

Text can only be added to GIF images. If you try to add text to any image format other than GIF, FrontPage will automatically convert your image to the GIF format. This can produce unexpected results and may even increase download time due to a larger file size.

To add text to images, follow these steps:

1. Open a new document in FrontPage. Insert the *Clouds.gif* image into your FrontPage document.

2. After you have inserted the image, click the Text icon in the Pictures toolbar, and a text box will appear inside the image. You can type anything you want inside that text box. The text can even be formatted while inside the image. (For more on formatting text, please see Module 2.)

3. In the text box, type **Clouds**:

Adjusting Contrast and Brightness

To use the More Contrast, Less Contrast, More Brightness, and Less Brightness icons, follow these instructions:

1. Open a new document in FrontPage. Insert the *Sun.gif* image into your FrontPage document.

2. After the image has been inserted, use the More Contrast and Less Contrast icons in the Pictures toolbar to increase and decrease the contrast, respectively. Likewise, use the More Brightness and Less Brightness icons to increase and decrease the brightness of your image, respectively.

3. The following shows an image before and after the More Brightness option was applied several times:

Before   After

Cropping an Image

To crop an image, follow these directions:

1. Open a new document in FrontPage. Insert *Disk.gif* into your FrontPage document.

2. Select the image, and click the Crop icon on the Pictures toolbar.

3. After you click the Crop icon, a box with handles will be superimposed on your image. Using the mouse pointer, drag the handles of the box until you encompass the portion of the image that you wish to keep:

4. To crop out all the sections that are not inside the box, click the Crop icon on the Pictures toolbar again. All of the image that is outside of the box will be deleted.

4

Applying Transparency

When you look at something transparent, the things behind are visible. In an image, you can allow the background of a page to be visible through certain portions of an image. When you apply transparency to an image, you are changing the image so that anything behind the image such as a background image is seen through. To make an image transparent, a color from the image is removed to have the background be seen through. FrontPage only supports one color per image to be made transparent.

To make a color transparent, follow these directions:

1. Open a new document in FrontPage. Insert *Transparent.gif* into your document.

2. After you insert the image, click the Set Transparent Color icon on the Pictures toolbar.

3. After you have clicked the Set Transparent Color icon, hover the mouse pointer over the image. Notice that the mouse pointer changes to an eraser so you can select a color to make transparent.

4. Select the light blue color by clicking the cloud in the image. The following image shows the *Transparent.gif* before Set Transparent Color was applied and after Set Transparent Color was applied:

Note

Sometimes when you make a color transparent, the edges of the entire image may get blurry. To remove the blurry edges, I recommend that you use an image-editing program to edit the image and blend the outside edges of the image with its surroundings.

Adjusting Alignment

Just like text, images can be aligned in different ways. You can align images using the Align Left, Center, Align Right, and Justify icons on the Formatting toolbar, but there are even more image alignment options in the Picture Properties window.

To align images using the Picture Properties window, follow these directions:

1. Open a new document in FrontPage. Insert any image into your FrontPage document. Right-click the image and select the Picture Properties command.

2. In the Picture Properties window, select the Appearance tab. In the Appearance tab you can adjust the alignment of an image by choosing an option from the Alignment drop-down menu. Figure 4-1 shows the Picture Properties window and the options available in the Alignment field.

3. After you have chosen an option, click OK to close the Picture Properties window, and the image will align according to your selection.

1-Minute Drill

● What path would you take to launch the Picture Properties window?

● How can the blurry edges of an image color that has been made transparent be removed?

Positioning Images

While HTML was at first very limited in its capability to place objects accurately, the development of Cascading Style Sheets 2 (CSS2) enabled HTML to place images with pixel precision anywhere on the page. Because positioning is a Cascading Style Sheets 2 (CSS2) specification, many older browsers do not support it. FrontPage makes it easy for you to use this advanced capability.

● Right-click an image and select the Picture Properties command.
● By removing the blurry edges in an image-editing program.

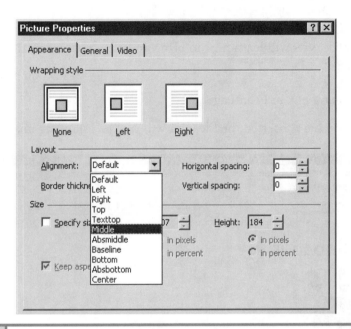

Figure 4-1 Alignment options in the Picture Properties window.

To position an image, follow these directions:

1. Open a new document in FrontPage. Insert the *Globe.gif* into your document.

2. Select the image using the mouse pointer. From the Pictures toolbar, click the Position Absolutely icon.

3. After you have clicked the Position Absolutely icon, hover the mouse pointer over the image. The mouse pointer will be replaced with the move pointer, and the move pointer will enable you to drag the image around the screen. Click the image and drag it to another location; you will be able to place it anywhere on the screen.

Stacking Objects

As we know, CSS2 enables positioning an image anywhere on a page, but it also enables you to place images on top of each other. Placing images on top of each other is called *stacking*.

Stacking Objects Above

In this exercise, you will learn how to bring an image forward so that it is over another image:

1. Open *above.htm* in FrontPage.

2. After you have inserted the file, you will see the following image:

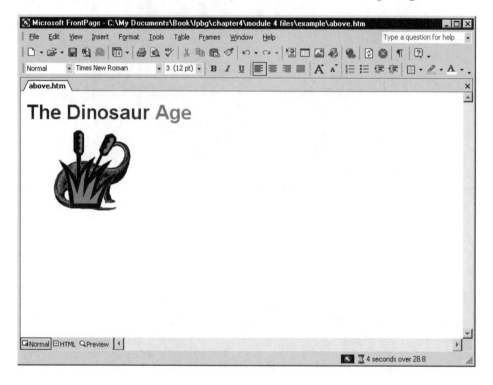

3. Select the dinosaur with the mouse pointer. Make sure that you do not select the grass. Once you have selected the dinosaur, click the Bring Forward icon on the Pictures toolbar.

4. The dinosaur will now be visible over the grass image:

Keep this file open because we will be using it in the next section.

Stacking Objects Below

In this exercise, you will learn how to move an image so that it is behind another image:

1. Open *stacking.htm* in FrontPage.

2. To move the dinosaur behind the grass, select the dinosaur with the mouse pointer and click the Send Backward icon on the Pictures toolbar.

3. After you have clicked the Send Backward icon, use the mouse pointer to drag the dinosaur towards the grass. You will notice that when it reaches the grass, the dinosaur image will go behind the grass:

Modifying Vertical Position

In FrontPage, the vertical arrangement of an image is determined by a number called the z-order. Z-order refers to the number assigned to an image in a 3-D plane. Because you are able to position an image vertically as well as horizontally, you are in fact arranging images in a three-dimensional space. When you try to position a lot of images on the screen, it is useful to know how to arrange the images vertically. That is where z-order plays a large role. In a nutshell, the larger the z-order number, the higher the image will be in comparison to other elements on the page. The lower the z-order number, the lower the image will be in comparison to other elements on the page.

Follow these directions to learn how to use z-order to position images in your pages:

1. Open the file *zorder.htm* in FrontPage. You will see three different geometric objects.

2. Before we use the z-order number to arrange the images, use the Position Absolutely command to stack each image:

Z-Order

3. After you have arranged the shapes, click the image on top and select Format | Position. The Position window will open (shown in Figure 4-2). Because you clicked on the image on top, the Position window corresponds to that top image.

Note

It does not matter which image is above the other images right now. Because the images will be rearranged several times, you may stack the images in any order you would like.

4. At the bottom of the Position window is the Z-Order field where you specify how images will be arranged vertically using numbers. Because there are three images, you will be using the numbers 1, 2, and 3. Please enter 1 into the Z-Order field:

Z-Order: 1

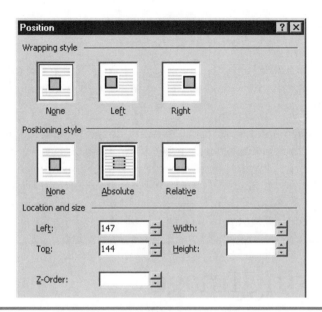

Figure 4-2   Using the Position window to arrange shapes

5. Click OK to close the Position window. The images should not have changed their vertical position.

6. Select the image in the middle and open the Position window (which means that the Position window corresponds to the middle image). Enter **2** into the Z-Order field. Click OK to close the window. You can now see that the middle image has moved to the top position, and the image that was on top is now in the middle.

7. Select the bottom image and open the Position window (which means that the Position window corresponds to the bottom-most image). Enter **3** into the Z-Order field. Click OK to close the Position window. The last image should now be on top.

Note

If you do not enter a z-order value for all images, the images will be stacked in the order in which they were inserted. You are not confined to using positive values. If you decide to add an image to go behind other images, you can enter a negative value.

Ask the Expert

Question: After I modify my images, I am asked if I want to overwrite the existing image while saving my document. Should I or should I not overwrite the existing image?

Answer: Do not overwrite the existing image. When you click Save, you will see the Save Embedded files window if any images were modified. To avoid overwriting an image, use the Rename icon from the Save Embedded files window and add an extra character to the original filename. This ensures that if you do not like the new version of the image, you can easily revert back to the older version.

Hyperlinking Images

In Module 3 you learned how to hyperlink text. The method of hyperlinking an image is almost the same. The only difference is that you are selecting an image instead of text to hyperlink.

Follow these directions to hyperlink an image:

1. Open a new document in FrontPage. Insert *image_hyperlink.htm* into your document. You will see some text and one image:

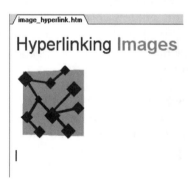

2. Right-click the image with the mouse pointer and select the Hyperlink command from the menu that pops up. This will open the Insert Hyperlink window.

3. In the Address field, enter **http://www.osborne.com**:

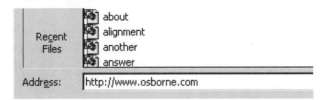

4. Click OK to close the Edit Hyperlink window. Preview the page in your browser. Now you can visit Osborne's Web site by clicking the image.

The following is the HTML code applied to the image we have hyperlinked:

```
<a href="http://www.osborne.com/"><img border="0"
src="temp/square.gif" width="128" height="128"></a>
```

─┼Note ──────────

As with text, you can make the hyperlinked image open a new browser window, send an e-mail, target a bookmark, and more. If you do not remember how to do these things, please refer back to Module 3.

Creating Hot Spots

You may have seen Web sites where you can visit different areas of a site or other sites by clicking different locations in a image. The hyperlinked locations in images are called *hot spots* (also sometimes called *image maps*). Hot spots enable you to create custom locations on an image and hyperlink them to different pages. There are three hot spot icons, the Rectangular Hotspot, the Circular Hotspot, and the Polygonal Hotspot.

─┼Note ──────────

Hot spot refers the shapes you create within the image that hyperlink to other things, not the image itself.

Creating Rectangular Hot Spots

1. Open a new document in FrontPage. Insert the file *imagemaps.htm*.

2. You will see a large map of the United States with some famous landmarks marked by graphic images. We are going to create a hyperlink for the Statue of Liberty.

3. Click the map with your mouse pointer, and the Pictures toolbar will appear if it is not already there. On the Pictures toolbar, click the Rectangular Hotspot icon.

4. After the Rectangular Hotspot icon has been selected, your mouse pointer will change to look like a pencil. Use the pencil to draw a rectangle that encompasses the Statue of Liberty so that it is all within the rectangle:

5. After you have finished drawing the rectangle, the Edit Hyperlink window will appear automatically. In the Edit Hyperlink window, enter **http:// www.newyork.com/** into the Address field. Click OK to close the Edit Hyperlink window.

Keep the page with the map of the United States open, as we will add to this map in the next section.

Creating Circular Hot Spots

Using the same map of the United States that we just added a rectangular hot spot to we will now learn how to create a circular hot spot:

1. Select the Circular Hotspot icon on the Pictures toolbar.

2. After you have selected the Circular Hotspot icon, use the cursor to draw a circle around the umbrella in the lower-right corner of the map. Make sure that the umbrella is within the boundaries of the circle:

3. In the Edit Hyperlink window that appears after the circular hot spot has been drawn, enter **http://www.miami.com/** into the Address field. Click OK to close the Edit Hyperlink window.

Please keep the map of the United States open, as we will add to this map in the next section.

Creating Polygonal Hot Spots

Now let's add a polygonal hot spot to the map of the United States. The polygonal hot spot is a little different than the other hot spots; when drawing the polygonal hot spot, you will need to click each time to create each side of the shape:

1. Select the Polygonal Hotspot icon on the Pictures toolbar.

2. After you have selected the Polygonal Hotspot icon, use the cursor to draw around the trees in the upper-left corner of the map. You will need to click each time you want the hot spot edge to angle to conform to the shape of the trees. Try to draw along the edges of the trees, and make sure that all of the trees are within the polygon:

Note

The Edit Hyperlink window will appear automatically after the polygonal hot spot has been drawn. In the Address field, enter **http://www.microsoft.com**. (Get it? Because Microsoft is located in Washington.)

Note

You can edit the hyperlink properties of a hot spot by right-clicking the hot spot and selecting the command for Picture Hotspot Properties.

3. Preview your page, and go ahead and test the three hot spots you've created in the last three sections.

Tip

If you cannot see the hotspots ever after selecting the image, select the image and press the Highlight Hotspot icon from the Pictures toolbar. FrontPage will display only the hotspots by not displaying the image. Press the Highlight Hotspot icon to see the image again. Your Web site visitors will see your images as normal. The Highlight Hotspot feature is used only during the editing of the image.

Inserting and Modifying Background Images

In designing a site, you can use images as the background of the site. Not only do background images provide a welcome change from solid colored backgrounds, background images look good as well.

Inserting Background Images

The instructions below will show you how to insert a background image:

1. Create a new document in FrontPage.

2. Right-click anywhere on the page and select the Page Properties command.

3. After you select the Page Properties command, the Page Properties window will appear. In the Page Properties window, click the Background tab:

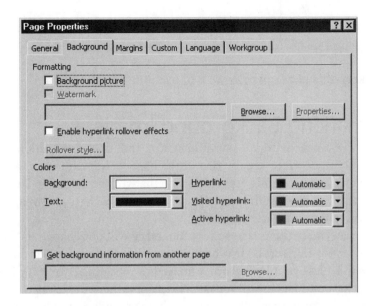

4. In the Background tab, check the Background picture box next. After you have checked that box, the empty field right below the Watermark box will become active:

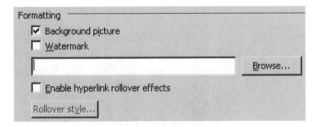

5. Click the Browse button to the right of the empty field, and browse until you find the *background.gif* image from the source files you downloaded.

6. After *background.gif* has been selected, the full path of the image will be shown in the empty field:

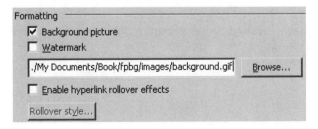

7. Click OK to close the Page Properties window. You will now see a background image in your page.

Please keep this page open, as we will use it in the next section.

Watermarking Background Images

When you have a page with a lot of information that doesn't fit on one screen, you need to scroll down to see the rest of the page. When you scroll a page, information on the page scrolls in the direction that you are scrolling. Background images also scroll along with the page. To prevent your background image from scrolling, you will watermark the image.

You can watermark the image so that the image will not change its position, even if the page is being scrolled. When a page is scrolled, the background image scrolls as well. Unless your background image is a repeating pattern or it is really large, the background image will repeat. The places where the background image repeats itself often produces a line that clearly marks where the background image ends and the where the same background image repeats. That line that is produced, which often ruins the look of your page and background, can be avoided by watermarking the background.

Follow these instructions to watermark an image:

1. Using the page that you just added the background image to. Right-click that page and select the Page Properties command. The Page Properties window will appear. Select the Background tab and check the Watermark box:

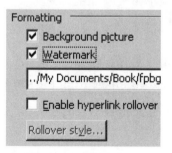

2. After you have checked the Watermark box, click OK to close the Page Properties window.

3. To see how the watermarked background image works, press ENTER a few times while in the page. You need to press ENTER because you will need to scroll in the page to see the watermarked image work. Keep pressing ENTER until you have to scroll down to see the last part of the page.

4. Preview the page and use the scroll bars to take you to the bottom of the document. You will see that the background image stays stationary while text or other elements move.

Inserting Background Colors

Follow these directions to insert a solid background color instead of an image:

1. Create a new page in FrontPage.

2. Right-click anywhere on the page and select the Page Properties command. From the Page Properties window, click the Background tab.

3. In the Colors section, click the Background drop-down menu and select a color that you like:

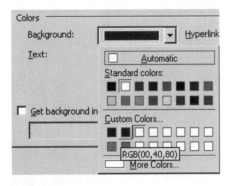

4. After you have selected a color, click OK to close the Page Properties window. The new background color will be visible in your page.

Note

If you are in a page that already has a background image, before you select a background color, you must uncheck the Background picture box in the Page Properties window. Only after the Background picture box has been unchecked will the background color be visible.

Ask the Expert

Question: When I use a smaller image as the background of my page, the image repeats itself over and over in the page. Is there a way I can prevent that?

Answer: No. When background images are smaller than the width and height of the page, they will repeat themselves until all empty spots are filled. You can either use a tiled (repeating) background image or use an image large enough to fit the width and height of your page, but remember that it will take your visitors longer to download and display larger images in their browsers.

Using Clip Art

FrontPage provides free images called clip art. Clip art can vary from simple lines and arrows to drawings of food, animals, symbols, and more. You can download even more clip art from Microsoft and/or other Web sites.

Inserting Clip Art

1. Open a new document in FrontPage.

2. From the Standard toolbar, select Insert | Picture | Clip Art:

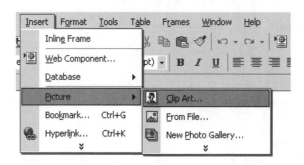

3. After you have selected Clip Art, the Insert Clip Art pane will appear to the right of your page. In the Search text field, type **internet**:

4. After you have typed **internet**, click the Search button, and the Insert Clip Art pane will display boxes with clip-art images for you to choose from.

Note

If you have an active Internet connection while you search, more images will be displayed in the Insert Clip Art Pane. The clip-art images are download from Microsoft's Web site, and with an active internet connection, the search results from Microsoft's Web site will be displayed.

Note

To search for more specific images using the Insert Clip Art pane, click the Modify button, and you will then be able to search for images using the Search field.

5. To add a clip-art image to your document, you can do one of two things:

- Place the mouse pointer over the image of your choice. When you place your mouse pointer over the image, an arrow will appear

4

directly to the right of the image. Click that arrow and select Insert from the drop-down menu:

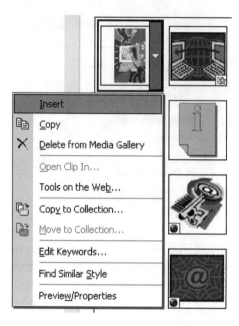

- Select the image of your choice, and drag and drop the image directly into your document.

6. If the image is too large for your Web page, you can resize it by going to the corner of the image and dragging the sizing handles until the image is the size you want.

7. If you want the image to look clearer and/or you want to remove any jagged edges, click the Resample icon on the Pictures toolbar. Clicking the Resample icon will automatically make the image clearer and remove any jagged edges.

Using the Clip Organizer

The Clip Organizer offers another way to search for clip art:

1. Open a new document in FrontPage. Display the Clip Art pane by selecting Insert | Picture | Clip Art.

2. At the bottom of the Clip Art pane, in the See also section, click the command for Clip Organizer.

3. After you have clicked Clip Organizer, the Clip Organizer window will open, as shown in Figure 4-3. To search for clip-art images, enter a word into the Search field. Once you enter a word into the Search field, click the Search button, and the Clip Organizer will display clip art that matches your search word.

4. To insert clip art into your document, place the mouse pointer over an image and use the arrow that appears on the right to choose Copy. After you have copied the clip art, paste it into your document by right-clicking in your document and selecting the Paste command.

Note

There is an easier method of inserting clip art images into your documents: select the image of your choice, and drag and drop the image directly into your document.

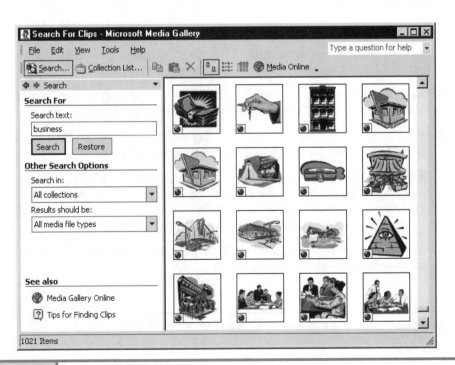

Figure 4-3 Searching for clips is easy.

1-Minute Drill

- Do clip-art images from the Web get displayed along with your standard search results?

- Can the Media Gallery be used to insert clip-art images into your documents?

project.htm

Project 4-1: Adding Images

The following are the goals for this project:

- Add an image

- Align the image in relation to text

- Add a background image

- Add transparency

- Position an object

Step by Step

1. Open a new document in FrontPage. Open the *project.htm* file in your document.

2. Insert the image *Fish.jpg* in front of the text: the image should go right below "Ocean Life" and before "A rich" in the first line.

3. Once the image has been placed, click the Left Align icon on the Formatting toolbar. This will align the image toward the left side of the document.

4. Now, let's add the background image. Right-click anywhere on the page and select the Page Properties command; the Page Properties window will appear.

5. In the Page Properties window, select the Background tab and check the Background picture box. Click Browse and browse for *back.jpg* from the source files you downloaded. After you have found and selected *back.jpg*, click OK to close the Page Properties window.

6. Now we will insert an image that will be positioned absolutely. Insert the *transparent.gif* file into your document.

- Yes. If you are connected to the Internet, you will automatically see online clip art displayed in the Insert Clip Art Pane with your search results.

- Yes. You can either copy and paste or drag and drop the clip art images.

7. Once the *transparent.gif* image is in place, select the image. From the Pictures toolbar, click on the Transparency icon. Your mouse pointer will change to an eraser. Click on the white space surrounding the goldfish with your mouse pointer.

8. After the transparency has been applied, click the Position Absolutely icon on the Pictures toolbar.

9. Drag the *transparent.gif* image toward the beginning of the copyright text: "Text Copyright Encarta Online." Use either the Send Backward icon or z-order to make the fish go behind the text.

10. You may add a highlight color and text color to the copyright text. (You learned how to do that in Module 3.) This step is optional, but it does increase the readability of the copyright text.

11. Your page is now finished and should look like Figure 4-3.

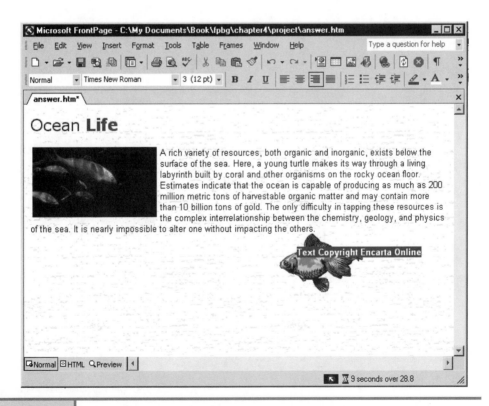

| **Figure 4-4** | The finished page for Project 4-1 |

Summary

Using images is a great way to enrich your site. FrontPage makes it easy to insert and edit images. You can position images exactly on screen, make an image color transparent, and more. By using clip art, you can add a variety of images to your site.

☑ Mastery Check

1. What file extensions will FrontPage automatically convert your images to?

_____

_____

2. Will the Pictures toolbar automatically appear when you select an image? If it does not, what steps should you take to display the Pictures toolbar?

_____

_____

3. When you crop an image, does the image resize?

_____

_____

4. What underlying Web technology/language is fundamental for positioning and stacking elements?

_____

_____

5. Why would you use the Highlight Hotspots icon?

_____

_____

6. How would you watermark a background image?

_____

_____

7. Is clip art confined to only images such as banners and arrows?

_____

_____

4

Module 5

Drawing and Using Multimedia

The Goals of This Module

- Draw using the Drawing toolbar
- Learn how to use WordArt
- Include sounds in your documents
- Incorporate videos into your documents

The major disadvantage of Hypertext Markup Language (HTML) is its inability to enable full creativity in design. In the previous module, you learned how to use Cascading Style Sheets (CSS) to position an image anywhere on the screen. In this module you will learn how to draw simple and complex shapes, incorporate sounds, and offer video files.

Drawing in FrontPage

With the advent of a Web technology called Vector Markup Language (VML), developers are able to draw lines and shapes directly by using mathematical conversions within the HTML code itself, and the supporting images and files are created and saved automatically. FrontPage enables you to draw lines and shapes without your having to know VML. Because VML is part of HTML code, FrontPage writes the necessary VML code in the background for the shapes and lines you draw. Best of all, FrontPage enables you to make all your shapes three dimensional with numerous customizations.

Note

Extensible Markup Language (XML) is used to link portions of a shape together. As usual, FrontPage handles all the XML tags, along with VML, automatically.

The Drawing Toolbar

Just as there is a Pictures toolbar for adding pictures, there is a Drawing toolbar for drawing. To launch the Drawing toolbar, select View | Toolbars | Drawing.

The Drawing toolbar will appear at the bottom of your FrontPage window. The following is an illustration of the Drawing toolbar:

Note

If at anytime you would like the Drawing toolbar to be closer to what you are working on for easier access to the icons, remember that you can move the toolbar anywhere you would like on your screen.

Table 5-1 shows each option on the Drawing toolbar and gives its name and function.

Note

Bookmark this table, as I will be referring back to it as we progress through this module.

Icon	Name	Function
Draw ▾	Draw	Draws and modifies simple shapes
▷	Select Object	Selects objects using the mouse pointer
AutoShapes ▾	AutoShapes	Offers predrawn lines, shapes, arrows, and more
╲	Line	Draws a line
↘	Arrow	Draws a line that has an arrow
▭	Rectangle	Draws rectangular shapes
◯	Oval	Draws circular shapes
▤	Text Box	Inserts text as an object
◢	Insert WordArt	Enables you to add custom, styled text
▣	Insert Clip Art	Inserts custom images
▧	Insert Picture From File	Inserts pictures

Table 5-1   The Drawing Toolbar

Icon	Name	Function
	Fill Color	Specifies the fill color of an object
	Line Color	Specifies the color of the line
	Font Color	Specifies the color of the text
	Line Style	Customizes the thickness of a line
	Dash Style	Customizes the dash style of a line
	Arrow Style	Customizes the type of arrow in an arrow line
	Shadow Style	Adds a drop shadow to any object
	3-D Style	Adds a three-dimensional effect to your shapes and designs

Table 5-1   The Drawing Toolbar (*continued*)

Using the Drawing Tools

Now that you are familiar with the Drawing toolbar, let's learn how to use the various drawing tools.

Drawing Arrows and Lines

Sometimes you may need to point out something in your Web page. A great way to do that is to draw lines using the Line and Arrow icons on the Drawing toolbar. I will teach you how to draw a line with an arrow and from this you can easily infer how to draw a line; a line is drawn the same way as a line with an arrow, except the arrow doesn't appear at the end of the line:

1. Open a new document in FrontPage. Open the *arrowline.htm* file. (That file is included with the source files you should have downloaded from http://www.Osborne.com or http://www.kirupa.com/frontpage.)

2. After you have opened the *arrowline.htm* file, you will see a set of questions and answers:

5

arrowline.htm*

Matching
Match the correct answer with the problem.

a. 2 x 3   **7**

b. 9 + 3   **6**

c. 6 / 2   **12**

d. 12 - 5   **3**

3. Launch the Drawing toolbar, and click the Arrow icon (see Table 5-1).

4. After you have clicked the Arrow icon, place the mouse pointer over the document, and you will see that the cursor is now replaced with a crosshair. A crosshair looks like a plus sign.

5. If we look at the questions and answers, we can see that the answer to d is 7. To draw a line with an arrow from d to 7, click after the formula 12–5 and hold down the mouse button. While holding down the mouse button, move the crosshair toward the 7; you will see that dashed lines follow the crosshair. Drag the crosshair from the first point to the 7 and click. The line and the arrow will be drawn from d to 7:

Matching

Match the correct answer with the problem.

a. 2 x 3   7

b. 9 + 3   6

c. 6 / 2   12

d. 12 - 5   3

Note

When you draw arrow lines from one point to another point, the arrow will point in the direction you are going to. If you are going from point A to point B, the arrow will point toward point B.

6. Repeat this for a, b and c. Once you have finished, your example should look like this:

Matching

Match the correct answer with the problem.

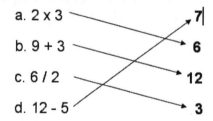

a. 2 x 3   7

b. 9 + 3   6

c. 6 / 2   12

d. 12 - 5   3

Drawing and Moving Rectangles and Circular Shapes

In addition to straight lines, you can also draw rectangles and circular shapes (circles and ovals) in FrontPage. These two features can be used for decorative purposes or to emphasize something on your Web page. To learn how to draw shapes and move them to create an exclamation point, follow these directions:

1. Create a new document in FrontPage.

2. Once you have opened the new page, make sure the Drawing toolbar is displayed.

3. To draw the period of the exclamation point, click the Oval icon on the Drawing toolbar. After you have clicked the Oval icon, click anywhere in your document and, while holding down the mouse button, drag the crosshair until the silhouette image of a circle is the size you want. Release the mouse button. Your circle should look similar to this:

4. To draw the rectangle that we will use in our exclamation point, click the Rectangle icon on the Drawing toolbar. Click anywhere in your document to set the first point of the rectangle. Once you have clicked, drag the mouse cursor until you get a rectangular shape:

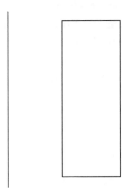

5

5. Because we want to make an exclamation mark, we need to move the circle and rectangle so that it creates an exclamation mark. To move either of the elements into position, move the cursor so that it is inside the shape. When you move the cursor to the inside of the shape, the cursor will change to a mouse pointer arrow with four arrows pointing outward below it; when you click in the shape and hold the mouse button down, the mouse pointer will disappear and only the outward pointing arrows will be visible. These arrows indicate that you may move the shape in any direction. After you have clicked inside the shape, hold the mouse button down and drag the shape to its new location to create an exclamation point:

Using AutoShapes

FrontPage comes with predrawn lines, shapes, arrows, and more that you can use for common tasks. You can see all of the available options by clicking the AutoShapes icon on the Drawing toolbar and browsing the options of lines, shapes, and so on.

To insert the Lightning Bolt into a document, follow these steps:

1. Open a new document in FrontPage.

2. After you have opened a new document, click AutoShapes on the Drawing toolbar. From the AutoShapes menu, select Basic Shapes and the Lightning Bolt:

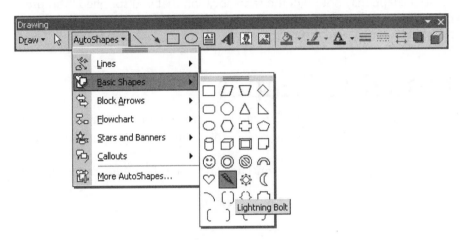

3. Once you have selected the Lightning Bolt, click anywhere in your document and drag. The lightning bolt will appear as you drag. When the lightning is the shape and size that you want it to be, release the mouse button. Your lightning bolt will look something like this:

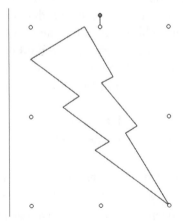

Note

Because shapes drawn in FrontPage are positioned absolutely, you can place it anywhere in your document. Because of that, when viewed under various monitor sizes, your shape may not be in the same location that you specified. This problem becomes more apparent when the shapes are added along with regular elements such as text, images, and more.

Customizing Shapes

The shapes and elements you draw can be customized in numerous ways. In this section you will learn how to resize, rotate, and skew drawn elements:

1. Open a new document in FrontPage and open the *rotate_resize.htm* file:

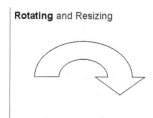

Rotating and Resizing

2. Select the arrow in the document. When you select the arrow, a small green circle(s), white circle(s), and yellow diamond(s) will appear, surrounding the arrow. These are called the rotate, resize, and skew features, respectively, and they are used to configure the orientation and size of the object once it has been drawn. Table 5-2 shows each feature and identifies its color, name, and function.

Image	Color	Name	Function
●	Green	Rotate option	Rotates the object
○	White	Resize option	Resizes the object; each white circle resizes a different portion of the object
◇	Yellow	Skew option	Modifies certain characteristics of the object; this feature varies according to the object, as some objects do not feature this symbol when selected

Table 5-2   The Rotate, Resize, and Skew Features

3. Returning to our document, to rotate the arrow, move the mouse over the green circle. Click the green circle, hold down the mouse button, and drag in a circular motion. You will see that an outline of the arrow previews how it will look when rotated

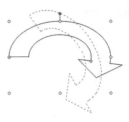

5

4. To apply the changes, release the mouse button.

5. To resize the arrow, move the mouse over the white circle. When you move the mouse over a white circle, the mouse cursor will change to show you in what directions the object can be resized. Click a white circle, hold down the mouse button, and drag to resize. To apply the change, release the mouse button:

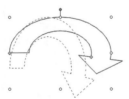

6. To skew the arrow, click a yellow square, hold down the mouse button, and drag in any direction. When you drag, you will notice that some characteristics of the arrow change. The action of this feature varies, depending on the shape you are working with:

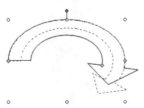

Adding Colors to Shapes

Besides the shape and size of an object, another characteristic that can be modified is the color of the object. There are two ways in which you can change the color of an object. You can change the color of the inside of the object by using the Fill Color icon, and/or you can change the color of the outline of the object by using the Line Color icon.

Changing Fill Color

The fill color of a shape is the color that it is filled with. To change the fill color of an object, follow these directions:

1. Open *color.htm* in FrontPage (it may look familiar to you).

2. Select the rectangle that is above the circle. Click the arrow to the right of the Fill Color icon (see Table 5-1) in the Drawing toolbar. From the color menu that appears, choose the color navy blue.

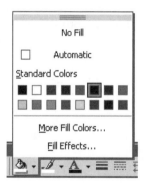

3. After you release the mouse button, the rectangle will be filled with the navy blue color.

4. Follow steps 1 and 2 to add a fill color to the circle. Once both the rectangle and the circle have a color applied to them, your screen should look something like this:

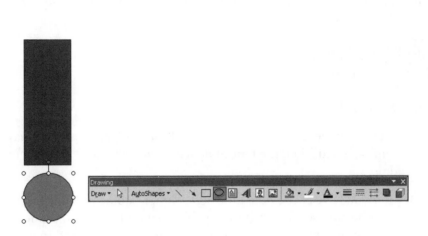

Keep the *color.htm* file open, as we will use it in the next section.

Changing Line Color

In this section, you will learn how to modify the outline color of a shape:

1. Using the same *color.htm* file we worked on in the previous section, select the circle with your mouse pointer.

2. Click the arrow to the right of the Line Color icon (see Table 5-1) on the Drawing toolbar. From the color menu, choose any color that contrasts with the color you chose to fill the circle with.

3. When you release the mouse, the circle will be outlined with the color you selected. Your circle will look something like this:

5

Changing Line Characteristics

Along with the shape, size, and color of an object, you can also change its line characteristics. When a shape is drawn in FrontPage, the default black, ¾ pt width line is drawn. FrontPage enables you to modify a line in numerous ways beyond the default setting.

Modifying Line Style

To change the style of a line, follow these directions:

1. Open the *lines.htm* page, and select the circle.

2. When you select a shape, the line is selected as well. Once you have the shape selected, click the Line Style icon (see Table 5-1) on the Drawing toolbar.

3. After you have clicked the Line Style icon, a submenu will appear. From the submenu, select 6 pt (pt is an abbreviation for "point," which is a unit of measurement equal to about 1/72 of an inch and is used to measure type; in this case, it is used to measure the width of the line):

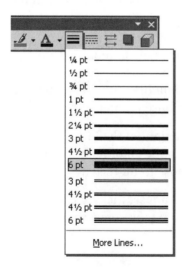

4. After you have selected 6 pt, the circle's outline will be thicker.

Please keep this file open, as you will use it in the next section also.

Adding Dashes

Lines always do not have to be solid. Dash styles in FrontPage enable you to be more creative with lines. By changing dash styles, you can use differently spaced dashes instead of the default, solid line. Follow these directions to add a Dash style to the circle we worded with in the previous section:

1. In the same file from the previous section, select the circle and click the Dash Style icon (see Table 5-1) on the Drawing toolbar.

2. From the Dash Style menu that appears, select Long Dash Dot. This illustration shows the circle with the Long Dash Dot style applied:

Applying Special Effects

You have already learned now to modify the shape, color, and outline of an object, but there are still other ways to modify objects. FrontPage enables you to add text, texture, patterned lines, and more to the inside of objects.

5

Adding Text

1. In Module 4 you learned how to place text on top of an image. In this section you will learn how to create a text box, which is text with a border surrounding it. Create a new document in FrontPage. Click the Text Box icon (see Table 5-1) on the Drawing toolbar. Once the Text Box icon has been clicked, draw a rectangular box in your document:

2. Inside the box, enter my name (or you can use your name, if you'd like). If your name is long like mine, it may be too long to fit completely inside the text box you created. To make it fit, resize the text box by dragging the handles until your entire name fits.

3. Just like shapes, you can modify the text box's line characteristics, dash style, fill colors, and more just like any regular shape. In the following illustration, you can see how my name looks inside a text box that I formatted:

Note

You can edit the text's font, font style, color, and more by using the Formatting toolbar just as you would for regular text.

Adding Shadows

To create the illusion of shapes floating on screen, you can add shadows. The add a shadow to a shape, follow these directions:

1. From a blank document in FrontPage, draw a shape.

2. Select the shape you just drew and click the Shadow Style icon (see Table 5-1) in the Drawing toolbar. From the shadow menu that appears, select a shadow style, as in Figure 5-1.

3. After you release the mouse button, the shadow style you selected will be applied to the shape.

Adding Fill Effects

In this section, you will learn how to go beyond simple fill and line styles by using custom patterns that are built in:

1. Open the *specialeffects.htm* file in FrontPage. Select the rectangle, and click the Fill Color icon (see Table 5-1) on the Drawing toolbar.

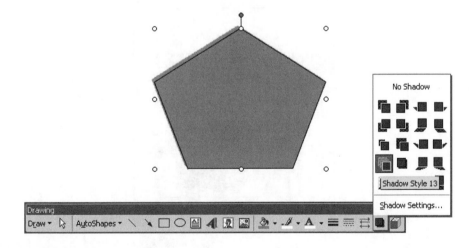

| **Figure 5-1** | Adding a shadow effect to a shape |

5

2. From the Fill Color menu that appears, select the Fill Effects command :

3. Once you have clicked the Fill Effects command, the Fill Effects window will appear. In the Fill Effects window, select the Texture tab.

4. In the Texture tab, select the Denim texture.

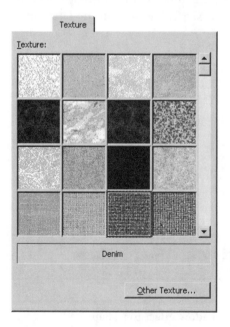

5. Click OK to close the Fill Effects window, and your shape will be filled with the Denim texture.

Keep this file open, as we will add to it in the next section.

Adding Patterned Lines

To add patterned lines to your shape, follow these directions:

1. In the same file from the previous section, click the circle and select the Line Color icon from the Drawing toolbar.

2. From the menu that opens, select the command for Patterned Lines. The Patterned Lines window will open.

5

3. Select the solid diamond pattern from the Patterned Lines window. After you select the solid diamond pattern, press OK. The circle will have the solid diamond line pattern applied.

1-Minute Drill

● Can line styles be applied to lines, as well as shapes?

● Can a shape have custom fills and patterns?

● Yes. Because lines and shapes both contain lines, line styles can be applied to them.
● Yes. To add custom fills and patterns, use the Fill Effects and Patterned Lines command found in the Fill Color and Line Color icons, respectively.

Using 3-D

All of the shapes you have worked with so far have been in 2-D. A nice way to enhance shapes in your site is by converting the shapes into 3-D. We will now learn how to convert 2-D shapes into 3-D shapes and then learn how to adjust the new 3-D shapes.

Converting 2-D into 3-D

To convert a 2-D shape in to a 3-D shape, follow these directions:

1. Open the *3d.htm* file in FrontPage.

2. Select the square with the mouse pointer. On the Drawing toolbar, click the 3-D Style icon (see Table 5-1).

3. From the 3-D Style menu that appears, select 3-D Style 3:

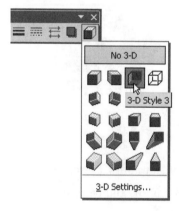

4. After you have selected 3-D Style 3, your square will now be three-dimensional:

─┤*Note* ───────────────────────────

3-D styles can be applied to any shape, whether created by you or created with the AutoShapes icon. The only exception is WordArt. You cannot make WordArt 3-D by using 3-D styles.

Adjusting 3-D Settings

There are numerous ways in which you can customize the 3-D styles that FrontPage supplies.

Adding Tilt

To rotate a 3-D shape, follow these directions:

1. Open the file *3dsettings.htm* in FrontPage. You will see a pentagon.

2. Select the pentagon with the mouse pointer. On the Drawing toolbar, select the 3-D Style icon. From the 3-D Style menu, select 3-D Settings:

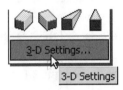

3. After you have selected 3-D Settings, the 3-D Settings toolbar will appear in your FrontPage window:

   Table 5-3 shows each icon on the 3-D Settings toolbar and gives its name and function.

4. Go back to your document, and select the pentagon with the mouse pointer. On the 3-D Settings toolbar, click the Tilt Down icon (see Table 5-3). Your entire shape will tilt downward slightly. You can keep clicking the Tilt Down icon until the shape is tilted as far as you would like. The Tilt Up icon (see Table 5-3) works the same way except in the opposite direction. The

Icon	Name	Function
![icon]	3-D On/Off	Toggles the selected shape from 3-D to 2-D or vice-versa
![icon]	Tilt Down	Incrementally turns a 3-D object downward
![icon]	Tilt Up	Incrementally turns a 3-D object upward
![icon]	Tilt Left	Incrementally tilts a 3-D object to the left
![icon]	Tilt Right	Incrementally tilts a 3-D object to the right
![icon]	Depth	Specifies the depth of a 3-D object
![icon]	Direction	Orients a 3-D object to face a different direction
![icon]	Lighting	Adjusts the light source and darkness or brightness of the 3-D object
![icon]	Surface	Adjusts the surface of the 3-D object
![icon]	3-D Color	Changes the color of the 3-D areas in your shape only

Table 5-3　The 3-D Settings Toolbar

following image shows our pentagon before and after the Tilt Down command was applied:

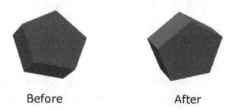

Before　　　　　　　　After

Note

The Tilt Left and Tilt Right icons work the same way as the Tilt Up and Tilt Down icons, except the Tilt Left and Tilt Right icons to rotate the 3-D shape horizontally.

Keep this page open, as we will use it in the next section.

Adding Depth

To add depth to your 3-D shape, follow these directions:

1. Using the same page from the previous section, select the pentagon with the mouse pointer and click the Depth icon (see Table 5-3) on the 3-D Settings toolbar.

2. A menu will appear that offers various point (pt) values. Select the 72 pt from the list. Your 3-D shape will increase in depth to the new value of 72 points:

Before   After

Please keep this document open, as we will use it in the next section.

Adding Light

The Lighting icon is used to adjust how the light hits your 3-D shape

1. Using the same page from the previous section, select the pentagon with the mouse pointer and click the Lighting icon (see Table 5-3) on the 3-D Settings toolbar.

5

2. From the menu that appears, choose the option for lighting all sides of the shape evenly:

The following image shows the pentagon with this option applied:

Please keep this document open, as we will use it in the next section.

Changing the Surface

The Surface icon changes the surface of your 3-D shapes. Changing the surface of a 3-D shape changes how light and color will reflect.

Follow these directions to change the surface of your shape:

1. Using the same page from the previous section, select the pentagon with the mouse pointer and click the Surface icon (see Table 5-3) on the 3-D Settings toolbar.

2. From the menu that appears, select Plastic:

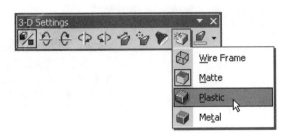

The following image shows the pentagon with the plastic surface effect applied:

Please keep the document open, as we will add to it in the next section.

Changing the Color

Earlier in the module, you learned that the Fill Color icon on the Drawing toolbar changes the overall color of a shape. That is not true when adding a Fill Color to a 3-D shape. The 3-D Color icon on the 3-D Settings toolbar changes the 3-D areas of your image only, which means that only the sides of the shape will change color.

Follow these directions to change the color of a 3-D shape:

1. Using the same page from the previous section, select the pentagon with the mouse pointer and click the 3-D Color icon (see Table 5-3) on the 3-D Settings toolbar.

2. From the menu that appears, select Lime:

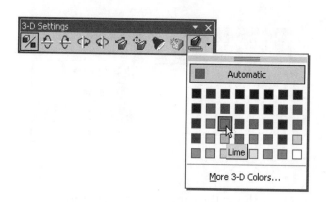

The following image shows the pentagon with the 3-D color lime applied to it:

Using WordArt

FrontPage comes with a handy tool that enables you to add custom text effects to regular text. This feature, appropriately dubbed WordArt, is found on the Drawing toolbar.

To learn how to use WordArt, follow these directions:

1. Open the *wordart.htm* file in FrontPage.

2. Highlight the word "FrontPage." Once it has been highlighted, click the Insert WordArt icon (see Table 5-1) on the Drawing toolbar. After you have clicked the Insert WordArt icon, the WordArt Gallery window will appear:

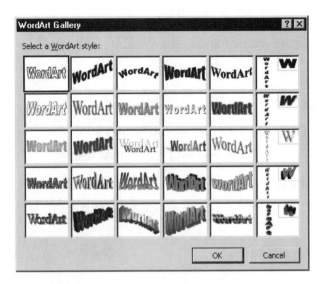

3. Select a WordArt Style from the WordArt Gallery and click the OK. After you have clicked OK, the Edit WordArt Text window will appear. In this window, you may change the font, text, point size, and text style:

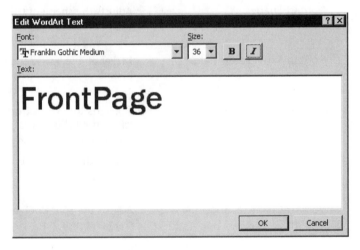

4. When you are finished in the WordArt Text Window, click OK and "FrontPage" will appear in the document in the style(s) you chose.

5. After "FrontPage" appears in the document with the style(s) that you chose applied, the WordArt toolbar will appear. You can click any of the icons in the WordArt toolbar to modify certain characteristics of your WordArt. Table 5-4 shows each option on the WordArt toolbar and gives its name and function.

1-Minute Drill

- Can WordArt be applied to any text in FrontPage?
- Are 3-D effects limited to only simple geometric shapes?

Icon	Name	Function
	Insert WordArt	Inserts WordArt text
	WordArt Gallery	Offers WordArt styles
	Format WordArt	Customizes various options such as line, shape, color, and so on
	WordArt Shape	Adjusts the shape of the text
	WordArt Same Letter Heights	Makes all the letters the same height
	WordArt Vertical Text	Converts the words from reading left to right (horizontal) to reading top to bottom (vertical)
	WordArt Alignment	Adjusts the alignment
	WordArt Character Spacing	Adjusts the space between each character or letter

Table 5-4   The WordArt Toolbar

- Yes
- No. 3-D effects can be applied to any shape drawn or inserted into FrontPage.

Using Sound

Before you add sound to your site, you should consider the advantages and disadvantages. One advantage is that short sound clips are a great way to keep your visitors entertained, though, in most cases, sound should be used sparingly. The following are some of the disadvantages associated with using sound:

● Increased download times for your visitors

● May distract visitors from reading the information on your site

● Some sounds may not play back properly on your visitor's computer

5

Adding Background Sound

Follow these directions to add background sound to your site:

1. Open the file *sound.htm* in FrontPage. Once the page has been opened, right-click any empty part of that page and select the command for Page Properties. In the Page Properties window, select the General tab. In the General tab, you will see an area marked "Background sound":

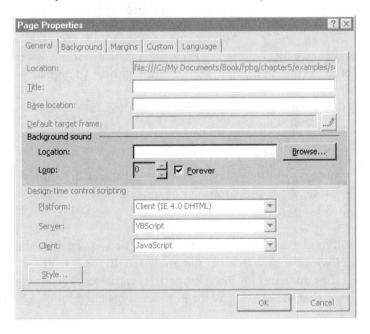

Ask the Expert

Question: What sound formats can be played as background music on a Web page?

Answer: You may use any sound format for your background music. Widely used sound formats include Audio Interchange File Format (AIFF), Wave (WAV), Musical Instrument Digital Interface (MIDI), MPEG Audio Layer-3 (MP3), and many more. The two most common formats for sounds in a Web page are WAV and MIDI. For background sounds, MIDI files are preferred because of their compact size. A difference between background sounds and regular sounds is that you do not control background sounds.

2. Using the Browse button in the Background sound section, locate the *stars.mid* file and insert it into the Location field:

3. Once you have the sound file located and inserted, click OK to close the Page Properties window.

4. Preview the page by clicking the Preview command in the lower-left corner of the FrontPage window, and you will hear the music play.

Keep this document open, as we will use it in the next section as well.

Managing Sound

By default, FrontPage will keep playing the music forever until the visitor closes the page. To customize the exact number of times the sound should play, follow these directions:

1. While still in our document from the last section, go back to the Page Properties window by right clicking anywhere in the document and selecting the command for Page Properties. In the Background sound area, you will see that the check box for Forever is checked; uncheck that box.

2. To the left of the Forever check box is the Loop field; enter **3** into the Loop field. The number that you enter into the Loop field corresponds to the number of times you want the music to play (loop):

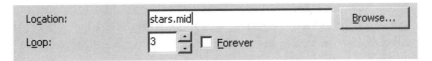

3. After you have entered **3** into the Loop field, click OK to close the Page Properties window.

4. Preview the page; the sound will play three times and stop.

The following is the HTML code that FrontPage uses to incorporate Background sound files. You can see in the code that the loop value is set to 3. A value of –1 is assigned to a sound clip that plays forever:

```
<bgsound src="stars.mid" loop="3">
```

Note

Sometimes your visitors may not have the required software on their computer to hear music playing from a browser. If your visitors do not have the required software, the will be unable to hear the music on your site. You can provide links to sites where they can download free music-playing software. Two links that you can point your visitors to download music-playing software are Beatnik's Audio Player (http://www.beatnik.com/) and Microsoft's Windows Media Player (http://www.microsoft.com/windows/windowsmedia/)

Using Video

With the number of users having fast Internet connections growing rapidly, an increasing number of Web sites use video to engage and inform the visitors. FrontPage enables the use of video in your pages without having to use another program. You should provide links to sites where your visitors can download the software that they may need to view the video on your Web site. Two links that you can refer your visitors to are Windows Media Player (http://www.microsoft.com/windows/windowsmedia/) and Apple QuickTime (http://www.apple.com/quicktime/download/).

5

Adding Video

Follow these directions to add video to your page:

1. Create a new document in FrontPage. From the Standard toolbar, select Insert | Picture | Video. You may have to expand the list by clicking the small down arrow in the submenu if you do not immediately see the Video command.

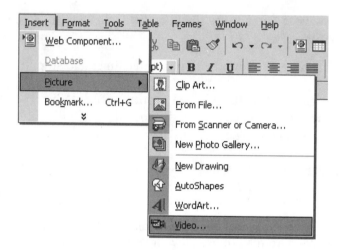

2. From the Video window that appears, browse to and select the *video.avi* file you downloaded earlier.

3. Once you have located the file, click OK, and the video file will be displayed in FrontPage. You can view the video by clicking the Preview command in the lower-left corner of the FrontPage window.

Managing Video

You can decide when and for how long the video should play. By default, the video clip will play automatically when the page is viewed in a browser and will play only once.

Determining Video Play

To change it so that the video will play only when the mouse pointer is moved over the video, follow these directions:

1. Right-click the video and select the command for Picture Properties. From the Picture Properties window, select the On mouse over option in the Start area:

2. Click OK to close the Picture Properties window. Preview the page and move the mouse cursor over the movie, and the movie will play.

Please keep this document open, as we will use it in the next section as well.

Setting a Video Loop

Just like looping sound, you can loop video as well:

1. In the same document we used in the last section, open the Picture Properties window.

2. In the Picture Properties window, there is a section marked "Repeat." In the Repeat section, there is a Loop field. The Loop field determines the number of times a video will play. Enter **2** into the Loop field.

3. Below the Loop field is the Loop delay field. The Loop delay field determines the number of milliseconds between the looping of the video. Enter **3** into the Loop delay field:

The following is the HTML code that FrontPage outputs to display video. In the code you can see the video options we selected:

```
<img border="0" dynsrc="video.AVI" start="mouseover" width="320"
height="240" loopdelay="3" loop="2">
```

1-Minute Drill

- What is the maximum number of times a sound will play by default?
- Does the Loop Delay action cause any changes in the initial playback of the video?

index.htm

Project 5-1: Adding Sound, Video, and Shapes

In this project you will learn how to incorporate and format sound, video, and shapes. The following are the goals for this project:

- Hyperlink to other pages
- Add background sound
- Use lines
- Insert a video

Step by Step

1. Create a new FrontPage Web (see Module 2). Import the entire Project folder from the source files you downloaded. Once the entire Project folder has been imported into your FrontPage Web, open the *index.htm* file.

2. Once you have opened the *index.htm* file, you will see three bulleted items below General Information. You need to hyperlink these items to an existing

---

- Forever or a limited number that you choose
- No. The Loop delay only effects the amount of time between the loops of a video, not before the first time it is played.

file: hyperlink "Australia" to the file *australia.htm*, hyperlink "Video of a Kangaroo" to the file *video.htm*, and hyperlink "Take the Australia Quiz" to the page *quiz.htm*.

3. Now, you need to add background music to the *australia.htm* file. Go to the Folders menu (View | Folders) and open the file *australia.htm*.

4. Once *australia.htm* has been opened, go to the Page Properties window and add the sound file *australia.mid*. The sound should loop only once.

5. From the *australia.htm* file currently open, add a hyperlink to the text "Return to the Main Page." You should link to the file *index.htm* for it is your main page.

6. Save this page, and open the file *video.htm*. Place your mouse pointer in the line below the first line of text. Insert the video file *video.avi* into this location. This file is included along with the example files. Do not make any modifications to the video properties:

5

7. Hyperlink the text "Return to the Main Page" to the *index.htm* page.

8. Save this file, and open the file *quiz.htm*. When the *quiz.htm* file has been opened, you will see some scrambled words and answers. Using the Arrow icon on the Drawing toolbar, draw an arrow line from the scrambled word to the answer:

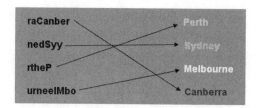

9. Hyperlink the text "Return to the Main Page" to the *index.htm* page. Save this file, and reopen the file *index.htm*. From the menu bar, select File | Preview in Browser. The Preview in Browser window will appear. Click the Preview button in the Preview in Browser window, and your site will be viewable in your default browser. You can now click the links and see how your site will look to visitors.

To see the final version of your project should look like, open the file *index_answer.htm* from the Answer folder.

Summary

A great way to liven up your site is by using FrontPage's multimedia tools. From creating simple lines to complex 3-D shapes, you can create a variety of shapes in FrontPage. By using sound and video in your site as well, your visitors will be provided with a complete, multimedia experience.

☑ *Mastery Check*

1. What language is largely responsible for the use of shapes in FrontPage?

_____

_____

2. Can text inserted using the Text Box icon be modified and formatted like regular text?

_____

_____

3. What is the difference between an arrow line and a regular line?

_____

_____

4. Can 3-D shapes be modified and rotated like regular shapes?

_____

_____

5. What is WordArt?

_____

_____

6. What are the two most popular file formats for sound on the Web?

_____

_____

7. What is the default number of times videos will play when inserted in FrontPage?

_____

_____

5

Module 6

Using Tables

The Goals of This Module

- Place tables in your document
- Add, remove, and modify cells
- Format tables
- Use nested tables

A problem many Web developers had with the first versions of the Hypertext Markup Language (HTML) was organizing content on their pages: combining text, images, and other objects on the same line was very difficult. The introduction of tables to the HTML language gave the developer more control of the placement of content on their pages.

Using Tables

FrontPage enables you to use tables extensively, and it also gives you full control over a table's attributes such as color and style; furthermore, you can control the individual parts (the cells) of the table as well.

Tables Toolbar

The Tables toolbar provides easy access to the majority of the functions related to tables. You will use this toolbar often when working with tables in FrontPage. You can access the Tables toolbar by going to View | Toolbars | Tables. The following image shows you the Tables toolbar:

Table 6-1 shows each icon found in the Table toolbar and gives its name and function.

If you forget which icon is which while going through the instructions, you can refer back to Table 6-1.

Tip

You can also access most of the Tables toolbar's functions by selecting Table | Table from the menu bar.

For the directions in this module, please download the various images and sample source files for Module 6 from http://www.kirupa.com/frontpage or http://www.osborne.com.

Icon	Name	Function
	Draw Table	Creates a new table
	Eraser	Erases all cells or cell walls by merging the selected cells
	Insert Rows	Inserts rows of cells above the currently selected cell
	Insert Columns	Inserts columns of cells to the left of the currently selected cell
	Delete Cells	Deletes highlighted cells from your table
	Merge Cells	Combines many selected cells into a single cell
	Split Cells	Splits a cell into several cells horizontally or vertically
	Align Top	Aligns all content within a cell to the top of the cell
	Center Vertically	Aligns all content within a cell to the vertical center of the cell
	Align Bottom	Aligns all content within a cell to the bottom of the cell
	Distribute Rows Evenly	Evens the height of the selected cells or tables to a consistent value
	Distribute Columns Evenly	Evens the width of the selected cells or tables to a consistent value
	AutoFit	Changes the width and height of a table to conform to the content contained within the table
	Fill Color	Sets a background color for the entire table or selected cells
None	Table AutoFormat Combo	Adds custom design/color styles to your table

Table 6-1   The Tables Toolbar

Icon	Name	Function
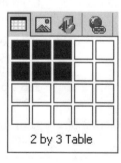	Table AutoFormat	Provides various selections for you to use to format your table with custom designs
	Fill Down	Copies the contents of the selected cell to all other cells selected vertically
	Fill Right	Copies the contents of the selected cell to all other cells selected horizontally

Table 6-1   The Tables Toolbar (*continued*)

Adding Tables

As mentioned earlier, FrontPage enables you to create, format, and modify tables easily. There are two ways of creating tables in FrontPage: One way involves drawing the table using the Draw Table icon on the Tables toolbar. The easier way involves using the Insert Table icon on the Standard toolbar. Because it is easier to use, I recommend that you use the Insert Table icon on the Standard toolbar.

When you click the Insert Table icon, a menu will appear with a graphical representation of how your table may look. You can move your mouse over the boxes to create the number of cells in your custom table. For example, the following image shows how you would create a 2 × 3 table:

Creating a Table

In this lesson you will learn how to add and customize a table:

1. Open a new document. Click the Insert Table icon on the Standard toolbar. From the menu that appears, drag the mouse cursor over the boxes until you have a 2 × 2 table highlighted. Once you have highlighted the 2 × 2 table, release the mouse button. A 2 × 2 table will be inserted into the page you created:

The following is the HTML code FrontPage outputs for creating the 2 × 2 table:

```
<table border="1" cellpadding="0" cellspacing="0" width="100%">
  <tr>
    <td width="50%" height="19">Cell 1</td>
    <td width="50%" height="19">Cell 2</td>
  </tr>
  <tr>
    <td width="50%" height="19">Cell 3</td>
    <td width="50%" height="19">Cell 4</td>
  </tr>
</table>
```

6

Formatting Table Dimensions

Most users spend extensive amounts of time formatting tables. Tables have numerous features such as width, spacing, padding, and so on that can be modified. In the next few sections, you will learn how to modify the size and spacing properties of a table.

Manually Adjusting Cell Width and Height

By default, FrontPage sets the width of your table to be 100 percent of the screen, and the height varies according to the content in the pages. Follow these directions to adjust the size of a table:

1. Open the file *table_size.htm*. (That file is included with the source files you should have downloaded.)

2. To adjust the width of the table, move the mouse pointer toward the vertical middle border of the table. When you see the mouse cursor change to a doubled-pointed arrow pointing left and right (the resize cursor), press and hold down the left mouse button and drag the resize cursor to the right. Release the mouse button after the table is the size you want. The table will adjust its dimensions accordingly:

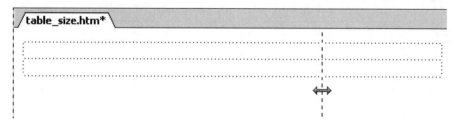

Keep this document open because we will be using it in the next section.

Adjusting Cell Width Using the Cell Properties Window

When working with tables, you may choose to set an exact width for the cells. When content is entered inside a table, the table adjusts its size to accommodate the content. When you enter an exact value for the table width and height, the content has to adjust itself to the dimensions of the table. To enter an exact value for the width and height of a cell, you need to use the Cell Properties window.

To adjust cell width, follow these directions:

1. Right-click inside the table and choose Cell Properties. In the upper-right corner of the Cell Properties window, there is a box into which you can enter an exact value for the height and/or width of a cell:

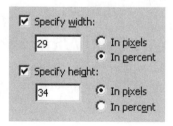

2. When you enter a value, you will need to select if the number will be percents or pixels by clicking the percents or pixels option button.

- **Pixels**   When you enter a number and select the option for pixels, the width of the cell will be static: the value you entered. A cell that has a width defined as pixels will not change its size, even when the browser is resized.

- **Percent**   It is recommended that you use the percent value for most tables and cells in a Web site. A cell with a percent value will automatically adjust its size when the browser is resized. When a value is entered and the percent option is selected, the cell will resize accordingly to the size of the browser window. A table with a value of 100 percent that is viewed on a large screen monitor with a high resolution will look differently than when it is viewed on a small screen monitor with a low resolution. In the larger monitor, more content will be displayed in one line of the table than will be displayed in the smaller monitor. Thus, the table in your larger monitor will be able to fit more content in fewer lines than the smaller monitor. You should note that unless you want the user to scroll horizontally, the percentage value for a table should not exceed 100.

Adjusting Table Width Using the Table Properties Window

To enter an exact value for the width and height of a table, you need to use the Table Properties window. The Table Properties window is similar to the Cell Properties window.

To adjust table width, follow these directions:

1. Right-click on a table and select the command for Table Properties. In the upper-right corner of the Table Properties window, there is a box into which you can enter an exact value for the height and/or width of a cell. Notice how similar the Table Properties window is to the Cell Properties window.

2. When you enter a value, you will need to select if the number will be percents or pixels by clicking the Percent or Pixels option button.

6

Tip

To adjust the width and height of multiple cells in one table, you will need to select all the cells in the row or column.

Cell Padding and Cell Spacing

When text is entered into a table, it is automatically placed very close to edge of the table. Having text that is very close to the edge or border of a table can make the text difficult to read. To overcome this problem, you can adjust the table's padding and spacing.

The following are brief explanations of cell padding and cell spacing:

- **Padding**   The padding of an cell refers to the amount of space between the borders of the cell and its contents.

- **Cell Spacing**   The cell spacing of a table refers to the space between adjacent cells.

The following image shows you tables with the padding and spacing adjusted differently in each:

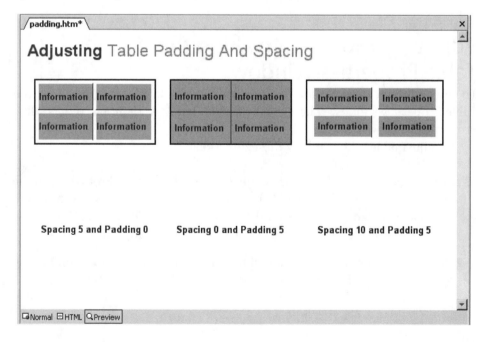

To adjust the padding and spacing of a table, follow these directions:

1. Open the file *padding_spacing.htm*. Once the page has been opened, right-click the table and choose Table Properties.

2. In the Table Properties window, there is a field for both Cell padding and Cell spacing. You can use the up and down arrows to increase or decrease the padding and spacing. Another method of adjusting the cell padding or spacing is by entering a value in the Cell padding and Cell spacing fields. Enter **5** into the Cell padding field, and enter **10** into the Cell spacing field:

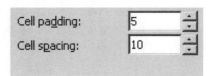

3. Click OK to close the Table Properties window. Your table should look like this:

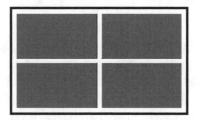

Adjusting Table Padding And Spacing

6

The following is the HTML code FrontPage outputs for adjusting the padding or spacing of a table. The numbers next to the words cell spacing and cell padding in the code refer to the value for both spacing and padding you entered in the Table Properties window:

```
<table border="0" cellspacing="10" cellpadding="4">
  <tr>
    <td width="14" style="border-style: none;
border-width: medium"></td>
  </tr>
</table>
```

Ask the Expert

Question: Which method of increasing space in a table is better: cell padding or cell spacing?

Answer: In most cases, cell spacing should not be used. Many developers would rather have the buffer space created by cell padding than a space between cells in a table. The disadvantage with cell spacing is that when you add custom styles such as borders and fill colors, cell spacing displays the actual space between the cells. That produces blank space and any colors applied to cells look separated from the other cells. Cell padding will not interfere with any styles that are applied to your table, and it will still create extra space between the contents in your cell and the cell border.

Adding, Splitting, Merging, and Deleting Cells

When tables are created, FrontPage enables you to add, split, merge, and delete cells easily. These functions can be accessed using the Tables toolbar, but they can also be accessed by right-clicking the table and choosing the appropriate command from the menu that appears.

For the next four sections make sure that the Tables toolbar is displayed. If it is not, launch it by selecting View | Toolbars | Tables from the Standard toolbar.

Adding Rows

To add a row to a table, follow these directions:

1. Open the file *modifycells.htm*, which is a page with a 1 × 1 table:

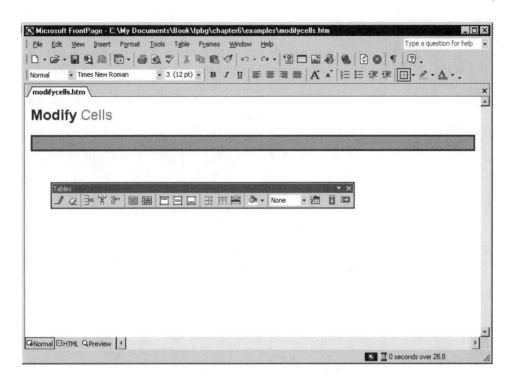

6

2. To add an extra row to the existing table, select the table by clicking anywhere in the table. After you have selected the table, click the Insert Rows icon on the Tables toolbar.

3. Each time you click the Insert Rows icon, a row will be added to your table. Click the Insert Rows icon until you have three rows of cells in your table:

Modify Cells

Tip

There is another way to add extra rows to your tables. If you place the mouse pointer somewhere in the last row of the table and press the TAB key, a new row of cells will be added.

Adding Columns

In the previous section, you learned about adding rows. Now, we will learn to add columns:

1. Open the file *column.htm*. Once the file has been opened, you will see that there are four rows in the table.

2. Place your mouse pointer in the first row. On the Tables toolbar, click the Insert Columns icon.

3. After you have clicked the Insert Columns icon, a column will appear to the right of all the rows in that table. Use the mouse pointer to resize the cells manually so that they look even and centered:

Add Columns

When you clicked the Insert Columns icon, you may have noticed that the columns extended toward all the rows in your cell. From the previous example, notice that when you clicked the Insert Columns icon from the top row, the columns extended down to the fourth row as well. To divide a cell so that a column runs through only one or a selected number of cells, you will need to split rows.

Splitting Rows

You can divide a cell that runs all the way down the width of the table by using the Split Cells option. Unlike the Insert Column option, the split cells will not cut through all the rows; when you split cells, only the row or selected rows are split. The remaining rows will remain unchanged.

To split a row, follow these directions:

1. Open the file *column_2.htm*. Once that file has been opened, place the mouse pointer in the second row and click the Split Cells icon on the Tables toolbar.

2. After you have clicked the Split Cells icon, the Split Cells window will appear. In the Split Cells window, select the Split into columns option and enter **2** in the Number of columns box:

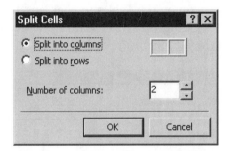

3. Click OK to close the Split Cells window.

4. After you have closed the Split Cells window, you will see that the second row has been split. Place the mouse pointer over the split cell divider in the second row and drag the edge of the split cell toward the left a little bit.

5. Place the mouse pointer in the fourth row and select the Split Cells icon from the Tables toolbar. You will see that the split cell divider appears exactly in the middle of the fourth row (just as it did in the second row) and that the second row has moved from its position toward the left and aligned itself in the middle also. When you split additional rows, the other cells that have been split follow the alignment of the newly split cell. If you move the split cell divider in the fourth row toward the left, the second row will move toward the left too:

6

Splitting Columns

To split a column, follow these directions:

1. Open the file *splitrow.htm.*

2. Once the file *splitrow.htm* has been opened, place the mouse pointer in the first cell of the second row.

3. Click the Split Cells icon on the Tables toolbar, and the Split Cells window will appear. Select the Split into rows option. To break the cell into three rows, enter **3** into the Number of rows box:

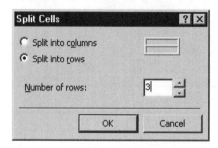

4. Click OK to close the Split Cells window. You will now see extra rows inside one cell:

Figure 6-1 shows you the various ways cells can be split. As you can see, cells can be split numerous times, and various split cells can exist within another split cell.

┼ *Tip*

There is another way to split cells. You can split by clicking the Draw Table icon on the Tables toolbar and clicking the cell with the mouse pointer to define the edges of the cell that needs to be split.

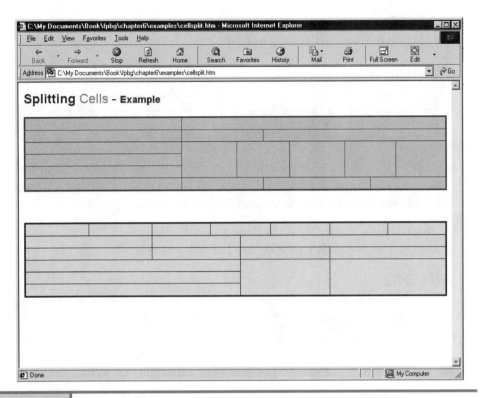

Figure 6-1   Example of split cells within cells

Merging Cells

When you merge cells, you are combining two or more cells together into one cell.

Follow these instructions to merge cells:

1. Open the file *merging.htm*. Once the file has been opened, you will see a table with various cells inside it.

2. The cells that you will merge are colored yellow and orange. To merge the yellow cells in the top row, place the mouse pointer in the first yellow cell. Once you have the pointer in the first yellow cell, click and drag to your right until all the yellow-colored cells are highlighted.

3. When the cells are highlighted, click the Merge Cells icon on the Tables toolbar. All the highlighted cells will now become just one cell:

Merging Cells

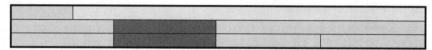

4. You can also merge cells vertically. To merge the two orange cells in the second and third row, place the mouse cursor in the top orange cell and drag down until the second orange cell has been highlighted too.

5. With the cells highlighted, click the Merge Cells icon on the Drawing toolbar. The two cells will merge to become one cell:

Merging Cells

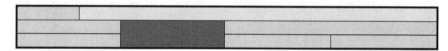

Keep this file open, as we will use it in the next section as well.

Deleting Cells

To delete cells, follow these instructions:

1. In the *merging.htm* file that we've been working in, highlight the two cells in the top row.

2. Once the cells have been highlighted, click the Delete Cells icon on the Tables toolbar. The top row of the table will be deleted:

Merging Cells

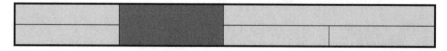

1-Minute Drill

- What are the two ways you can increase the distance between information contained in a cell?
- Can cells be split horizontally and vertically?

Content and Tables

Tables are commonly used to display information in an organized format. The information displayed in a table can be as simple as text or as diverse as images or video clips. In this section you will learn how to convert text into tables, how to align table content, how to distribute rows and columns evenly, how to AutoFit, and how to wrap text.

Converting Text to Tables

If you have a series of words and/or numbers that you would like to convert to a table, there are two ways you can accomplish this in FrontPage: automatically and selectively.

Letting FrontPage Automatically Convert Text to a Table

To let FrontPage automatically create a table for you, follow these directions:

1. Open the file *text.htm*. After you have opened the file, you will see a series of words. We will convert all those words into a table.

- By increasing cell padding and cell spacing
- Yes

6

2. Starting with the heading *VegeTables Inventory*, highlight all the words. Once the words have been highlighted, from the menu bar, select Table | Convert | Text to Table:

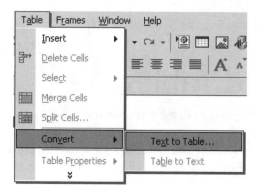

3. After the Text to Table command has been selected, the Text to Table window will appear. Select the option for commas and click OK. The series of words will now be in a table:

VegeTables Inventory							
Name	Okra	Squash	Zucchini	Eggplant	Potatoes	Pumpkin	Tomatoes
In Stock	Yes	No	Yes	No	No	No	Yes
Color	Green	Orange	Yellow	Purple	Brown	Orange	Red

Selectively Converting Text to Table

Instead of converting a series into a table by allowing FrontPage to convert them automatically, you can selectively choose which words will be converted into a table. By using any character to separate items in a series, you can convert the items in that series into a table by entering the character used to separate the items.

The following instructions will help you to selectively convert a series of text into a table:

1. Open the file *computer.htm*. Once the file has been opened, you will see information regarding antique computers. Notice that the information is separated by colons (:) instead of commas That minor observation is key to converting the series of text into a table.

2. Highlight all the words below the black line. Select Table | Convert | Text to Table, and the Convert Text To Table window will appear:

The following is a list of each option in the Convert Text To Table window and what each option does:

- **Paragraphs**   Creates a table with a row for each paragraph highlighted for conversion.

- **Tabs**   Creates a table with a column for each word in the series separated by a tab space.

- **Commas**   Creates a table with a column for each item in the series separated by a comma.

- **None**   Creates a table with all of the highlighted contents inside a single cell.

- **Other**   Enables you to enter a character to separate the series of words. For example, if you used a question mark to separate each word in the series, you would enter a question mark in this box.

3. Because the words in the *computer.htm* series are separated with colons (:), in the Convert Text To Table window, select the option for Other and enter a colon (:) in the box:

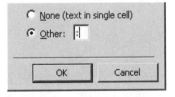

4. Click OK to close the Convert Text To Table box, and the text in the series will be placed in separate cells in a table. Figure 6-2 shows what the table should look like.

6

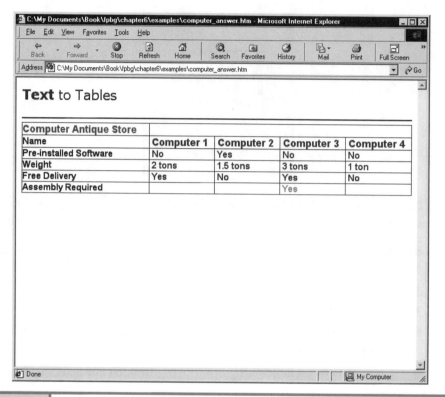

Content Alignment

In cells, graphics, text, video, and more can be aligned vertically, as well as horizontally.

In this section, you will learn how to vertically align information in a table:

1. Open the file *alignment.htm*. Once the file has been opened, you will see a table with three cells.

2. To vertically align the contents of the first cell, place your mouse pointer in the first cell. From the Tables toolbar, select the Align Top icon. After you have selected the Align Top icon, the text in the cell will move to the top.

3. We want the contents of the second cell to be vertically aligned in the middle. Because FrontPage's default setting for vertical content alignment in a cell is center, you will not have to modify this cell.

4. To vertically align the contents of the third cell, insert your mouse pointer in the third cell and click the Align Bottom icon on the Tables toolbar. The following is an illustration of what your page should look like:

Content Alignment

Align Top	Center Vertically	Align Bottom
Information in this cell should be Top aligned.	Information in this cell should be Center aligned.	Information in this cell should be Bottom aligned.

6

Tip

You can horizontally align the content of tables by using the Align Left, Center, Align Right, and Justify commands found on the Formatting toolbar.

Distributing Rows and Columns Evenly

When adding or removing text, copying and pasting whole tables, and more, the cells in a table are resized by FrontPage. To make the width or height of cells in a table even, FrontPage provides two useful commands: the Distributing Rows Evenly and Distributing Columns Evenly icons in the Drawing toolbar.

To distribute rows and columns evenly, follow these instructions:

1. Open the file *distribute.htm*. Once the file has been opened, you will see a table with several rows and columns of uneven cells.

2. Highlight all the cells in the table. You can do that by clicking the upper-left cell and dragging the mouse until all the cells have been highlighted.

3. With all the cells highlighted, select the Distribute Rows Evenly icon on the Tables toolbar. All the rows in your table will now be evenly sized:

Cell Distribution

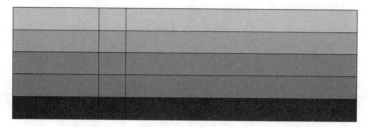

4. Now that the rows are even, let's distribute the columns equally: highlight all the cells in the table again, and this time, select the Distribute Columns Evenly icon on the Tables toolbar. The columns in your table will now be evenly divided just like the rows:

Cell Distribution

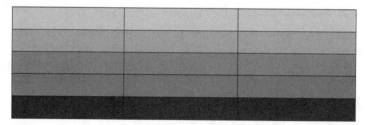

Note

You do not have to distribute all the rows or columns in a table evenly. If you choose to evenly size only a few cells, you may select only those cells and the size of the unselected cells will not be affected.

AutoFit to Contents

FrontPage includes a tool that customizes the size of the table according to the content within it:

1. Open the file *autofit.htm*. Once the file has been opened, you will see that there is a word centered in each cell. Because there is a lot of space between words, we will use FrontPage's AutoFit to Contents tool to remove some of the extra space.

2. Highlight all the cells in the table. After all the cells in the table have been highlighted, select the AutoFit to Contents icon on the Tables toolbar. After the AutoFit to Contents icon has been selected, the table will resize accordingly to incorporate the text:

AutoFit to Contents

Birmingham	Paris	New Delhi
Toronto	Zurich	Rome

Because all the words are close to the edge of the cell, I added a cell padding value of 5 to all the cells. If I did not increase the cell padding, the words would be difficult to read. To see my version of this example, please open the file *autofit_answer.htm*.

Text Wrapping

You may have noticed that when your tables are viewed in a smaller-sized screen, the entire table resizes to accommodate that change. Some of the text might be displayed on two lines instead of one line. Sometimes you do not want lines (such as titles and main headings) to flow onto two lines. To solve that problem, you can use the No Wrap command found in the Cell Properties window.

To prevent the wrapping of text in a cell, follow these directions:

1. Right-click the cell you do not want to flow onto two lines and choose the command for Cell Properties.

2. In the middle-left of the Cell Properties window, check the box for No Wrap.

Figure 6-3 shows a table before No Wrap was applied and after No Wrap was applied.

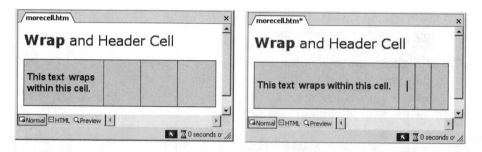

An example of a cell before and after the No Wrap option was selected

In Figure 6-3, notice that the window did not change size. Instead, the other cells changed their widths to accommodate the text in the first cell moving onto one line. You should understand that No Wrap should primarily be used for titles and headers. Adding No Wrap to a large sentence will cause many users with smaller monitors to have to scroll horizontally to read the content. You should try to avoid making users scroll horizontally to see information on your pages because it is annoying to the visitor.

Formatting Tables with Colors and Styles

Now that all the basic functions of tables and cells has been covered, we will learn about adding colors and custom styles to enhance the look of the table. The various cosmetic features of tables include color, background images, custom styles, and borders.

Adding Color to Tables

Follow these instructions to add color to a table:

1. Open the file *color.htm*. After the file has been opened, right-click the table and choose the command for Table Properties. In the Table Properties window, click the menu for Color in the Background section. From the Color menu, select a color:

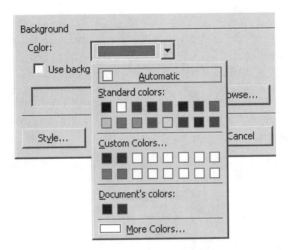

2. After you have selected a color, click OK to close the Table Properties window. When you close the window, the color that you select will be applied to the entire table.

The following is the HTML code FrontPage outputs for adding color to a simple, one-column table:

```
<table border="1" cellspacing="0" style="border-collapse:
collapse; border-width: 0" bordercolor="#111111" width="100%"
cellpadding="0">
  <tr>
    <td bgcolor="#004080" style="border-style: none; border-width:
medium"> </td>
  </tr>
</table>
```

Adding Color to Cells

There are two methods of adding color to cells: one method for a single cell and one method for two or more cells.

Adding Color to a Single Cell

1. Open the file *cell.htm*.

2. To add a color to the first cell, right-click it and select the command for Cell Properties from the menu that appears. After you have selected Cell Properties, the Cell Properties window will display.

3. In the Cell Properties window, under the section marked Background, click the Color menu and select a color. Click OK to close the Cell Properties window.

4. The color you selected will be applied to the first cell only:

Cell Color

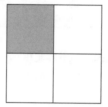

5. Now, I want you to add a background color to another cell. Follow the previous instructions and add a color to the first cell on the second row:

Cell Color

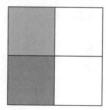

Adding Color to Two or More Cells

1. Highlight both cells on the right using the mouse pointer. While both cells are highlighted, click the arrow to the right of the Fill Color icon on the Tables toolbar.

2. From the menu that appears, choose a color that you would like to use. After you have selected a color, that color will be applied to both cells:

Cell Color

Tip

To modify the fill for a single cell or multiple cells, you can also use the Highlight icon on the Formatting toolbar. Select the cells that you would like to add color to and click the Highlight command to apply the color.

6

Adding Background Images

Another way to liven up tables and cells is to add background images.

There are two types of background images that you can add: single images and tiled images.

Adding a Single Image Background

1. Open the file *background.htm*. Once the file has been opened, you will see a table with a blue cell and a blank cell.

2. We will add a background image to the colored cell first. Right-click the colored cell and choose Cell Properties. In the Cell Properties window, in the Background section, check the Use background picture box:

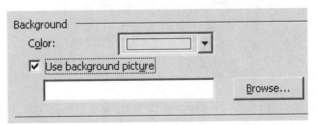

3. Using the Browse button, find and select the *clouds.jpg* file. Click OK to close the Cell Properties window.

4. After you have closed the Cell Properties window, the *clouds.jpg* image will be applied to the top cell:

Cell Color

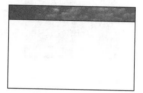

Please leave this page open, as we will add to it in the next section.

Adding a Tiled Image Background

A background gets tiled when a single image doesn't completely fill the inside of a cell or table; the browser repeats the image to fill up the space. Note that using images that are not meant to be tiled will produce undesirable results. Images meant for tiling should repeat evenly without the viewer actually seeing the single image that is being repeated.

To add a tiled image, follow these directions:

1. In the same page from the previous section, right-click the blank cell and choose Cell Properties.

1. In the Cell Properties window, check the Use background picture box and browse for the file *lines.jpg*:

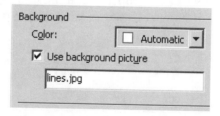

2. Click OK to close the Cell Properties window. The second cell now has a tiled background image as well because the image repeats itself:

Cell Color

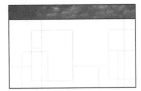

To see my version of the example you just completed, open the file *background_answer.htm*.

Note

To add a background image to a table, you would follow the same steps, except you would select Table Properties when you right-click.

Adding Custom Styles

A way to enhancing the look of your entire table is to add custom styles.

There are two features to that enable you to add custom styles to a table: Table AutoFormat Combo and Table AutoFormat.

Using Table AutoFormat Combo Drop-Down Menu

Follow these directions to learn to use the AutoFormat command:

1. Open the file *autoformat.htm*.

2. In the *autoformat.htm* file, select the table with the mouse pointer. From the Tables toolbar, select the Table AutoFormat Combo icon.

3. From the styles that appear in the drop-down menu, select Classic 4. Your table should look like the following image:

Top 5 Elements in Human Body

Element Name	Percentage %
Oxygen	65
Carbon	18
Hydrogen	10
Nitrogen	3
Calcium	1.5

Keep the *autoformat.htm* page open, as we'll use it in the next section as well.

Using Table AutoFormat

Use the Table AutoFormat icon to exert more control over the custom style of your table:

1. In the same page we used for the last section, place the mouse pointer inside the table and click the Table AutoFormat icon on the Tables menu. After you have clicked the Table AutoFormat icon, you will get the Table AutoFormat window:

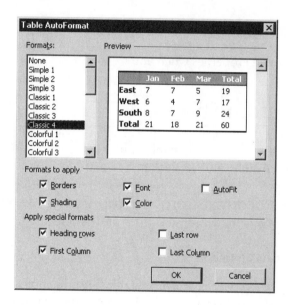

Table 6-2 lists the options found in the Table AutoFormat window and gives a brief explanation of its function.

When you click any of the various check boxes or select a format style from the Formats box, the table is displayed in the Preview window with those changes. Once you find a look that you like, click the OK button to close

Option	Function
Borders	Applies formatting to the borders of a table
Font	Adjusts the font and font styles for text inside a table
AutoFit	Modifies the size of the table so that its content fits inside it
Shading	Applies colors to create a three-dimensional (3-D) look for your tables
Color	Applies background colors to cells
Heading Rows	Applies formatting to the first row of a table
Last Row	Applies formatting to the last row of a table
First Column	Applies formatting to the first column in a table
Last Column	Applies formatting to the last column of a table

Table 6-2   The Table AutoFormat Window

the Table AutoFormat window, and the format(s) you chose will be applied to your table.

6

Borders

When creating tables in FrontPage, you may have noticed that a thin black line separates the cells. That thin black line is the default border that FrontPage applies to all tables and cells:

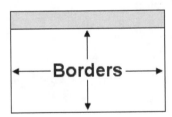

In the next sections you will learn to change the border from the default, change the thickness and color of the border line, and change the light border and dark border.

Changing Borders

In this lesson you will learn how to adjust the borders for a table:

1. Open the file *border.htm*. You will see a simple 2 × 2 table.

2. Select all the cells with the mouse pointer. After all the cells have been selected, click the arrow to the right of the Outside Borders icon on the Formatting toolbar:

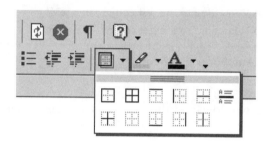

3. From the Border menu, select the choice for No Border. The No Border command is the border choice with dotted lines all around it. Once you have selected the No Border command, your table should look like the following image:

Border Styles

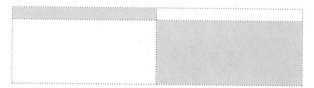

4. To add borders, select all the cells and click on the Borders icon from the Formatting toolbar. You may select as many border choices as you would like.

Note

Borders do not have to be applied to the entire table. You can assign borders to a single cell or many cells. To assign borders to only certain portions of a table, highlight the cell(s) that you would like to have borders and use the Border icon on the Formatting toolbar.

Changing Border Thickness and Color

When you create a table, the default thickness FrontPage assigns to the border is 1. To adjust the border thickness of a table, follow these instructions:

6

1. Create a new document in FrontPage and draw a 2 × 2 table. Adjust the width of the table to 30 percent and the height of the table to 150 pixels. Make sure the value for Cell spacing is 0. Your Table Properties window should look like the following image:

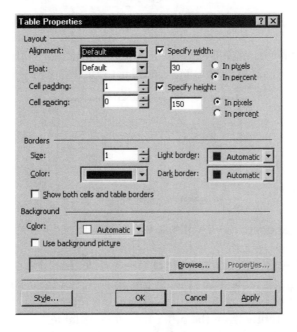

2. In the same Table Properties window, look in the Borders area. In the Size field, enter 5. Entering a value in that box adjusts the border size of the table. Do not close the Table Properties window yet.

3. Right below where you entered a value for the border size, there is a menu for Color. Click the Color menu and choose a color:

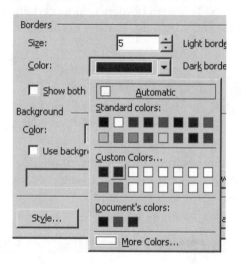

4. After you have chosen a color, click OK to close the Table Properties window. Your table should look similar to the following image:

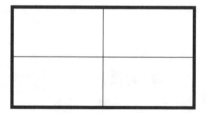

Keep this page open, as we will use it in the next section as well.

Changing the Light Border and the Dark Border

The light border of a table is the table's top and left borders. The dark border of a table is the bottom and right borders. Changing these borders will color half of your table differently from the other half of your table.

To change the light border and dark border, follow these directions:

1. Go back to the Table Properties window by right-clicking the table and choosing Table Properties. On the right of the Borders area, you will see the Light border and Dark border options with their corresponding menus.

2. From their menus, select two different colors:

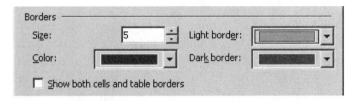

3. Click OK to close the Table Properties window, and the colors you selected will be applied to the outer borders of the table:

Border Size and Color

To see my version of this example, open the file *bordersize.htm*.

Note

The cells of your table will be colored the same as the color you specified for the light border of the table. The colors for the light and dark borders are useful to simulate a 3-D effect.

1-Minute Drill

● What are the three ways content can be vertically aligned in a cell?

● Should No Wrap be applied to large sentences?

● What are two background elements you can add to a table or cell?

● Top, Center, and Bottom
● No
● Background color and background images

6

Nested Tables

Now that you have a basic understanding of creating and formatting tables in a Web site, we will learn to apply this knowledge to the actual Web developing. Most developers use tables extensively. Tables are used for the organization of content, and they should be one of the first elements added to a Web page.

An important feature of laying out information on a page is the use of nested tables. Nested tables are tables that are contained within a cell of another table. Most Web sites, such as Microsoft's page shown in the following image, use a table for navigation, a table for links, and more:

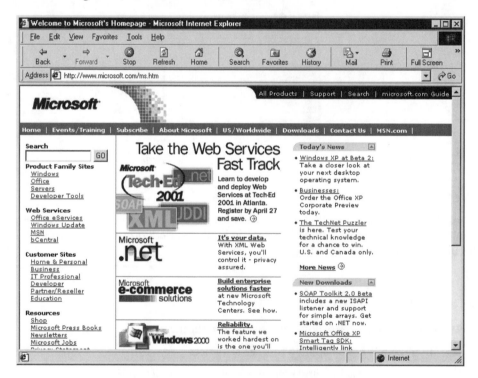

Creating a Nested Table

To create a page with a nested table, follow these directions:

1. Open the file *nested.htm*. You will see a one-column table.

2. Place the mouse pointer inside the table and add a 3 × 2 table using the Insert Table icon on the Standard Toolbar.

3. After the 3 × 2 table is inserted, you will see that the original table is still visible. The is because I set the spacing on the original table to 5. Now, right-click the table you just inserted and from the Table Properties window set the border to 0.

4. You have just created a nested table:

Nested Tables

Figure 6-4 is an example of a more complex layout created using only tables.

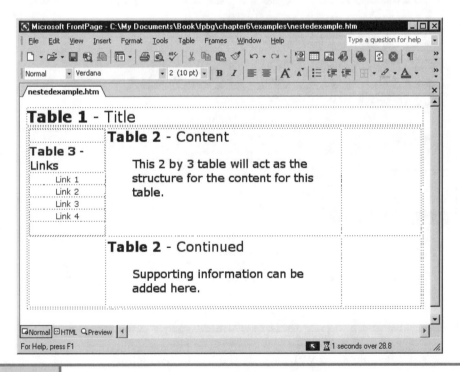

| **Figure 6-4** | Example of a page created entirely with nested tables |

To see how examine the image in Figure 6-4, open the file *nestedexample.htm*; notice that I started my page by creating a table first.

Creating a Layout Using Nested Tables

As you have learned, creating nested tables is not very complicated, but in creating nested tables, design must also be considered. How you organize the information on the page can attract or repel visitors and can help the visitor to use your site.

When creating a nested table, try to design the tables in a way that does not look cluttered. As always when developing pages, you should try to make sure that your pages look acceptable on smaller monitors. Figure 6-5 and Figure 6-6 shows how a page looks different when viewed on a large monitor versus a small monitor.

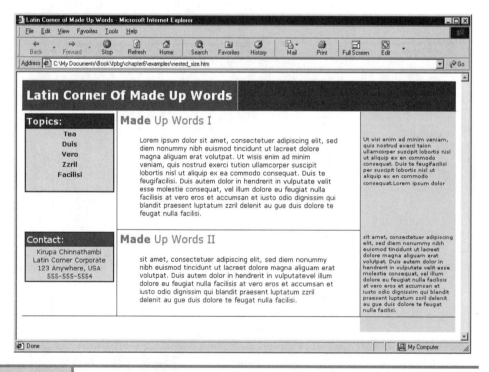

Figure 6-5   Example of a Web page viewed in a large monitor

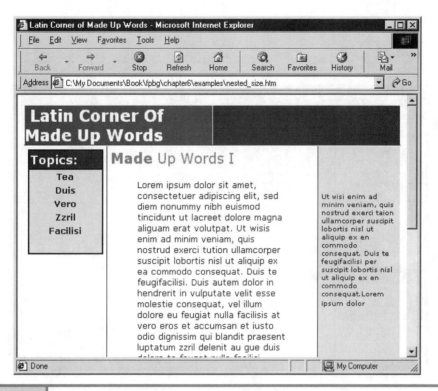

Figure 6-6   Example of the same Web page viewed in a small monitor

The best way to solve the problem of a site that is too large to be viewed on a small monitor is to make the fonts smaller and remove extraneous space such as spacing and padding. When removing spacing, make sure that the information in the table is still legible without the extra space.

Nested Table Guidelines

The following guidelines will provide some valuable information on creating an effective layout using nested tables. These guidelines can really enhance your site's overall look:

● **Remove Table Borders**   When you create your layout, make sure to set the value for Table borders to 0. Figure 6-7 shows you an example of how using full borders makes the information difficult to follow.

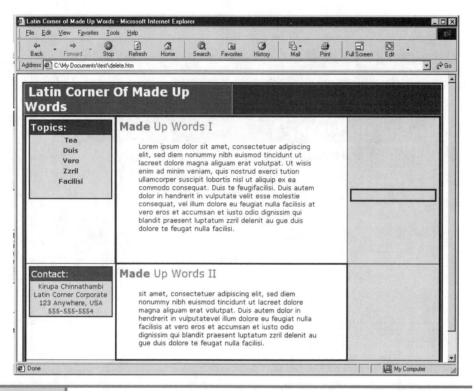

Figure 6-7   Using full borders

- **Set Table Spacing to Zero**   For a better layout, you should set the value for table spacing to 0. When you add cell colors, background images, and more, the use of cell spacing will degrade the flow of information. For the spacing of information, increase cell padding instead.

- **Use Cells**   Sometimes you may want to split existing cells to create new areas for content. The fewer tables you use, the easier it will be to adjust the page's layout in the future.

- **Set Table Width in Percents**   As I mentioned earlier in this module, set the width of your table in percents instead of pixels. The reason for this is that a table layout that has its width in percents automatically adjusts the content within the table to different monitor sizes. When you set a pixel width for your table that is larger than 800, many visitors to your Web site will have to scroll horizontally to view the rest of the content.

- **Always set a Background Color**   When you use tables, make sure you always set a background color. The default color of Automatic that FrontPage applies is interpreted differently by various browsers. Internet Explorer interprets Automatic as white, while some versions of Netscape interpret Automatic as gray. If the background color is going to be white, set the background color to white. Various visitors may have set their default background color in their browser different than that of white, but as long as you set a background color to your site, your site will show properly on your visitors' screen.

index.htm
trees.htm

Project 6-1: Tables and Cells

The following are the goals for this project:

- Create a table

- Convert text to a table

- Format a table

- Adjust table borders

- Add a nested table

Step by Step

1. In your Projects folder, open the file *index.htm*. That page will act as the home page for the fictitious company, Imaginary Numbers.

2. We will start by converting text to a table. From the Projects folder, open the file *trees.htm*. Press CTRL and click the link Number of Trees on Mars to open the page in FrontPage.

3. Once the *trees.htm* file is displayed in FrontPage, highlight all the text starting with the single exclamation point (!) and ending with the last line "Week 4...". After you have highlighted the text, select Table I Convert I Text to Table.

4. Because the series in the table is separated by exclamation point (!), select the option for other and enter an exclamation point (**!**) in the box:

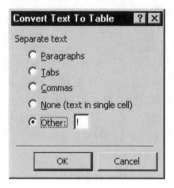

5. After the text has been made into a table, set cell spacing to 0. Right-click the table and choose Table Properties. Enter **0** in the Cell Spacing box.

6. After cell spacing has been set to 0, add a custom AutoFormat to your table. From the Table AutoFormat Combo menu in the Tables toolbar, select the Elegant option. After you have applied the AutoFormat, highlight the cells that contain numbers under the tree types. Select the Center icon from the Formatting toolbar:

Trees on Mars: Official Census Report

	Apple Trees	Sequoia Trees	Eucalyptus Trees
Week 1	14	35	2352
Week 2	35	35	375
Week 3	451	34	562
Week 4	1762	39	463

7. You should have three main cells: The left cell is blank, the middle cell has your table and other text, and the right cell is blank with a background color. In the left cell that is blank, insert the image file *mars.gif*. Right-align the image using the Align Right command on the Formatting Toolbar.

8. Hyperlink back to the home page. Highlight the words "[Return to Home Page]" and hyperlink it to the file *index.htm.* Your *trees.htm* page should look like Figure 6-8.

9. Save and close *trees.htm.*

10. Open the file *footsteps.htm.* You will see that a table has already been created. You need to modify this table to make it easier to read.

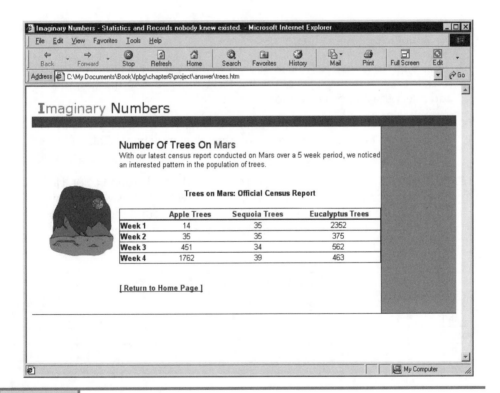

Figure 6-8   Result of hyperlink

11. Right-click the table and choose Table Properties. Check the Specify width box and enter **100**. Make sure In percent is selected:

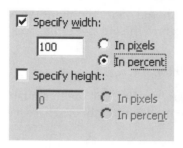

12. Click OK to close the Table Properties window, and your table will now span the entire length of the cell.

13. We will now add borders to the table. Highlight all the cells inside the table. Click the arrow to the right of the Borders icon on the Formatting toolbar and select the All Borders option.

14. To help space the information on the table, we will increase the value for cell padding. Right-click anywhere on the table and choose Table Properties. Enter **2** in the Cell Padding field. Click OK to close the Table Properties window.

15. To enhance the look of the table, you should add a background color. Highlight the entire second row of cells and go to the Cell Properties window by right-clicking and choosing Cell Properties. In the Background section, choose a color from the Color menu. Try to make the color light enough so the text can be seen clearly:

Treasure Island: Footsteps			
	The Parrot	Jim Hawkins	Long John Silver*
Month 1	1578	1244	235
Month 2	4463	6572	678
Month 3	346	9084	905

* The infamous pirate only had one leg.

16. Insert the image file *map.gif* into the left cell. Make sure the map is aligned toward the right, as seen in Figure 6-9.

17. The last step is to hyperlink back to the home page. Remember, you will hyperlink the links to *index.htm*. Save this file, and we will continue with the remaining two pages.

18. Open the file *population.htm*. You will need to make some minor modifications to this table. From looking at the table, you can see that some borders are missing.

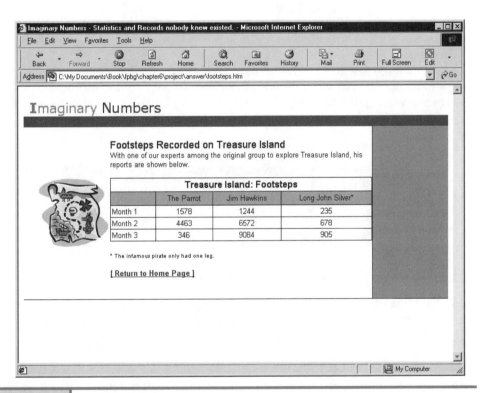

Figure 6-9 Inserting the *map.gif*

19. Insert your mouse pointer in the first cell. Click the Border command from the Formatting toolbar and select the option for Top Border.

20. Look at the first column of cells on the left. You can see that this information is shown on two rows. You will add the No Wrap property to these cells. Highlight the three cells on the left and go to the Cell Properties window by right-clicking and choosing Cell Properties. Check the No Wrap box:

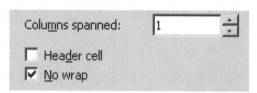

21. Click OK to close the Cell Properties window, and the first column of cells should now be displayed on one single line. To alleviate the problem of overcrowding of information, increase the cell padding to **4**. Also, center all the numbers in the table. Your table should look like the following image:

Census Data: Atlantis			
	Census 1	Census 2	Census 3
15-30 Age Group	1578	1244	235
30-100 Age Group	4463	6572	678
100-350 Age Group	346	9084	905

22. In the left cell, insert the file *atlantis.gif*. Right align that image.

23. Hyperlink the words "[Return to Home Page]" to the home page, *index.htm*. Save the file. Your final page should look like Figure 6-10.

24. Open the file *founding.htm*. You will add a nested table by adding a table inside the existing table.

25. Place your mouse pointer in the existing table. Using the Insert Table icon on the Standard Toolbar, insert a 3 × 2 table. After the table has been inserted, right-click the table and choose Table Properties.

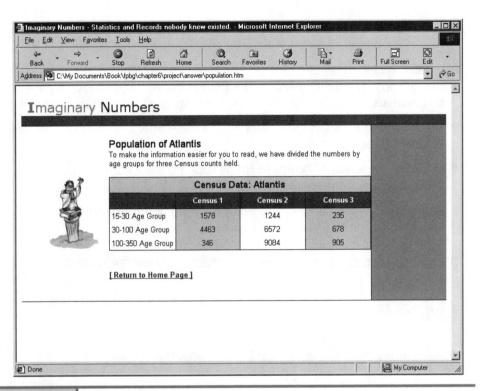

Figure 6-10	The final page

26. From the Table Properties window, set cell spacing and border size to 0. Click OK to close the Table Properties window. You will get the following image:

27. In the first cell, insert the picture file *newton.gif*. In the second cell, insert the picture file *galileo.gif*. In the third cell enter the picture file *copernicus.gif*.

28. In the first cell of the second row, type **Newton**. In the second cell of the second row, type **Galileo**. In the third cell of the second row, type **Copernicus**. You may want to adjust the font styles to suit this document.

29. Highlight all the cells in the table and click the Center command on the Formatting toolbar.

30. Hyperlink the words "[Return to Home Page]" to the home page, *index.htm*. Your page should look like Figure 6-11.

Your project is now finished. To see my version of this project, open the file *index.htm* from the answers folder.

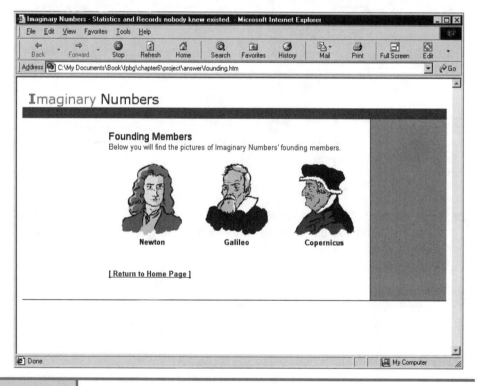

Figure 6-11   Hyperlinked images on the page

Summary

Tables are great assets to the Web developer. As you have learned, the organization of information on a page is much easier because of tables. From the project is this module, you learned how to combine various elements of a table into one site. Tables are invaluable when creating sites and should be used to their utmost extent.

☑ Mastery Check

1. Is table background color independent of cell background color?

_____

_____

2. What are the ways you can access table commands in FrontPage?

_____

_____

3. What is the difference between cell padding and cell spacing?

_____

_____

4. Can cells be split within another cell?

_____

_____

5. What is the difference between pixel and percent when adjusting the size of a table or cell?

_____

_____

☑ Mastery Check

6. What happens when you merge two cells?

_____

_____

7. Why should you not apply No Wrap to large pieces of text?

_____

_____

8. How would you horizontally align content in a table?

_____

_____

9. What does the Table AutoFormat icon do?

_____

_____

10. What are nested tables?

_____

_____

11. If you set your table's width to 900 pixels, will visitors on resolutions lower than 1024 × 768 have to horizontally scroll to view the entire table?

_____

_____

Module 7

Using Frames

The Goals of This Module

- Create frames
- Save frame pages
- Customize frame properties
- Create inline frames

U p until this point, the links we created were the type of links that when clicked, would open a whole new page. This module introduces you to a feature called *frames,* which enables you to create links that update portions of your page while keeping other, already open portions of your page static. Frames enable you to view two or more Hypertext Markup Language (HTML) pages in a single window at the same time. With frames, when you click a link in a Web site, the link loads in one part of the current page.

The following images of Oracle's site are examples of a page with frames in action. Figure 7-1 shows the top page containing the navigation links, and Figure 7-2 shows bottom page containing the content. You can see that scrolling the content page does not affect the top part of the Web page:

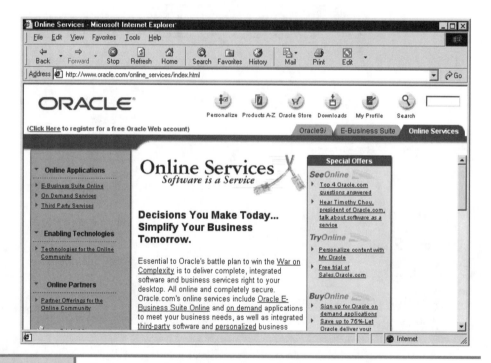

Figure 7-1   The top part of the Oracle site shows frames in action.

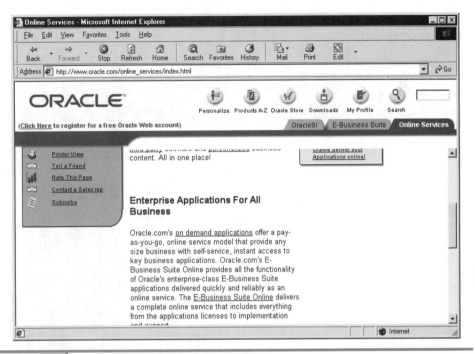

Figure 7-2 The bottom portion of the Oracle site shows content.

A *frameset* is a set of several HTML pages displayed in the browser at the same time. When you view a site that contains frames, you will not see the frameset page. The frameset page contains only HTML code. What you will see are the pages contained in the frameset.

The following image shows how a page containing frames is structured. This page is composed of four HTML files. The frameset is *index.htm*. The supporting files are each linked to the frameset file.

For the directions in this module, please download the various images and sample source files for Module 7 from http://www.kirupa.com/frontpage or http://www.Osborne.com.

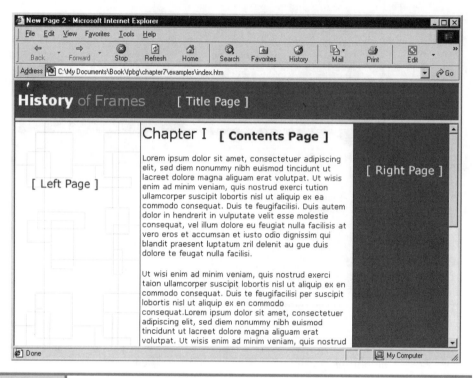

Figure 7-3   A page containing frames has this structure.

Creating Frames

Now that you have had a brief introduction to frames, you are ready to create a page in FrontPage that uses frames:

1. Open a new document in FrontPage. Select to File | New | Page or Web. After you have selected the Page or Web command, the Task pane will appear on the right of your window. From the Task pane, click the command for Page Templates:

New from template

   Narrow, Left-aligned Body
   One-column Body with Contents
   Page Templates...
   Web Site Templates...
   Templates on Microsoft.com

2. After you click the command for Page Templates, the Page Templates window will appear. At the top of the Page Templates window, select the Frames Pages tab, as shown in Figure 7-4.

3. In the Frames Pages tab, click the template for Header and click OK to close the Page Templates window. Your screen should look like the following image, which is the basic structure for a page that contains frames. You can tell from looking at the image that there will be two frames in the frameset. Select the top frame using the mouse pointer and click the button for Set Initial Page; see Figure 7-5.

7

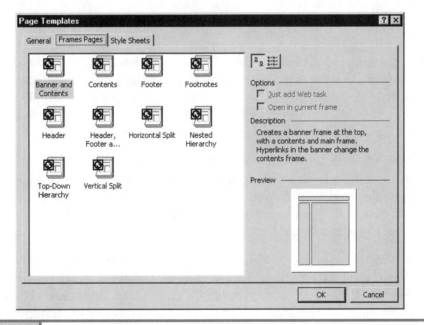

Figure 7-4 Set frames options using the Frames Pages tab in the Page Templates window.

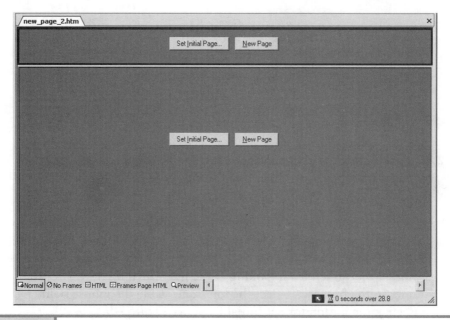

Figure 7-5   The basic structure for a page with frames

4. In the Insert Hyperlink window that appears, browse to select the file *top.htm*. (That file is included with the source files you should have downloaded from http://www.Osborne.com or http://www.kirupa.com/ frontpage.) Click OK to close the window. After you have closed the window, the top frame of your page will now display the *top.htm* file.

5. Now, click the Set Initial page button in the lower frame. From the window that appears, browse and select the file *main.htm*. Click OK to close the window. After you have closed the window, the *main.htm* file will now be displayed in your FrontPage window. Figure 7-6 shows you what your page should look like.

6. To see how your page would look when someone views the page in a browser, click the Preview command at the bottom of the FrontPage window. When you are previewing the page, you will see that when you move the scroll bars, the top frame does not move. The top frame does not move because it is a HTML page that is independent of the HTML page of the second frame.

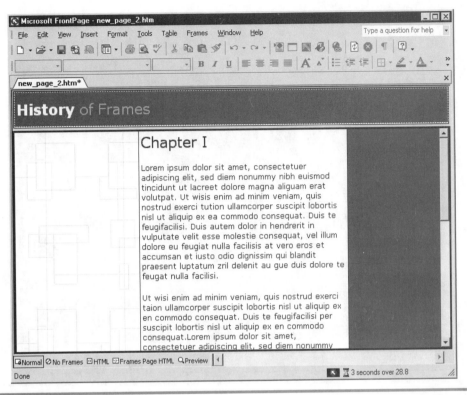

Figure 7-6   A page made up of two frames

Creating a New Frameset

In the previous section, you set an initial page for the frames pages in the frameset. In this section, you will learn to create a new frames page to be used in your frameset:

1. Open a new document in FrontPage. Select File | New | Page or Web. From the Task pane that appears to the right of your window, click the command for Page Templates. In the Page Templates window, click the Frames tab. Select the Banner and Contents frame template and click OK. Your screen should look like that shown in Figure 7-7.

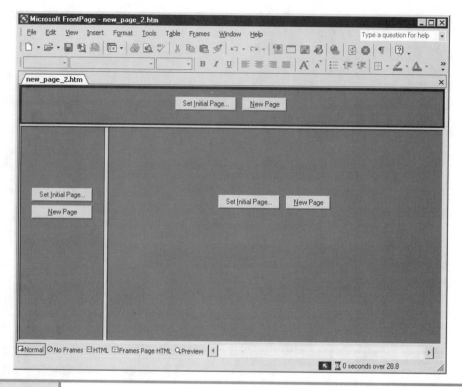

Figure 7-7 Selecting the Banner and Contents frame template

2. Click the button marked New Page in each of the frames. After you have clicked New Page for all the frames, you should see three frames with a white background and borders separating each frame. Two of the frames will have scrollbars as shown in Figure 7-8.

3. Generally, the top frame is used as the heading or title of your page, the main or right frame is used to display the site's information, and the left frame is used for navigation. In the top frame, type **Frame 1**. In the left frame, type **Frame 2**. In the main or right frame, type **Frame 3**. If you

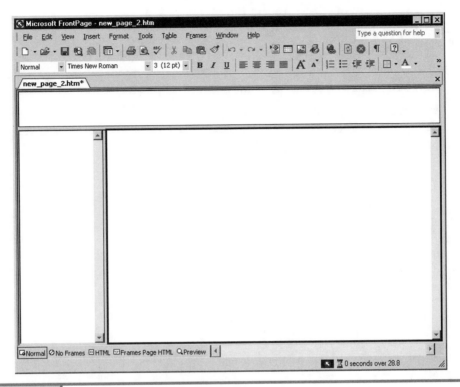

Figure 7-8   Two frames with scrollbars

wish, you may adjust the font size and color of the words you entered. Your frameset should look something like that shown in Figure 7-9.

Do not close this page, as we are going to use it in the next section.

Tip

You can delete or split frames by clicking Frame I Split Frame or Delete Frame on the menu bar.

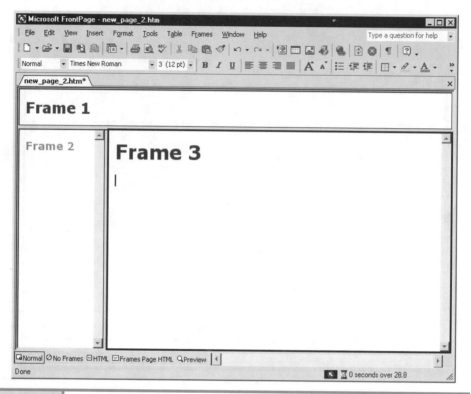

Figure 7-9   A frameset contains more than one frame.

Saving Frames

As I mentioned at the beginning of this module, a frames page is comprised of several HTML pages. Because a frames page is composed of several HTML pages, each HTML page will need to be saved individually.

Follow these directions to save the frameset you created in the previous section:

1. Using the frameset we created in the last section, click the Save icon on the Standard toolbar. When you click the Save icon, the Save As window will appear. Figure 7-10 shows the Save As window when using it to save frames.

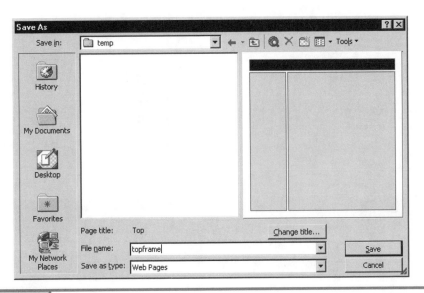

Figure 7-10 The Save As window for saving frames

2. As you can see in Figure 7-10, a graphical representation of your current frameset is shown to the right of the Save As window. Because saving several files can get confusing, FrontPage highlights the frame that is about to be saved as an HTML file. In Figure 7-10, the top frame is highlighted. That means the file name you enter to save this file is the name that will correspond to the HTML page in the top frame.

3. To save the top frame as an HTML file, in the File name field, type **frame1**:

4. After you have typed **frame1** into the File name field, click Save, and the Save As window will appear again. This time you will need to save the left

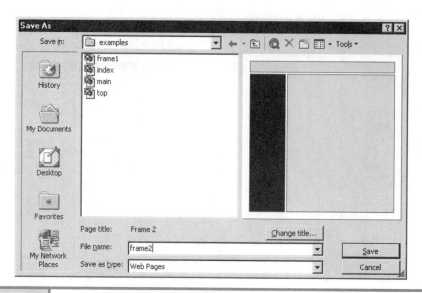

Figure 7-11   Saving the left frame of the frameset

frame because the left frame is highlighted in the frameset preview area. In the File name field, type **frame2** and click the Save button.

5. Now it is time to save the third frame. As you can see, the right frame is now highlighted. In the File name field, type **frame3** and click the Save button.

6. After you clicked the Save button for the third frame, you would expect to be done saving all the files in your frameset, but remember that I mentioned that there is always an extra HTML page in the frameset that links all the frames together. This file does not contain any useful content for the reader, but this file is necessary to display your frameset correctly. You can tell that the extra HTML page needs to be saved because in the preview area (on the right) of the Save As window, the border that surrounds all the frames is highlighted, as shown in Figure 7-12.

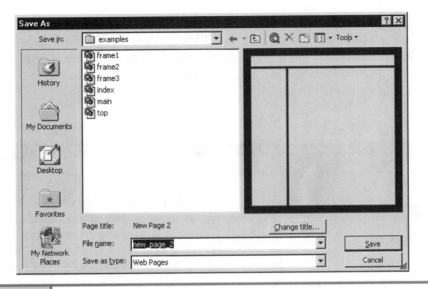

Figure 7-12 Saving the extra HTML page

7. Type the file name **frame** into the File name field:

8. After you have entered the file name, click Save and you will be taken back to FrontPage's normal view. Notice that *frame.htm* is displayed in the file name tab instead of each frame page's file name:

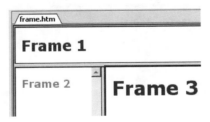

9. To preview your frameset in a browser, go to File | Preview In Browser. Select a browser from the list, and click Preview. Your frameset should look like that in Figure 7-13. In Figure 7-13, three separate HTML pages compose the frameset, but only the frameset name (*frame.htm*) is displayed in the browser.

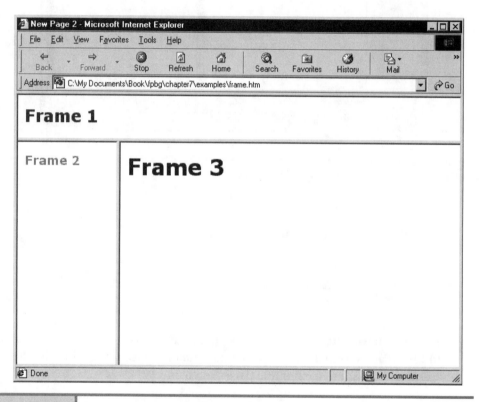

Figure 7-13 The frameset you created

Formatting Frames

FrontPage enables you to modify many characteristics of frames, from adjusting borders to setting page margins. Follow these directions to learn to modify frames:

1. Open the file *format.htm*. This is the same file that you opened used in the previous section.

2. Click anywhere on the top frame. Then right-click the top frame and choose Frame Properties. The Frame Properties window will open.

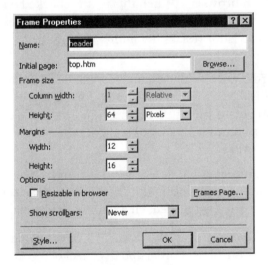

The following is a list of the options found in the Frame Properties window with a brief description of each:

- **Name**   The name FrontPage assigned to your frame. You may modify the name, but you will need to remember the name you assigned to the frame when you hyperlink to it.

- **Initial page**   The file name shown is the page you are currently editing.

- **Column width**   Frames can contain columns. In frames, a column is a vertical frame spanning down a page. You can adjust the width of the frame's column from this location.

- **Height**   This is the box in which you enter how tall you want your frame to be. You can enter a pixel value, a percent value, or a relative value. A relative value is a number that resizes the frame in relation to other frames currently in your frameset.

- **Width**   Width is the horizontal space that separates content in the frame from the borders of your HTML page. This is similar to cell padding, which you learned about in Module 6.

- **Height**   Height is the vertical space that separates the information in the frame from the borders of your HTML page. This is similar to cell padding, which you learned about in Module 6.

- **Resizable in browser**   When this box is checked, visitors will be able to resize each frame. It is recommended that this box not be checked because if a visitor resizes the frame, it might degrade the overall look of your site for them.

- **Show scrollbars**   In this menu, you can decide whether or not you want to display scrollbars. Generally, for the top or header frame that may contain very little information, this value should be set to Never. For frames with a lot of content, you should use either If Needed or Always.

3. In the Frame Properties window, click the Frames Page button. The Page Properties window will appear with the Frames tab selected. If the Frames tab is not automatically selected, click on the Frames tab.

4. To adjust the border size, enter a value of **1** in the value of Frame Spacing field. Make sure the Show Borders box is checked.

5. Click OK to close the Page Properties window. After you have closed the window, the border property will be assigned to your page. Because the border property is a value assigned to all the frames, you will not have to reapply the setting for all the frames.

6. You would think that when you modified the border, you would have to resave all the pages, but you actually only have to save one file. Remember that I said that there is one master HTML file that links all the frames together and controls all the attributes of the frameset; therefore, in this case, only the *frame.htm* file needs to be saved. To save that file, select File | Save.

7. If you are curious to know what the master frameset HTML file looks like, you can examine the master frameset HTML file by clicking the Frames Page HTML command at the bottom of the FrontPage window:

> ⬜Normal ⊘No Frames ⊡HTML ⊡Frames Page HTML �ΩPreview

Note

Not all browsers support the use of frames. If your site uses frames, a visitor using a browser incapable of viewing frames will see a message stating that the site cannot be seen using that browser. To edit the message that is displayed, click the No Frames command from the bottom of the FrontPage window.

Editing Frames Pages

Even though pages contained in a frame are displayed in FrontPage at the same time, each page in the frame can be edited individually. You can perform editing tasks such as adding text, inserting images, creating tables, and more on a frames page just as you would be able to for a regular, nonframed page.

To edit frames pages, follow these directions:

1. Open the file *format.htm*.

2. After the file *format.htm* has been opened, you will see three frames pages.

3. To edit the bottom frame, simply click on the bottom frame and perform common editing tasks. To edit the bottom frame page in its own separate view, right-click the bottom frame and select Open Page in New Window:

4. After you have selected Open Page in New Window, only the bottom frame (*main.htm*) will be displayed in FrontPage.

5. After you edited the *main.htm* page, close it by clicking the *x* in the upper-right corner or by going to File | Close. Any changes you made to *main.htm* will be displayed in the frameset.

An easier way to edit the information in frames pages is to edit the pages directly from the frameset itself. To edit a frames page directly from a frameset, click on the page you wish to edit from the frameset and edit that page as you would regular HTML pages.

Splitting Frames

Sometimes, after you have created frames, you may decide to split or delete extra frames. To split a frame into two frames, follow these directions:

1. Open *format.htm* in FrontPage

2. Select the bottom frame by clicking it with your left mouse button. After you have selected the frame, select Frames | Split Frame.

3. In the Split Frame window that appears, you can specify whether you want the frames to be split into rows or columns. Whichever method you choose, one of the frames will contain the content of the frame you just split, and the other frame will be new.

4. You can specify whether you want to create a new page or set an initial page. It is basically like creating a new frame entirely.

Keep the *format.htm* file open because you will be using it in the next section.

Deleting Frames

To delete frames, you would follow a similar procedure as you did for splitting frames:

1. Make sure the *format.htm* file from the previous section is displayed.

2. Select the frame that you would like to delete by selecting it with the left mouse pointer. After the frame has been selected, select Frames | Delete Frame.

3. The selected frame will be deleted.

1-Minute Drill

- What command can you use to modify the message that appears when a browser incapable of viewing frames visits your site?
- If a frameset has three frames, how many pages will be saved by FrontPage?

- The No Frames command located at the bottom of the FrontPage window
- Four: the three frames pages and the one frameset HTML page

Hyperlinking Frames

The best part about frames is that portions of your page can stay static while other portions of your page change. You learned how to hyperlink text in Module 3, and in this module we are going to build upon that knowledge and learn to hyperlink to frames within a frameset.

To hyperlink a frame to a frameset, follow these directions:

1. Create a new document, and open the file *hyperlink.htm*. After the file has been opened, you will see a frameset with three frames. The top frame is used for the title, the left frame is used for the links, and the right frame is used for holding the main content. Figure 7-14 shows the *hyperlink.htm* file.

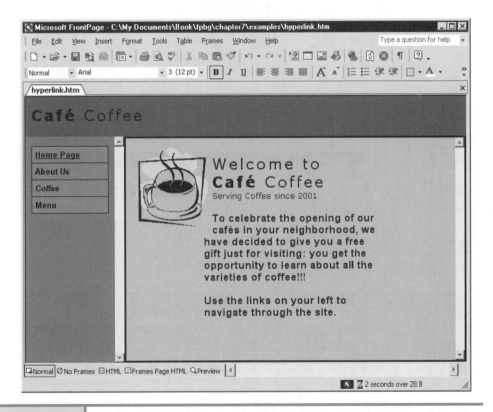

Figure 7-14   The *hyperlink.htm* file

2. To hyperlink the second link, About Us, (I already hyperlinked Home Page), highlight the words "About Us" and click the Insert Hyperlink icon on the Standard toolbar. (You may also right-click the selected words and choose Hyperlink.)

3. In the Edit Hyperlink window that appears, type **about.htm**. After you have entered the filename, click the Target Frame button:

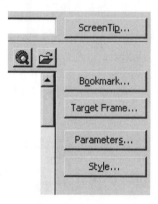

4. After you click the Target Frame button, the Target Frame window will appear, as here:

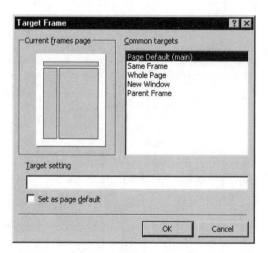

5. In the Target Frame window, you will see a graphical representation of your current frameset in the Current frames page area. Because you want the pages to load on frame on the right, select the right frame in the Current frames page area. After you have selected it, that area will be darkened and the name of the frame you have selected will appear in the Target setting field:

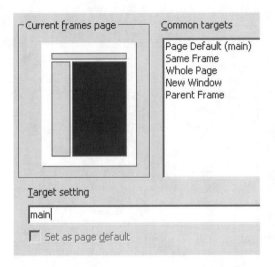

6. Click OK to close the Target Frame window. Click OK to close the Edit Hyperlink window.

7. Preview the page in your browser. Click the words "About Us," and the new information *(about.htm)* will load in the second frame, as shown in Figure 7-15.

8. To hyperlink the next link, highlight the word "Coffee" and open the Edit Hyperlink window by selecting the Insert Hyperlink icon on the Standard toolbar. Remember, you hyperlink by either right clicking and choosing the Hyperlink command or by clicking the Insert Hyperlink icon on the Standard toolbar.

9. In the Insert Hyperlink window that appears, type in *coffee.htm* and click the Target Frame button.

10. In the Target Frame window, select the frame with the mouse pointer. Click OK to close the Target Frame window and click OK to close the Edit Hyperlink window.

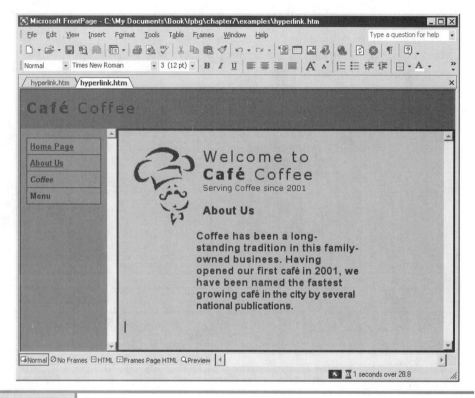

Figure 7-15   About Us information for Café Coffee

11. To hyperlink the word "Menu," highlight the word. Right-click on the highlighted word and choose Hyperlink. The Insert Hyperlink window will appear. Link to the file name *menu.htm*.

12. Select the frame in the Target Frame window.

13. Save the frameset and preview it in your browser (remember, to preview your page in a browser, go to File | Preview in Browser). Click the Preview button after you have selected the browser and resolution you would like to preview the page in. The *menu.htm* page displayed in your browser will look like that in Figure 7-16.

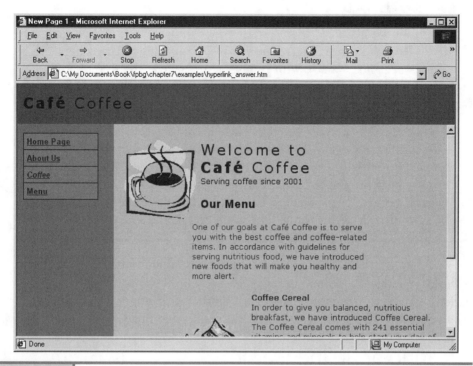

| **Figure 7-16** | The menu for Café Coffee |

14. You will now be able to hyperlink to pages contained in a frame. To see an example version of this exercise, open the file *hyperlink_answer.htm* in your browser or in FrontPage.

Note

When you hyperlink pages in a frame, you should test all the links to make sure they load in the correct frame, display properly and work in other browsers.

Inline Frames

Inline frames are just like frames, except they can be placed anywhere on a Web site. Instead of regular frames that take up either a whole row or a whole column on your screen, inline frames take up very little space—they can even

Ask the Expert

Question: I know that when a browser incapable of viewing a frames page visits a site with frames, a message is displayed informing them of that. Instead of displaying a message, would it possible to incorporate a simple navigation page?

Answer: Absolutely. When you select the No Frames command, you can edit the message that is displayed for browsers incapable of viewing frames. Not only can you edit the message that is displayed, you can insert tables, use images, and perform other tasks just as you would for a regular HTML page. You can even create an entire site with navigation links to provide your visitors with a method of still browsing your site.

be placed inside a table. To see an example of an inline frame and to see how it works, open the file *iframe_example.htm* in your Web browser. Click the various names and watch how the image on the left changes. (You can also see that I included the name of the HTML file in each image.)

Creating an Inline Frame

To create an inline frame, follow these directions:

1. Open the file, *inlineframe.htm*.

2. After you have opened *inlineframe.htm*, place the mouse pointer in the cell to the left of the names. With the mouse pointer in that cell, select Insert | Inline Frame from the Menu bar.

3. After you have selected Inline Frame, your FrontPage window will display the inline frame. In the inline frame, click the New Page button:

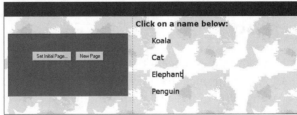

4. After you click the New Page button, the inline frame will display as a blank page.

5. Insert the mouse cursor inside the inline frame by clicking on the inline frame. With the mouse cursor is in the inline frame, type in big, bold letters, **Welcome:**

6. Save the page by clicking the Save icon on the Standard toolbar.

7. Because you created a new page for the inline frame, you will need to save the file you created. Click the Save icon from the Standard toolbar. In the File name field, enter **welcome:**

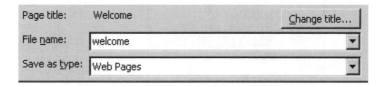

8. Preview the inline frame in FrontPage. You will only the see the word "Welcome" that you typed in.

The following is the HTML code FrontPage creates for the inline frame you just created:

```
<iframe name="name" src="welcome.htm">
    Your browser does not support inline frames or is currently
configured not to display inline frames.
</iframe>
```

7

Hyperlinking Inline Frames

To learn to hyperlink new pages inside the inline frame, follow these directions:

1. Open the file *inlineframe.htm* that you were working on.

2. Right-click the inline frame and choose Inline Frame Properties. You need to right-click exactly on the inline frame's border to display the Inline Frame Properties command, and it can be very tricky to find the inline frame's border. The easiest way to select an inline frame's border is to use the left mouse button to click as close to the border as you can. When you click exactly on the border, eight little squares will appear. When the eight little squares appear, you can then right-click the border of the inline frame and select the Inline Frame Properties command:

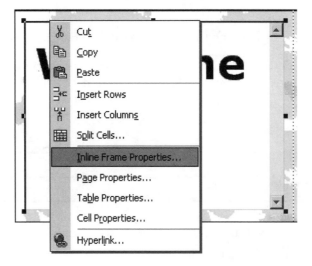

3. After you have selected the Inline Frame Properties command, the Inline Frame Properties window will appear:

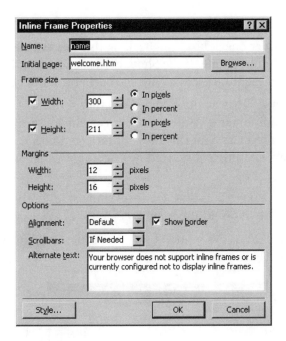

The following is a list of the commands found in the Frame Properties window with a brief description of each:

- **Name** This is the name of your inline frame. You will use this name when you hyperlink the inline frame. You should remember that you entered a name in this box before hyperlinking to it. Having a name specified will make it possible to target the inline frame in the Target Frame window that is found in the Edit Hyperlink window.

- **Initial page** This is the first page that is displayed when a user sees your inline frame. In this exercise, our initial page is the file *welcome.htm* that contains the word "Welcome."

- **Width and Height** This is where you adjust the size of your inline frame. You may enter a percent value to have your inline frame automatically readjust in size. You may also drag the handlebars of your inline frame, as we did in the previous section, to adjust the size.

- **Alignment** This enables you to choose how your inline frame will be aligned. You can select from the following alignment choices: Left, Right, Top, Top, TextTop, Middle, Absmiddle, Baseline, Bottom, Absbottom, and Center.

7

- **Show border** To the right of the alignment menu, you will see the Show border check box. Unchecking this box will remove the border for your inline frame. If the Show border check box is unchecked, you can blend the inline frame with the background of your page.

- **Scrollbars** This menu specifies whether scrollbars should be shown in your inline frame. Unless you are certain you want to display or not display scrollbars, you can allow FrontPage to decide whether scrollbars should be displayed by selecting the default choice of If Needed.

- **Alternate text** This text will display on older browsers that do not support the use of inline frames.

4. In the Name field of the Inline Frame Properties window, you should see "I1." Change I1 to **name:**

5. Click OK to close the Inline Frame Properties window.

Note

While it is not necessary to enter a new name for the inline frame, a unique and/or logical name does make it much easier to find the inline frame when hyperlinking.

6. Now, highlight the word "Koala" from the list of names. While the word "Koala" is highlighted, right-click the word and choose the command for Hyperlink. From the Edit Hyperlink window that appears, enter the file name, **koala.htm**, into the Address field (you may also browse for *koala.htm* by clicking the Browse button and browsing for the file):

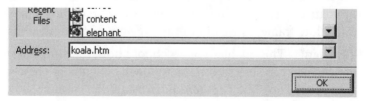

7. After you have entered **koala.htm** into the Address field, click the Target Frame button on the right side of the Insert Hyperlink window, and the Target Frame window will appear. From the list of Common targets in the Target Frame window, select name (name is the name you assigned to your inline frame).

Tip

In the Target Frame window, there is a Set as page default check box. When that box is checked, you will not have to go back to the Target Frame window to specify the frame you would like to load your pages to. By default, all pages you click will load in the frame that you set as the default target.

8. Click OK to close the Target Frame window. Click OK to close the Edit Hyperlink window.

9. Preview your file in FrontPage, and you will see that the word "Welcome" is displayed first in your inline frame. If you click the Koala link, the inline frame changes to display the image of the koala found in the *koala.htm* page.

10. To hyperlink the next link, highlight the word "Cat" and go to the Insert Hyperlink window. Browse for or enter the filename, **cat.htm**. Click the Target Frame button and select the name option from the Common targets list. Click OK to close the Target Frame window and click OK to close the Edit Hyperlink window.

11. Repeat the same steps for hyperlinking the word "Cat" as you did for hyperlinking the word "Koala," but hyperlink to the filename *cat.htm*.

12. For the word "Elephant," hyperlink in the same way you did "Koala" and "Cat," but hyperlink to the filename *elephant.htm*.

13. For the last word "Penguin," hyperlink it in the same way you did "Koala," "Cat," and "Elephant." The only difference is you should hyperlink to filename *penguin.htm*.

7

14. Now that you have all the words hyperlinked, preview your work. You should be able to click all of the names, and the appropriate animal or bird should appear in the inline frame:

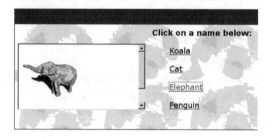

15. Click the Save icon.

—Note —————

If you look at your example, you can see that you have to scroll vertically in the inline frame to see the rest of the loaded page. You may remember that in my example, there was no vertical scrolling. In the next section, you will learn how to modify the properties of an inline frame and resize it so there will be no need for scrolling.

Formatting Inline Frames

In some pages, vertical scrollbars are necessary to display all the information. But in the page we have been working on in the previous sections, the loaded HTML pages do not take up much vertical space, so the best thing would be to resize the inline frame to get rid of the scroll bars.

Resizing Inline Frames

To resize the inline frames, follow these directions:

1. Make sure the *inlineframe.htm* file is open and displayed in FrontPage. Select the inline frame with the mouse pointer. When you select the inline frame with the mouse pointer, handles will appear that enable you to resize the inline frame. Drag the lower-center handle downward until the inline frame almost takes up the entire height of the cell:

2. Preview your page in FrontPage by clicking the Preview command at the bottom of the FrontPage window. Now, when you click the various links, the scroll bars have disappeared because you increased the height of the inline frame.

1-Minute Drill

● Can inline frames be placed anywhere on a Web page?

● What is the recommended setting in the Scrollbars field of the Inline Frame Properties window?

turtle.htm

Project 7-1: Using Frames

The following are the goals for this project:

● Edit an existing frameset

● Hyperlink between frames

● Remove frame borders

Step by Step

1. Open the file *turtle.htm*.

2. Right click any window and choose the command for Frame Properties. From the Frame Properties window, click the Frames Page button. After you have clicked on the Frames Page button, the Page Properties window will appear.

7

● Yes
● If Needed

If it is not already selected, select the Frames tab. Uncheck the Show Borders check box on the Frames tab:

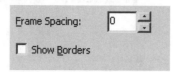

3. Click OK to close the Page Properties window. Click OK to close the Frame Properties window.

4. Highlight the words "Things to Bring" and click the Insert Hyperlink icon on the Standard toolbar. The Insert Hyperlink window will appear.

5. Click the Target Frame button. From the Target Frame window, use the mouse pointer to select the bottom frame in the Current frames page area:

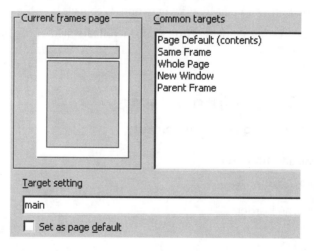

6. After you have selected the bottom frame, click OK to close the Target Frame window. Click OK to close the Edit Hyperlink window.

7. Highlight the word "Itinerary" and click the Insert Hyperlink icon on the Standard toolbar. You may also right-click the highlighted word and select the command for Hyperlink.

8. In the Edit Hyperlink window, enter **itinerary.htm** into the Address box. Click the Target Frame button and from the Target Frame window, target the bottom frame.

9. Click OK to close both the Target Frame window and the Edit Hyperlink window.

10. Save the file. Preview the file in your browser by going to File | Preview in Browser and clicking the Preview button. The following image shows what your page should look like:

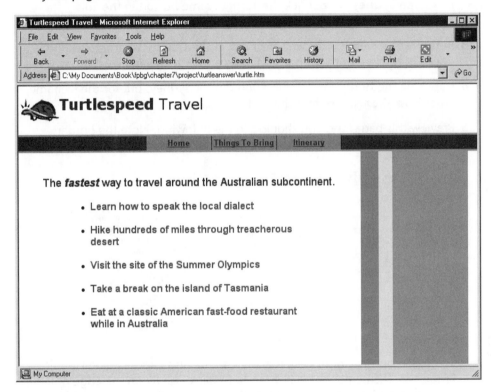

To see my final version of this project, open the *turtle.htm* file in the turtleanswer folder.

inlineproject.htm

Project 7-2: Using Inline Frames

The following are the goals for this project:

● Hyperlink to show another page inside a inline frame

● Format an inline frame by removing borders

7

Step by Step

1. Open the file *inlineproject.htm*.

2. I have already completed the first link for New York City, so start by highlighting Sydney, right-clicking, and selecting Hyperlink. In the Address box, type **sydney.htm**. Click the Target Frame button in the Edit Hyperlink window.

3. In the Target Frame window, select city in the Common targets section. Click OK to close both the Target Frame and Edit Hyperlink windows.

4. Hyperlink the Hong Kong just like you did for Sydney, but for the filename, enter **hongkong.htm** into the address box.

5. Preview this page, and you should see the following. Note the border surrounding the inline frame:

Population of Famous Cities

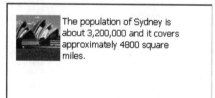

The population of Sydney is about 3,200,000 and it covers approximately 4800 square miles.

Click on any of the city names below to learn more about them.

New York City

Sydney

Hong Kong

6. To disable borders, right-click the inline frame and choose Inline Frame Properties. (Remember, you have to right-click exactly on the edge of the inline frame.) From the Inline Frame Properties window, uncheck the Show border check box.

7. Preview your page, and you will no longer see the border.

To see my example of this project, open the file *inlineproject_answer.htm*.

Summary

Frames and inline frames are great assets to the Web developer. They provide a way of organizing information while keeping the information dynamic and changing. By using FrontPage, the complexities of creating, linking, and formatting frames are removed. Not only can you create frames, you can control a frame's characteristics such as borders, colors, names, and more.

☑ Mastery Check

1. What is a frameset?

_____

_____

2. In a frameset, are the HTML pages independent of each other?

_____

_____

3. When saving pages contained in a frameset, how can you tell what page is currently being saved?

_____

_____

4. How can you open a frames page in a separate FrontPage window?

_____

_____

5. How do you insert an inline frame?

_____

_____

6. How do you assign a name to an inline frame?

_____

_____

7. What can you do to make the inline frame blend seamlessly with the surrounding background?

_____

_____

7

Module 8

Creating Lists

The Goals of This Module

- Use lists in your documents
- Format lists
- Create collapsible lists

One of the more common elements used to display information in an organized, structured format is a list. Lists play an important part in drawing attention to information on a Web page. While tables enabled you to organize information more easily, lists are useful to draw attention to short pieces of information.

FrontPage enables you to create and format lists easily. There are three types of lists you can create in FrontPage:

- Ordered

- Bulleted

- Collapsible

You will learn how to create the three list types in this module. Before we begin, let me introduce the icons that you will be using for this lesson. The icons that you will use to create lists are found in the Formatting toolbar, and Table 8-1 shows each icon and gives its name and function.

If you forget which icon is which while going through the instructions, you can refer back to Table 8-1.

For the directions in this module, please download the various images and sample source files for Module 8 from http://www.kirupa.com/frontpage or http://www.Osborne.com.

Icon	Name	Function
	Numbering	Creates numbered lists
	Bullets	Creates bulleted lists
	Decrease Indent	Decreases the indention of your list
	Increase Indent	Increases the indention of your list

Table 8-1 Icons for Creating and Formatting Lists

Creating Ordered Lists

Ordered lists are lists that are organized in a hierarchical way. In other words, the lists follow a pattern using either numbers or letters. Figure 8-1 shows an example of an ordered list in a Web browser.

Follow these directions to create an ordered list:

1. Open a new document in FrontPage. Once you have created a new document, click the Numbering icon on the Formatting toolbar.

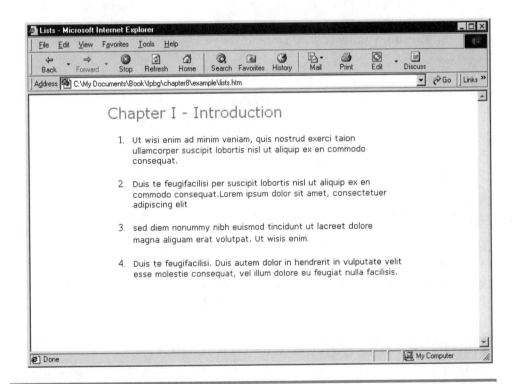

8

Figure 8-1   An ordered list

2. After you have clicked on the Numbering icon, you will see the number 1 appear in your document. Type Monday and press ENTER on your keyboard. You will see the following:

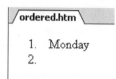

3. Notice that when you pressed ENTER, the mouse pointer moved to the next line and the list number increased sequentially in value. At the number 2, type **Tuesday** and press ENTER. Keep adding more days of the week to your list until you reach Friday. Your list will look like this:

Please keep this file open, as we will use it in the next section.

Formatting Ordered Lists

Just as many other things in FrontPage, you can format lists in various ways. FrontPage makes it simple to modify various characteristics of an ordered list.

Changing the Font and Font Color

Changing a list's font style may sound pretty simple. You would think you could simply highlight the words and select a different font style from the Font menu.

But, when you change the font color and style using the Font menu, the words change their font style, but the numbers of the list keep their default font. For example, the following image shows what would happen if we apply the font Arial to the entire list we just created:

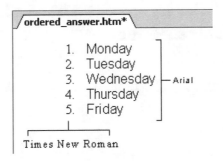

To change the font of the whole list, including the numbers, follow these steps:

1. In the page we used in the last section, right-click the list and choose List Properties. From the List Properties window, click the Style button:

2. After you click the Style button, the Modify Style window will appear. In the Modify Style window, click the Format button and choose Font.

3. After you have clicked Font, you will get the Font window. (This window should be familiar to you because we used the Font window when we covered modifying font styles in Module 3.)

8

4. Under Font, select Comic Sans MS, and under Font style, select Bold:

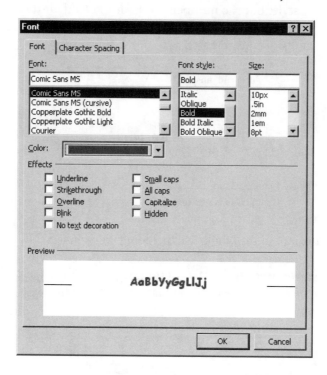

5. Click OK to close the Font window. Click OK to close the Modify Style window. Click OK to close the List Properties window. After you have closed those three windows, your list will look like that shown in the next illustration.

ordered_answer.htm*

1. Monday
2. Tuesday
3. Wednesday
4. Thursday
5. Friday

Note

If at this point you were to apply a font to the words in your list by using the Formatting toolbar, that font will take priority over the font selections you have made from the List Properties and Modify Style windows.

The following is the HTML code that FrontPage outputs for changing the font style of a list. Notice where the font name, color, and font style tags are in the following HTML code.

```
<ol style="font-family: Comic Sans MS; color: #CC3300;
font-weight: bold">
   <li>Monday</li>
   <li>Tuesday</li>
   <li>Wednesday</li>
   <li>Thursday</li>
   <li>Friday</li>
</ol>
```

8

Changing Ordering Style

We just learned how to create a numbered list, but you can also create lists with different formats including letters, Roman numerals, and more. To change the formate of the list, follow these directions:

1. Open the file *orderstyle.htm*. (That file is included with the source files you should have downloaded from http://www.Osborne.com or http://www.kirupa.com/frontpage.) After you have opened the file, right-click the list and choose List Properties. You should automatically be taken to the Numbers tab of the List Properties window. If you are not at the Numbers tab, click the Numbers tab:

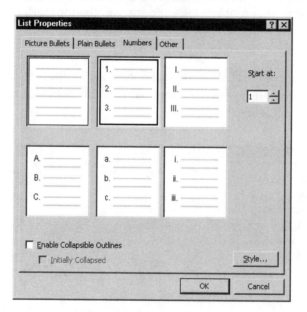

2. In the Numbers tab, you will see that there are six choices. Click the fifth choice with the lowercase letters.

3. After you have that choice selected, click the OK button to close the List Properties window. Your list will now be ordered using lowercase letters instead of numbers:

```
orderstyle_answer.htm*
    a.   Monday
    b.   Tuesday
    c.   Wednesday
    d.   Thursday
    e.   Friday
```

You may now modify properties such as font style and color in the same way as you did for a numbered list.

Continuing an Interrupted List

Oftentimes when you are creating lists, you may need to break in the middle of the list and add information that is not part of the actual list. When you break a list with information that is not part of the list and continue the list again, the numbers or letters will not be in order, but will start over again. The following image is a good example of what I am talking about:

```
numbering.htm*
    a.   Monday
    b.   Tuesday
    c.   Wednesday

The above lists the first three days of a 5-day work week.

    a.   Thursday
    b.   Friday
```

8

In the preceding image, you can see that the ordering of the list has been changed. Instead of continuing the ordering from the previous list, the portion of the list below the sentence starts over again.

To learn how to make the ordering of the list continue, follow these directions:

1. Open the file *numbering.htm*.

2. Right-click the list below the sentence "The above lists the first three days of a five-day work week" and choose the command for List Properties.

3. In the List Properties window, enter 4 in the Start at field, as shown next. (Because Thursday and Friday are the fourth and fifth days, respectively, the starting value for the list will be 4.)

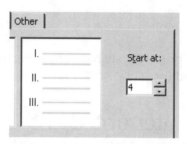

Note

Even though you entered **4** for the starting point of the second list, FrontPage interpreted it as a letter and started with a *d*.

4. After you have entered 4, click OK to close the List Properties window. Your list will now increase continuously from Monday to Friday.

Modifying a List Item

It is important to understand that a list is composed of two parts: the actual list and the list items. When looking at a list with five words, the five words are the actual list and each word is a list item. The following image should help you understand the parts of a list:

Modifying the Font of a List Item

In FrontPage, you can modify the properties of a single list item individually. Instead of using the commands from the List Properties window, you would use the List Item Properties window.

Follow these directions to modify the properties of a single list item:

1. Open the file *item.htm*.

2. Right-click Saturday and select the command for List Item Properties. The List Item Properties window will appear.

3. The List Item Properties window looks like the List Properties window and works in much the same way. To modify the font style for Saturday, you would follow the same steps as you did to modify the font style for a list: Click the Style button, and the Modify Style window will appear. From the Modify Style window, click Format and choose Font.

4. From the Font window, click the Bold option under Font style. Once you have selected the Bold option, choose Comic Sans MS under Font. I also want you to choose a different color for the list item. Your Font window should look something like the following image:

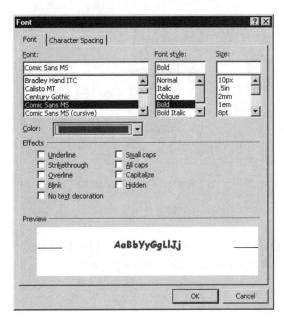

8

5. Click OK to close the Font window. Click the OK to close the Modify Style window. Click OK to close the List Item Properties window. Your example will look similar to this:

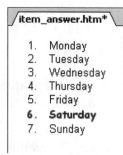

As you can see, only Saturday has been modified.

Modifying the Numbering Style of a List Item

You can modify other properties of a list item besides the font. For example, you can change the numbering style for one list item from numbers to letters or Roman numerals. The following image shows you an example of the numerous ways a list can be modified:

a. **Monday**
2. Tuesday
iii. Wednesday
D. **Thursday**
5. F r i d a y
6. **Saturday**
VII. Sunday

Follow these directions to modify the numbering of a single list item:

1. Open the file *item.htm*.

2. Right-click Friday and select the command for List Item Properties. The List Item Properties window will appear.

3. From the choices listed for the numbering, select a choice and press the OK button. The word "Friday" will have the list choice you selected from the List Item Properties window applied.

1-Minute Drill

● Is modifying a list property the same as modifying a list item property?

● What is the default starting value for an ordered list in FrontPage?

About Unordered Lists

In the previous sections, you learned about using ordered lists. In the next few sections, you will learn about unordered lists. Unlike ordered lists, unordered lists do not use numbers or letters to specify a certain order. Unordered lists use bullets and images instead of numbers and letters. The following image is an example of an unordered list created in FrontPage:

- Cars
- Ships
- Airplanes
- Trucks
- Bicycles

8

Creating Unordered Lists

In this lesson you will learn how to create an unordered list:

1. Open a new document in FrontPage. Once the blank document has been created, click the Bullets icon on the Formatting toolbar. After you click

---

● No. Modifying the list property modifies the entire list. Modifying the list item property only modifies the selected list item.

● 1

the Bullet icon, a bullet will appear in your FrontPage document. Type **Cars** after the bullet and press ENTER. Your example will look like the following image:

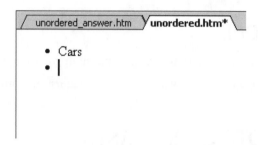

2. After you type **Cars**, add **Ships**, **Airplanes**, **Trucks**, and **Bicycles**, pressing ENTER after each word. Your example will look like the following image:

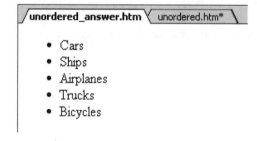

Please keep this document open, as we will use it in the next section as well.

Changing Unordered List Type

Just as you can change the type of numbering for an ordered list, you can change the type of bullet for an unordered list. The three types of bullet styles that FrontPage offers are the circle, the square, and the hollow circle.

To modify the bullet style, follow these directions:

1. Using the same document that we created in the last section, right-click the list and choose List Properties. Select the Plain Bullets tab in the List Properties window.

2. Click the box with the square bullets and click the OK button to close the List Properties window. Your list will now have boxes as the bullet style:

> unordered.htm*
>
> - Cars
> - Ships
> - Airplanes
> - Trucks
> - Bicycles

Changing Bullet Color

Sometimes, the black color FrontPage assigns your bullets can get bland. FrontPage enables you to change the color of your bullet easily.

To change the color of your bullet, follow these directions:

1. Open the file *color.htm*. Right-click the list and choose List Properties.

2. In the List Properties window, click the Style button; the Modify Style window will appear.

8

Ask the Expert

Question: I would like to break each sentence in a paragraph into a bulleted list. How can I do that?

Answer: To make each sentence in a paragraph into a bulleted list, select the entire paragraph and click the Bullets icon on the Formatting toolbar. Your entire paragraph will be made into one list. To break each sentence into a list item, place your mouse pointer at the beginning of second sentence and press ENTER; the sentence will now be made into a separate list item. Repeat that process for each sentence until they are all separate bulleted items.

3. Click the Format button in the Modify Style window. From the menu that appears, choose the command for Border:

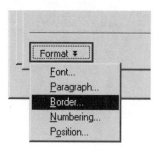

4. Once you click the command for Border, the Borders and Shading window will appear. Click the Shading tab.

5. In the Fill section of the Shading tab, click the command for Foreground color. From the menu that appears, choose a color that you want your bullets to have

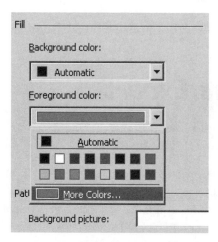

6. Once you have selected a color, click the OK button to close the Borders and Shading window. Click OK to the Modify Style window. Click OK to close the List Properties window. Your bullets will now have the color that you chose from the Borders and Shading window.

You can see that the text in your list became the same color as the bullet color you selected in the Borders and Shading window. Unless you applied a font color to the text in your list prior to modifying the list properties, the text will have the color you selected from the List Properties window. You can change the text color by highlighting the text and modifying the font styles by using the icons found in the Formatting toolbar.

Modifying Individual Unordered List Items

To create contrast between unordered list items, you might want to adjust each list item's property such as color, font, and so on. Just as you were able to modify individual portions of a list in ordered lists, you can do the same for unordered lists. I will only briefly cover a few of the features that can be modified because you are already familiar with most of these procedures.

To modify an individual unordered list item, follow these directions:

1. Open the file *individual.htm* in FrontPage.

2. Highlight Trucks and right-click it. From the menu that appears, choose the command for List Item Properties.

3. From the List Item Properties window, select the disc-shaped hollow circle as the bullet style.

4. Once you have the hollow circle style selected, click the OK button to close the List Item Properties window. Your example should look like the following image:

individual_answer.htm*

- Cars
- Ships
- Airplanes
- Trucks
- Bicycles

The following is the HTML code FrontPage outputs to modify the Trucks bullet. With the exception of the Trucks list item, all the other list items do not have a bullet style defined. The reason the other bullets do not have a style defined is because I accepted FrontPage's and the HTML language's default style. Most browsers interpret the default bullet style to be the solid circle:

```
<ul>
  <li>Cars</li>
  <li>Ships</li>
  <li>Airplanes</li>
  <li type="circle">Trucks</li>
  <li>Bicycles</li>
</ul>
```

Changing List Indention

Sometimes you may want to create a list that is in an outline format. In an outline format, some list items are indented further right than other elements:

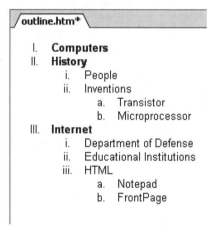

Follow these directions to indent a list item:

1. Open the file *indent.htm* opened in FrontPage. Highlight the word "Tuesday."

2. Click the Increase Indent icon on the Formatting toolbar twice.

┤Note

Indenting a list item by clicking the Increase Indent icon only once will cause that list item not to indent, but to skip a line. You need to click the Increase Indent icon twice to actually indent a list item.

3. Once you have clicked the Increase Indent icon twice, your example will look like the following image:

```
indent_answer.htm*

   1.  Monday
          1.  Tuesday
   2.  Wednesday
   3.  Thursday
   4.  Friday
   5.  Saturday
   6.  Sunday
```

4. Now select "Wednesday" and press the Increase Indent icon twice; "Wednesday" will align directly below "Tuesday."

8

5. As you can see, "Wednesday" and "Tuesday" have the same numbering font as the other words. Having indented list elements have the same numbering font can be confusing to the viewer. To change that, right click "Tuesday" and choose List Properties.

6. From the List Properties window, choose the sixth numbering style that uses lowercase Roman numerals:

7. Click OK to close the List Properties window.

8. Your list will now feature a distinct sublist containing the words "Tuesday" and "Wednesday." Notice how that when you changed the list property for "Tuesday," the list property for "Wednesday" also changed. That is because, as I mentioned earlier, FrontPage defines those two words as a separate list. To see my example of this exercise, open the file *indent_answer.htm*.

Difference in Line Breaks

When creating lists, you may decide that you want to break your list into two sections. For example, you may want to write one word and then write about that word on another line. The following image is an example of what I am referring to:

- **Archipelago**
  A group of islands scattered over a body of water.

- **Continent**
  A great division of land on the globe.

- **Territory**
  A geographical location under a government's authority.

To create a list with information divided over two lines, follow these directions:

1. Open the file *linebreak.htm*.

2. Place your mouse pointer after the last letter of the word "Archipelago." To move to the next line to enter text, press SHIFT-ENTER on your keyboard. You cannot just press ENTER here because doing so will only insert another list item below "Archipelago."

3. After you pressed SHIFT-ENTER, type **A group of islands scattered over a body of water**. Once you have typed that, press SHIFT-ENTER again. This will place a space between each list item in the list:

> ```
> / linebreak_answer.htm \ linebreak.htm* \
> ```
> - **Archipelago**
>   A group of islands scattered over a body of water.
>
> - **Continent**
> - **Territory**

4. Place your mouse pointer at the end of Continent and press SHIFT-ENTER. On the line that is created, type **A great division of land on the globe**. Press SHIFT-ENTER again after the end to create extra space.

5. Now, insert a line break after Territory and type **A geographical location under a government's authority**. You do not have to enter some blank space after this list item by pressing SHIFT-ENTER because there is no more information after this list:

> ```
> / linebreak_answer.htm \ linebreak.htm* \
> ```
> - **Archipelago**
>   A group of islands scattered over a body of water.
>
> - **Continent**
>   A great division of land on the globe.
>
> - **Territory**
>   A geographical location under a government's authority.

8

1-Minute Drill

- Can an unordered list's bullet style be modified?
- How many times should you press the Increase Indent button to have a list indent properly?

- Yes
- Two

Using Images for Bullets

Not only can you choose between several bullet styles, FrontPage also enables you to substitute bullets with images.

Follow these directions to change a bullet to an image:

1. Open the file *image.htm*.

2. Right-click the list and choose List Properties. From the List Properties window, click the Picture Bullets tab:

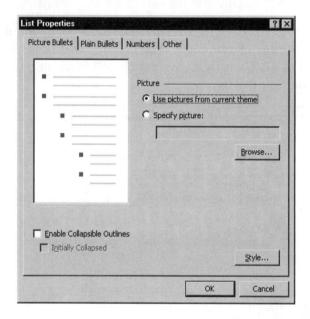

3. In the Picture Bullets tab, select the Specify picture option. Click Browse, which is under the Specify Picture field, and search and select *square.gif*.

4. Click the OK button to close the List Properties window. Your list will now have small squares as the bullet:

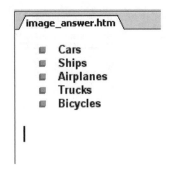

FrontPage has another way of applying bullet images to a document by using themes. You will learn more about using themes in Module 13.

Tip

Make sure you substitute an image that is about the size of the bullet you are replacing. Using a large image will make your list's spacing look disproportional to the other text and spacing in your document.

8

Creating Collapsible Lists

In FrontPage, you can create a special type of list called a *collapsible list*. In a collapsible list, you can click a list item to show more information below it. Figures 8-2 and 8-3 are examples of a collapsible list before it has been clicked and after it has been clicked.

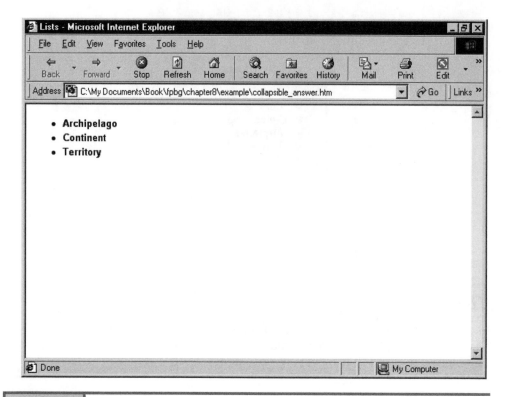

Figure 8-2   A collapsible list before it has been clicked

Now that you understand what a collapsible list is, it is time to create one yourself.

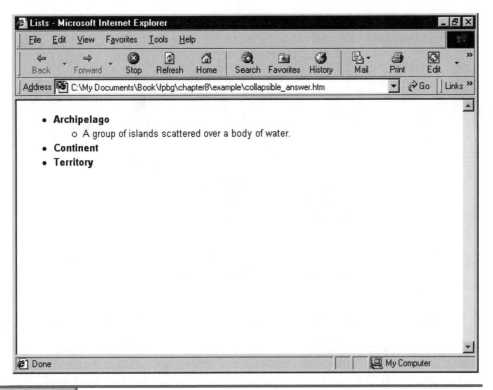

Figure 8-3   The same collapsible list after it has been clicked

1. Open the file *collapsible.htm*.

2. Right-click the list and choose List Properties. From the List Properties window, check the Enable Collapsible Outlines box:

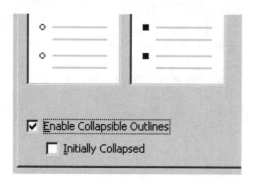

3. Check the Initially Collapsed box. When this box is checked, you will have to click the list item to reveal the extra information when the list is previewed in a browser.

4. Click the OK button to close the List Properties window.

5. You can now click a list item and watch it expand to show more information.

For this collapsible list to work, you will need to indent the supporting information. Simply pressing SHIFT-ENTER to create a line break, and then enabling the collapse list command will not allow your list to collapse.

Note

Most versions of Netscape browsers do not recognize the collapsible list and will display the list in its expanded state instead.

index.htm

Project 8-1: Modifying Lists

The following are the goals for this project:

- Indent a list
- Change a list's bullet style
- Make a list collapsible

Step by Step

1. Open the file *index.htm* from the Project folder in FrontPage.

2. Select all the words under "Vegetables" and click the Increase Indent icon twice.

3. Select all the words under "Other" and click the Increase Indent icon twice. Your page should look like the following image:

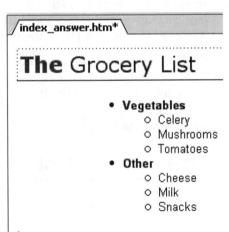

8

4. To number the headings, right-click "Vegetables" and choose List Properties. From the List Properties window, click the Numbers tab and select the second choice with the Arabic numerals for numbers. Press OK to close the List Properties window. Your page will now look like this:

1. **Vegetables**
   - Celery
   - Mushrooms
   - Tomatoes
2. **Other**
   - Cheese
   - Milk
   - Snacks

5. The final step is for you to make the list collapsible. Right click "Vegetables" and choose the command for List Properties. From the List Properties window, check the Enable Collapsible Outlines box. Make sure that the Initially Collapsed box is also checked. Click OK to close the List Properties window.

6. Preview your page. Click the "Other" list item, and the list items under the "Other" heading will be displayed. The following image shows you how your example will look after "Other" has been clicked:

> **index_answer.htm***
>
> # **The** Grocery List
>
> 1. **Vegetables**
> 2. **Other**
>   - Cheese
>   - Milk
>   - Snacks

Summary

Lists are great ways to display short pieces of information. Like other objects such as inline frames, tables, and so on, lists can be placed anywhere within a document. You can even allow your lists to be interactive, enabling the user to use the collapsible list option. Best of all, creating and formatting lists in FrontPage is easy.

8

✓ Mastery Check

1. What is the best way to change the font color for a whole list?

_____

_____

2. What is the difference between a list and a list item?

_____

_____

3. Do collapsible lists always have to be initially collapsed when created in FrontPage?

_____

_____

4. How large should the physical dimensions of an image be that will be used as a bullet?

_____

_____

5. What will happen when you try to enter a line break to your list by pressing ENTER instead of SHIFT-ENTER?

_____

_____

6. How many times should you click the Increase Indent icon to indent a list item?

_____

Module 9

Modifying and Publishing Your Site Online

The Goals of This Module

- Modify page settings
- Publish your site to a server supporting FrontPage extensions
- Use the Reports view
- Explore the Navigation view

U p until this point, you have created files as practice and stored them locally on your hard drive. Eventually, you will create files for sites that you want people around the world to see. In this module, you will learn how to send your site's files to a Web server and modify certain page properties.

For the directions in this module, please download the various images and sample source files for Module 9 from http://www.kirupa.com/frontpage or http://www.Osborne.com.

Modifying Page Properties

When you create a new Hypertext Markup Language (HTML) page in FrontPage, there are numerous settings and characteristics that are added and modified automatically, but there are also properties that you may want to modify yourself. The next few sections will help you to modify some of the more important properties regarding your Web site.

Adding Titles

The title of a page is the text that is displayed on the top of the browser window. Most Web sites that you visit on the Internet have titles that help you to quickly understand what the site is about. The title commonly includes the site's name, its slogan, and so on. This image shows Amazon.com's title:

To add a title to your page, follow these directions:

1. Create a new document in FrontPage, right-click the document, and select the Page Properties command. The Page Properties window will appear. In the Title field, type **Welcome to my home page**:

2. Click OK to close the Page Properties window.

3. Save this file.

4. Preview it in your Web browser. The title you specified will be visible in your browser's window.

Tip

When you save your HTML page for the first time and/or when you use the Save As command, you can add or change the title of the file by clicking the Change title button. When you click the Change title button, the Set Page Title window will appear. Enter the title for your site in the Set Page Title window and click OK to close the Set Page Title window.

Adjusting Margins

When you create a document and start inputting information, there is a small space between the information and the edges of your working area. When you preview a page that you have created in your Web browser, you will notice that there is also a small space between the information and the edge of your browser's window. This space is known as the *margin*:

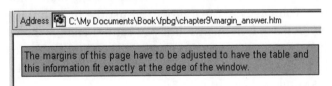

In this section you will learn how to adjust the margins of your page:

1. Open the file *margin.htm*. (That file is included with the source files you should have downloaded from http://www.Osborne.com or http://www.kirupa.com/frontpage.)

9

2. Once the file has been opened, right-click anywhere in the document and choose Page Properties.

3. From the Page Properties window, click the Margins tab. After you click the Margins tab, you will see two checkboxes: the Specify top margin checkbox and the Specify left margin checkbox. Check both boxes.

4. After the boxes have been checked, a value of 0 pixels will be displayed to the right of each checkbox. Because we wanted to remove all margin space, enter a value of 0 pixels for both the top and left margins. Click OK to close the Page Properties window.

5. After you have closed the Page Properties window, you will see that the table in the document is aligned directly next to the window's borders. Preview the page in your Web browser, and you will see that the table is aligned directly next to the border.

For the most part, you do not want to modify the margins FrontPage sets for your documents, but there are times when margins should be removed or used. Some sites look better without margins, and some sites look better with margins. Whether you decided to use margins or not, make sure the margins are consistent throughout your site.

Setting Hyperlink Color

When you hyperlink text, the default font color for the hyperlink is blue, the default color for a visited hyperlink is purple, and the default color for an active hyperlink is red. You have the capability to adjust the hyperlink color by using the Formatting toolbar's font menus, but you cannot change the visited and/or active hyperlink colors from there. To change the visited and/or active hyperlink colors, as well as the regular hyperlink color, you must use the Page Properties window.

Follow these directions to change the visited hyperlink color:

1. Create a new document. Right-click the document and select the command for Page Properties.

2. From the Page Properties window, select the Background tab. You will see three color drop-down menus with the captions Hyperlink, Visited Hyperlink, and Active Hyperlink.

3. The following is the description of each caption:

- **Hyperlink**   Sets the color for all the hyperlinks in your page.
- **Visited Hyperlink**   Sets the color for hyperlinks that have been visited.
- **Active Hyperlink**   Sets the color for hyperlinks that are selected or are active.

4. Click the color menu to the right of the Visited Hyperlink. Select the green color from the color menu.

5. Click OK to accept the visited hyperlink color and to close the Page Properties window.

To change the color of either the hyperlink or the active hyperlink, follow the preceding instructions, but select Hyperlink or Active Hyperlink in the Background tab.

Setting the Default Font

Usually, when you start writing any text in FrontPage, the font that will be used is Times New Roman. Unless you change the font using the Formatting toolbar, which you learned how to do in Module 3, the visitor will also see the Times New Roman font in their browser. There is an easier way to change the font for the entire document without having to use the Formatting toolbar, and the method for setting the default font for the whole page can be found in the Page Properties window.

The following instructions will explain how to set the default font for the document:

1. Create a new document in FrontPage. Right-click anywhere in the document and select the command for Page Properties.

2. In the Page Properties window, select the General tab. In the General tab, click the Style button.

9

3. After you have clicked the Style button, the Modify Style window will appear. Click the Format button and select the Font command:

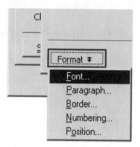

4. After you select the Font command, the Font window will appear. By now you should be rather familiar with this window. Choose a font and any font styles that you want to apply to your page, and click the OK button to close the Font window.

5. Click OK to close the Modify Style window. Click OK to close the Page Properties window.

6. After all the windows have been closed, type a sentence into your document. You will see that the sentence has the font and font style that you selected in the Font window.

7. Save your page, and preview it in your browser. You will see that your document has the same font style here as well.

Note

You will learn more about modifying font properties when we discuss Cascading Style Sheets (CSS) in Module 15.

1-Minute Drill

● From what two windows can the page title be set?

● What is a visited hyperlink?

● The Page Properties window and the Set Page Title window.
● A visited hyperlink is a hyperlink that has already been navigated through.

The Page Options Window

In the Page Properties window, we modified settings that affect how the Web page looks. On the other hand, in the Page Options window, we will modify options that customize the look and feel of FrontPage's features without greatly affecting the Web page itself.

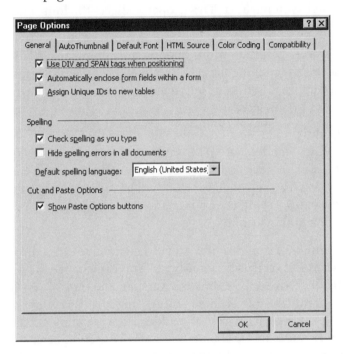

The following is a list of the tabs in the Page Options window with a brief description of some of the options found in each tab:

- **General**   In this tab, you can modify minor page elements such as spelling properties and HTML formatting of elements such as forms and positioned objects.

- **AutoThumbnail**   You may remember from Module 4 that you can thumbnail large images into smaller images within FrontPage by using the AutoThumbnail command. This tab deals with modifying certain properties of a thumbnailed image. You can specify the dimensions of a

9

thumbnailed image, adjust border thickness, and choose whether a thumbnailed image's edge should be beveled for a 3-D effect.

● **Default Font**   In this tab you can set the default font you want to see in FrontPage. You should understand that the changes you make would be visible in FrontPage only. Unlike setting a page font as you did in a previous section, users viewing your page in a Web browser will not see the font style you have set. This property affects the font style within FrontPage only.

● **HTML Source**   All the various options and commands in this tab deal with manually modifying the HTML code in FrontPage. Because FrontPage writes the entire HTML code automatically, you will not have to modify any options in this section.

● **Color Coding**   This section deals with editing HTML code in FrontPage as well. When you look at HTML code in FrontPage, it is color coded to make it easier for developers to modify the code. Here you can specify which HTML feature will have which color. Again, because FrontPage writes the entire HTML code automatically, you will not have to modify any options in this section.

● **Compatibility**   From this box, you can customize the compatibility issues regarding various browser types. You can change the settings for choosing the browser type, browser version, and type of server your site will use. Modifying any of these settings might cause certain menus and commands in FrontPage to stop working. It is recommended that all checkboxes under the Available Technologies section be checked because most people use Internet Explorer or a recent version of Netscape.

Publishing Your Site

Ask any Web developer what their goals are in creating a site, and many will say that one of their goals is to get as many people as possible to visit their site. I am sure that is one of your goals for your site as well. To get people from around the world to see your site, you will need a method of displaying your site to them. To do that, you will need to invest in a Web server and upload your files to it.

Tip

The words "publish" and "upload" both have the same meaning. When you are uploading or publishing files, you are sending files from your computer to another computer, which is called a server.

Choosing a Web Host

A Web server is a computer that is connected to the Internet. A Web host is the company or individual that you pay to maintain your Web server. A typical Web host charges from $15 to $30 (US dollars) for hosting a basic site, and there are thousands of Web hosts around the world that provide reliable Web hosting. You can set up a Web server yourself, but the complexities required to install and maintain it go far beyond the scope of this book.

It is not necessary for a Web host to be located near you; because most of the updates will be done over the Internet, the server can be located anywhere.

Before you invest in a Web server, there are some guidelines you should consider:

- **Reliability**   Find out if the Web host offers any protection against data loss. Most servers back up your site's information in case something happens that causes your data on your site to be lost. Many Web hosts provide a percentage that shows the reliability of their service, which includes the ease of data transfer, how long the servers have been operational without problems, and more.

- **Space**   Make sure you know exactly how much space your host allots for a Web site. All of your HTML pages take up space on your host's servers, and you may be charged extra for using more space than allowed by your Web host.

- **Bandwidth Usage**   Bandwidth is the amount of data transferred from your site. Bandwidth is usually measured in gigabytes (gigabyte is abbreviated as GB). The number of gigabytes is used by you and your Web host to analyze the amount of files transferred. When a visitor visits your site, your Web server transmits text, images, and more to display on their browser. All the transmitting of objects such as text and images can add up to several gigabytes for a fairly popular site. You should find out how

9

much bandwidth your host supports because you may be charged extra should you exceed their bandwidth limit.

● **FrontPage Server Extensions** FrontPage Server Extensions software is a set of tools that is installed on a Web server to help you publish your site and maintain it using FrontPage 2002. While many Web hosts support the use of the FrontPage Server Extensions, many do not.

Your potential host's Web site will usually provide you with plenty of information regarding their hosting services.

For an extensive list of Web hosts that support the FrontPage server extensions, visit http://www.microsoftwpp.com/, which is the link to Microsoft's Web Presence Provider site. From there you can search for a suitable Web host by providing information such as features you want, service plans, and more.

Publishing to a Web Server

In this section you will learn how to publish your Web site to a Web server. The method of publishing you will learn will work on both FrontPage- and non-FrontPage-compliant Web servers.

To publish your Web site to a Web server, follow these directions:

1. Open your FrontPage Web in FrontPage. If you do not have a FrontPage Web, you can easily create one by referring to Module 2.

2. Once the Web has been opened in FrontPage, select File | Publish Web. The Publish Destination window will appear.

3. In the Enter publish destination field of the Publish Destination window, enter the address of your Web server. The address of your Web server is the domain name or unique address of your host. In this example, I am publishing to a folder within the server:

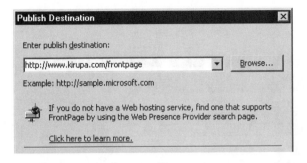

4. After you entered in the address, click OK to close the Publish Destination window. You might receive a window asking you if you want FrontPage to create a Web at that location. Click OK to enable it to create a FrontPage Web on your server. If you do not receive this message, go to the next step.

5. To authorize that you have permission to work on the Web server, you will be prompted to enter your user name and password in the Enter Network Password box. This is to make sure that only you or other people you authorize can have access to your Web server. Click OK to submit your user name and password. If you are not sure what your user name and password are, you need to contact your Web host:

6. After your user name and password have been accepted and verified by the Web server, the Publish Web window will display. This window contains

9

all the files contained in your FrontPage Web that you want FrontPage to publish:

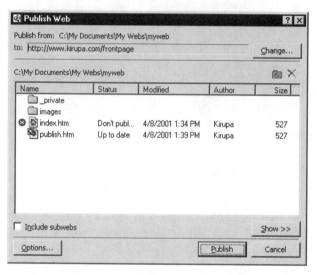

7. If you do not want a file to be published, right-click the file in the Publish Web window and select the command for Don't Publish. A small *x* will appear to the right of the filename, indicating that the file will not be published.

8. Click the Publish button to finalize all the files that will be uploaded to your server. You will see a progress bar showing the publishing status of your files. After all the files have been published to your new location, you will see a confirmation window. You can preview your published files by clicking the first link, Click here to view your published Web site:

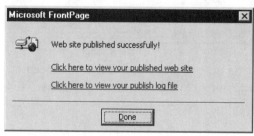

7. You can also preview your published files by typing the location of your Web site in your Web browser.

To see the file I uploaded for this example, go to http://www.kirupa.com/ frontpage/publish.htm.

Modifying Publishing Options

When you are publishing your Web, you can modify several settings to customize how your pages and files get published.

To modify publishing options, follow these directions:

1. Go to File | Publish Web. (If you are continuing from the previous example, you might not be prompted for a user name or password.) Click the Options button. The Options window will appear with the Publish tab selected. If the Publish tab is not selected, please select it:

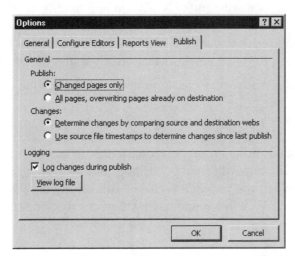

The following list describes each option found in the Publish tab of the Options window:

● **Changed pages only**   Checking this option will only publish those files on your hard drive that have been modified since the last time you published the files.

● **All Pages, overwriting pages already on destination**   When this option is checked, all the files in your Web get uploaded, whether they have been modified since the last publish or not. If you have a lot of files, publishing all the files will take some time.

- **Determine changes by comparing source and destination webs** When this option is checked, changes to the files are checked by comparing the files on your hard drive and the server.

- **Use source file timestamps to determine changes since last publish** When this option is selected, changes to the files are checked using timestamps. A timestamp is the time a computer records for a file. That time gets updated each time the file gets modified. If the timestamp for a file on your hard drive is the same as that same file on your Web server, that file will not be uploaded. If the timestamp is different, that file will get uploaded.

- **Log changes during publish** When you modify or publish files and folders in your server, your user name, time accessed, and other information are stored in a log file. Check this box to enable or disable FrontPage from logging information when files are published.

2. After you have made your selections, click OK to close the Options window.

Importing a Web

On servers that support the FrontPage extensions, you can import a Web directly into your site. While importing and publishing your Web are similar, importing a Web is easier. When you import a Web, you can specify the exact location you want to import your Web to without having to worry about existing files, folders, and more.

Ask the Expert

Question: How can I publish my FrontPage Web to a specific directory or folder on my Web server?

Answer: When you are selecting the location to publish the files, specify the exact path to your folder or subdirectory. If the folder you specified does not exist, FrontPage will automatically create it for you on the Web server.

Tip

On servers that support the FrontPage Server Extensions, the location where your site will be stored is known as a Web. Just as you were able to create and work with FrontPage Webs on your hard drive, you will be able to create and work with a FrontPage Web on your server.

To open an online FrontPage Web and import a Web, follow these instructions:

1. Click File | Open Web. Once you clicked the Open Web command, the Open Web window will appear.

2. In the Open Web window, enter the address of your server in the Web name field. The name of your Web will appear in the list of icons:

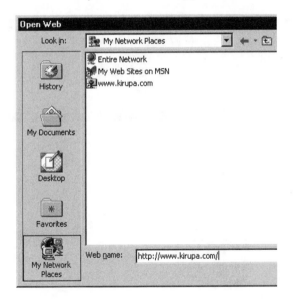

3. After you have entered the address of your server, click the OK button to close the Open Web window.

4. After you close the Open Web window, the Enter Network Password window will appear. Enter your server's user name and password. After the user name and password have been entered, click the OK button to close the Enter Network Password window.

9

5. After you have closed the Enter Network Password window, the folders of your server's Web will be displayed in the Open Web window. Click the Open button.

6. After you click the Open button, you will see your FrontPage background. Select View | Folders to see all the folders and files in your Web. (More than likely, you will not see as many folders as shown in Figure 9-1.)

7. To import an existing Web from your hard drive to your Web server, go to File | Import. You should be familiar with the Import window because you used it to import files and folders in Module 2. Click the From Web button in the Import window.

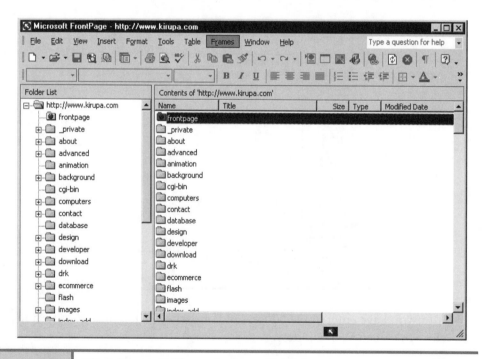

Figure 9-1   The folders and files in the example Web

8. After you have clicked the From Web button, the Import Web Wizard – Choose Source window will appear. Because your Web is located on your hard drive, select the From a source directory of files on a local computer or network option. In the Location field, enter the path of your Web. You may have to browse for your Web using the Browse button. After you have located the path for your Web, click the Include subfolders checkbox to make sure that your Web's subfolders get imported as well:

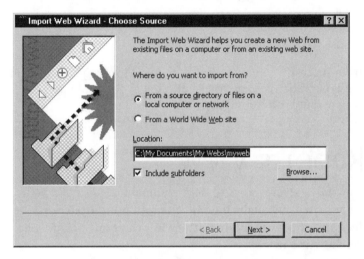

9. Click Next, and the Import Web Wizard – Edit File List window will appear displaying a list of files that will be imported to your Web. You can select any file and click the Exclude button if you choose not to import that file to your Web server.

10. Click Next, and the Import Web Wizard – Finish window will appear. Click the Finish button in the Import Web Wizard – Finish window, and the files from the Web would be loaded in your Web.

11. You will now be able to modify the files from your Web server itself. Because your Web supports the FrontPage extensions, you can make modifications to your page without having to download each file to your hard drive before modification.

9

Up until this point, you had been creating your pages on your hard drive. With your Web server, you can create and edit pages directly on your Web site. If you edit directly on the Web site, there is no need to copy the files to your hard drive to modify them.

Note

For more information on modifying pages contained in a FrontPage Web, please refer to Module 2.

Tip

After you have successfully loaded your Web into FrontPage, there is an easier way to open your FrontPage Web: go to File | Recent Webs, and you will be able to select and open your Web from there.

Using Reports View

FrontPage includes several ways to help you manage your site better. One way to manage your site is by analyzing information found in Reports view. The Reports view provides you with important information such as space usage, hyperlinked files, and more.

To access the reports for your site, select to View | Reports | Site Summary. If you are more comfortable with clicking on icons in a toolbar instead of using menus, you can launch the Reporting toolbar by going to View | Toolbars | Reporting.

Depending on how many files you have on your server, the results process will take anywhere from a few seconds to several minutes. After the results process is over, your FrontPage window should look similar to that shown in Figure 9-2.

In the following sections, I will provide a brief explanation as to what each underlined report item means. Report items that are not underlined do not provide in-depth information for you to analyze.

Tip

You can modify various report properties by selecting to Tools | Options | Reports View. From the Options window, you can change the values for reports, modify how the reports display, and more.

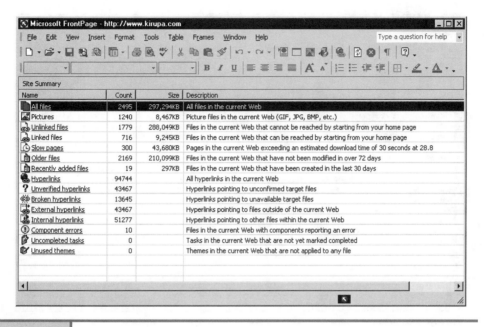

Name	Count	Size	Description
All files	2495	297,294KB	All files in the current Web
Pictures	1240	8,467KB	Picture files in the current Web (GIF, JPG, BMP, etc.)
Unlinked files	1779	288,049KB	Files in the current Web that cannot be reached by starting from your home page
Linked files	716	9,245KB	Files in the current Web that can be reached by starting from your home page
Slow pages	300	43,680KB	Pages in the current Web exceeding an estimated download time of 30 seconds at 28.8
Older files	2169	210,099KB	Files in the current Web that have not been modified in over 72 days
Recently added files	19	297KB	Files in the current Web that have been created in the last 30 days
Hyperlinks	94744		All hyperlinks in the current Web
Unverified hyperlinks	43467		Hyperlinks pointing to unconfirmed target files
Broken hyperlinks	13645		Hyperlinks pointing to unavailable target files
External hyperlinks	43467		Hyperlinks pointing to files outside of the current Web
Internal hyperlinks	51277		Hyperlinks pointing to other files within the current Web
Component errors	10		Files in the current Web with components reporting an error
Uncompleted tasks	0		Tasks in the current Web that are not yet marked completed
Unused themes	0		Themes in the current Web that are not applied to any file

Figure 9-2 Your FrontPage window after the results process is done running.

All Files

If you click the All files report item, FrontPage will go to the All Files view, which displays all the files currently stored in the FrontPage Web. As you can tell from looking at the results that it displays in Figure 9-3, the files can be anything from actual Web pages to sounds and images.

You can customize the files that are displayed by clicking the various category columns. For example, if you click the Size column, the files will then be organized according to size. From the All Files view, you can rename, delete, and modify all the files.

Unlinked Files

The Unlinked Files view is very similar to the All Files view, except that the Unlinked Files view only shows files that are not linked by other pages. The files listed in this view are not being used by FrontPage and are probably taking up disk space on your server. It is important to understand that some of these files might be incorrectly reported as not linked. Before deleting the files listed

9

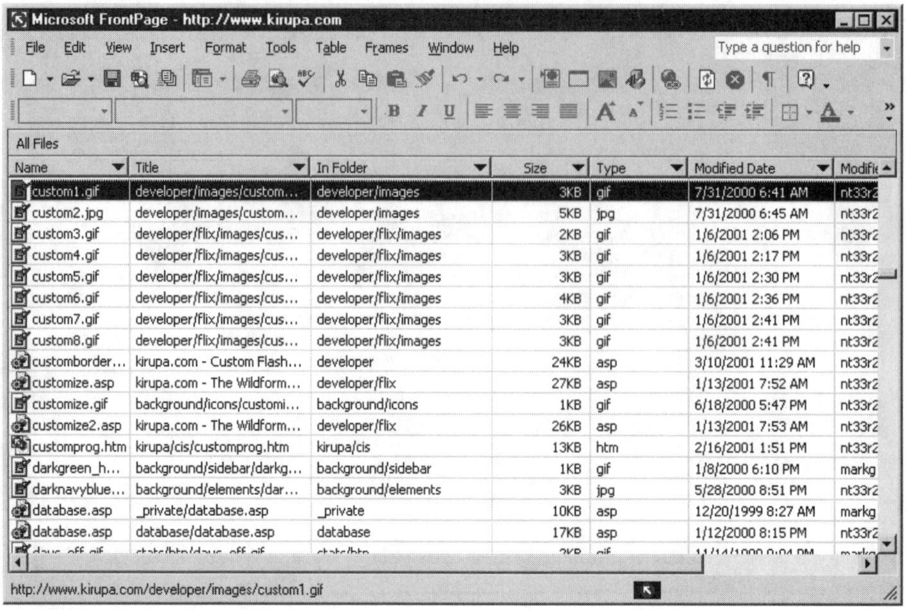

Figure 9-3 The FrontPage All Files view

in this view, you should double-check to make sure that the file is indeed not linked, so that you do not delete a file that is actually being used in your site.

Slow Pages

The Slow Pages view provides you with a detailed list of pages and files in your Web that take the most time to load using a standard 28.8K connection. The download time not only includes the actual HTML page, but it includes supporting files such as images, sounds, animations, and anything that is loaded to be displayed on your page. You can click the Download Time column heading, and the files will list according to the time they take to load.

I recommend that you reduce the download time of these pages by modifying them in FrontPage. Your site's visitors will not appreciate having to wait a long time for the site to load. If your site takes more than 30 seconds to display using a 28.8K modem, you should decrease the number of extraneous items such as large background images, background sounds, and other extraneous items that do not detract from the information the site is conveying.

Older Files

In FrontPage, files are considered older if they have been created or not modified more than 72 days ago. The Older Files view is useful to see whether you may need to update or modify information.

Recently Added Files

The Recently Added Files view provides a central location from which you can see all the files that have recently been added to your FrontPage Web. Any file that has been created within the past 30 days is displayed here.

Hyperlinks

The Hyperlinks view displays all the hyperlinks currently in your Web and displays the location where the hyperlinked files are stored.

Unverified Hyperlinks

FrontPage recognizes hyperlinks by following the hyperlinks contained in a page. Sometimes, you may add hyperlinks to files and objects that FrontPage cannot recognize: when you hyperlink to dynamically created pages that require a browser to view, to pages that are not located in your Site, or to pages on which information such as text or numbers are needed for the hyperlink to work. When FrontPage cannot recognize hyperlinks, the hyperlink addresses will be displayed in the Unverified Hyperlinks view:

9

Broken Hyperlinks

Broken hyperlinks are hyperlinks verified by FrontPage that link to pages or files that do not exist anymore. These links can be images that have been deleted, scripts that no longer work, other HTML pages, and so on. Most of the time, when you delete or modify HTML pages contained in your FrontPage Web, FrontPage will alert you to all the files that are hyperlinking to this file. FrontPage oftentimes automatically modifies the hyperlinks to the updated link locations so you do not have to. When FrontPage modifies hyperlink information, it will notify you with a message stating the changes that will be made.

To fix broken hyperlinks, follow these directions:

1. Double-click the file in the Broken Hyperlinks view. The Edit Hyperlink window will appear:

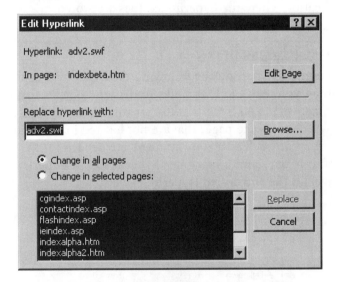

2. In the Edit Hyperlink window, you will see all the pages that are linking to that file. If you renamed the broken hyperlink, you can enter an updated name in the Replace hyperlink with field. If you do not know where the file is, click the Browse button to search for that file in your FrontPage Web or elsewhere.

3. After you have finished making the changes click the Replace button or the Cancel button to close the Edit Hyperlink window.

External Hyperlinks

The External Hyperlinks view provides information on hyperlinks that point to files outside your FrontPage Web. You can use this view to test the hyperlinks in the pages that contain links pointing to other sites. You can modify the link path and other small characteristics in the External Hyperlinks view.

Internal Hyperlinks

The Internal Hyperlinks view provides information on hyperlinks that point to files inside your FrontPage Web. This view can give you a good idea as to which files you are hyperlinking to the most, which files are not being linked to at all, and more. You can modify the link path and other small characteristics in the Internal Hyperlinks view.

Component Errors

The Component Errors view provides you with information on pages that contain errors with FrontPage components. FrontPage Components are small programs that automate tedious tasks for your site. You will learn more about components in Module 12. The Component Errors view provides the page the error is found in, and it also provides a brief explanation as to what may be causing the problem. In the following image, you can see that majority of the component errors in this Web result from the FrontPage Include component. To correct these errors, you will have to open the pages and manually fix them:

9

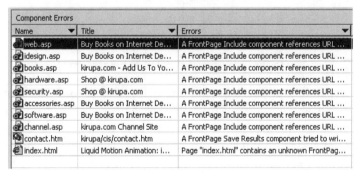

Uncompleted Tasks

In FrontPage, you can assign tasks for individuals to perform in your Web. This type of collaborative effort is very useful in completing a large set of updates and changes. In the Uncompleted Tasks view, you can check to see to whom you have assigned tasks and which tasks have been completed or not been completed.

Unused Themes

Themes are sets of predefined color and style schemes that you can use to enhance the look of your Web pages. The Unused Themes view provides you with a method of removing unused themes contained in your Web. You will learn more about themes in Module 13.

1-Minute Drill

● Can you modify pages from the Reports view?

● What does it mean to publish files?

Using Navigation View

When planning and organizing pages in your FrontPage Web, the Navigation view is a very helpful and versatile tool. The Navigation view is useful when you are creating navigational elements such as link bars and more. You will learn more about using link bars in Module 12.

To see the Navigation view, go to View | Navigation. You will see a graphical representation of your home page displayed in the center of your window.

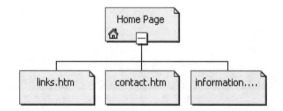

Because most of your pages in your site will follow an ordered manner, your supporting pages will branch out from the home page. To use the navigation view, you can drag a file from the Folder list menu on the left of the window toward the Home Page graphic in your Navigation view. You can add multiple pages to your list that way.

● Yes. Click each file from the Reports view to see the various modification options available.
● Publishing files is sending files from your computer to a Web server so that anybody in the world can see your site.

The Navigation view and features related to the Navigation view will be discussed in Module 12. The Navigation view is also used to create Navigation bars. Navigation bars are a series of links your user can use to navigate through your site. You will learn more about the Navigation features when we cover FrontPage components in Module 12.

Tip

You can attach more than one file from the Folder list to a page in the Navigation view.

index.htm

Project 9-1: Modifying and Publishing Pages

The following are the goals for this project:

- Modify page properties
- Add hyperlinks
- Publish to a Web server

9

Step by Step

1. Go to File | Open Web. Browse and select the Project9 Web from the source files. After you have found the Web, open it in FrontPage.

2. From the Project9 Web, open the file *index.htm*. You will need to add a title to that page. Right-click the page and choose the Page Properties command. In the Title field, enter **Welcome to Speedy Computer Club**. Click OK to close the Page Properties window.

3. Hyperlink the word "Home" to the file *index.htm*. Hyperlink the words "Our Locations" to the file *location.htm*. Hyperlink the words "Operating Hours" to the file *hours.htm*. For information on hyperlinking text, go to Module 3.

4. At this point, you can see that the hyperlinked text is not clearly visible because of the background cell colors. To modify the hyperlink colors, go to the Page Properties window by right-clicking anywhere on the document and choosing the Page Properties command. Click the Background tab. In the Hyperlink color menu, choose the color White. In the Visited Color menu, choose White again. Click OK to close the Page Properties window. All the hyperlinks should now be colored white, and they should be easier to see.

5. Save the *index.htm* file and open the file *location.htm*. To add a title to this page, open the Page Properties window and add the title **Location**. Make sure you hyperlink the links at the bottom of the page. Please refer to step 3 for the names of the files you will be linking to. Make sure that you change the hyperlink color in the Page Properties window.

6. Save the file *location.htm* and open the file *hours.htm*. Add the title **Operating Hours**. Again, hyperlink the words at the bottom of the page. Refer to step 3 for the names of the files you will be linking to. Do not forget to modify the hyperlink color so the links will be clearly visible. Save the file *hours.htm*.

7. We will now publish this Web to a Web server. If you do not have a Web server, you may skip the next few steps.

8. Go to File | Publish Web. From the Publish Destination window, enter the address of your Web server. To ensure that the file names in your Web do not conflict with the files in the imported Web, you may want to upload this project to a separate folder on your Web server; this is to ensure that the project does not disrupt your existing site's file structure.

9. After you specified the location, click OK to close the Publish Destination window. The Enter Network Password window will appear; enter your user name and password there. After you have entered them, click OK to close the Enter Network Password window. You will see all the files that will be uploaded to your server. Once you have verified the files that are going to be uploaded or published, press the Publish button.

10. Your Web should now be published to your Web server. You may view your uploaded files by clicking the first link in the window that pops up confirming that your page has been published successfully.

11. To see the final version of this project in FrontPage, open the Answer Web folder. You can also see the final version on the Internet by going to http://www.kirupa.com/frontpage/a/index.htm.

Summary

In this module, you learned how to modify page elements such as hyperlink colors, page titles, and properties, and you learned how to publish your FrontPage Web. With the knowledge you have acquired so far in this book, you have mastered the basics of using FrontPage. We will now go beyond the basics to explore how to enhance your site using some of FrontPage's advanced tools.

☑ *Mastery Check*

1. What are the two ways the title of a page can be modified?

_____

_____

2. What is the difference between changing the page font from the Page Properties window and modifying the Default font in the Page Options window?

_____

_____

3. What are the FrontPage Server Extensions?

_____

_____

4. What are some of the benefits of using the Reports view?

_____

_____

5. What is the best way to delete files that have been found unused by the Reports view?

_____

_____

6. How do you access the Navigation view?

_____

_____

9

Part

Making Your Site Interactive

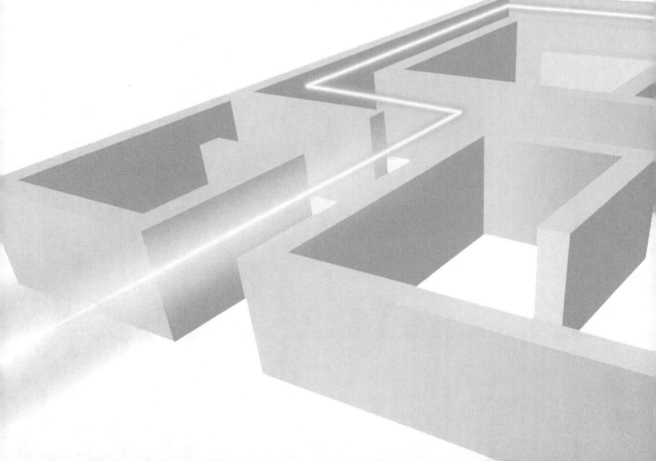

Module 10

Using Forms

The Goals of This Module

- Learn to use forms
- Validate information entered into a form
- Modify how data gets received
- Save and retrieve information from a database

A great benefit of having your own Web site is the ability to interact with people all around the world. While e-mail can be used to communicate with people, there are more effective means of receiving feedback from a Web site. One such method is by using forms. Forms enable your site's visitors to communicate with you directly through a Web browser. A form is an area in which form elements such as checkboxes, buttons, and more collect and transmit information.

FrontPage uses HTML to submit information from a form to a location you specify. Information submitted through forms can be E-mailed to you, saved on a file, stored on a database, and other methods. Forms are also customizable. You can adjust a form's layout, colors, font style, data type, and more by modifying a few settings. In this module, you will learn to create and customize forms for your Web site.

Understanding Forms

Forms that you see on a Web site are no different than forms that you use in everyday life: you fill out the required information on the form and you submit it.

The Form Submenu

All of the form options in FrontPage are conveniently located in the Form submenu. You can access the Form submenu by selecting Insert | Form. Table 10-1 lists the icons found in the Form submenu, as well as their name and their function.

Icon	Name	Function
	Form	Inserts a form
	List Form	Inserts a list form
	List Field	Inserts a list field
	Textbox	Inserts a text box
	Text Area	Creates a scrollable text box

Table 10-1 The Form Icons

Icon	Name	Function
	File Upload	Provides a method in which visitors can transmit files to you
	Checkbox	Creates a checkbox
	Option Button	Creates an option button
	Group Box	Provides a method of grouping form elements
	Drop-Down Box	Groups portions of a form together
	Push Button	Creates a button
	Advanced Button	Formats a button
	Picture	Substitutes a picture for a button
	Label	Specifies a label that can be used to access your form via HTML or other Web technologies such as JavaScript, CGI, and more.
	Form Properties	Modifies form properties

Table 10-1   The Form Icons (*continued*)

Tip

To make it easier for you to access the form icons, you can float the Form submenu by dragging the gray top edge of the Form submenu away from the Insert menu. Doing so will create a toolbar containing the form icons described in Table 10-1.

Introduction to Forms

To introduce you to forms, you will edit a simple form and test it to see how it works on your Web browser. I recommend that you create the form directly on your Web server instead of your hard drive. Forms will not work, and, therefore, you will not be able to test them, unless they are located in a Web server equipped with the FrontPage Server Extensions. If you do decide to create the form on a

FrontPage Web stored on the hard drive, you will have to publish the FrontPage Web to your Web server in order for it to work and be tested. Please refer to Module 9 for information on publishing a FrontPage Web to a Web server.

To become familiar with using forms, follow these directions:

1. Import the file *form.htm* into your FrontPage Web. (That file is included with the source files you should download for this module from http://www.Osborne.com or http://www.kirupa.com/frontpage.) Open the file *form.htm* that you just imported in FrontPage. You will see the following image:

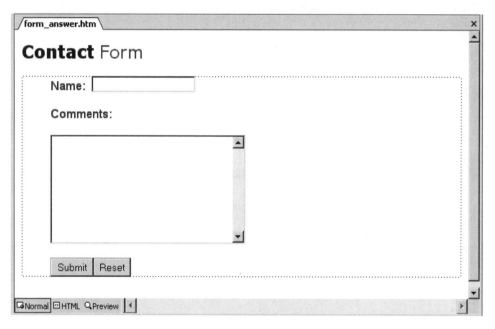

2. Before we can modify the form, you need to identify the form in the *form.htm* page. The form is all the contents within the dashed lines. Right-click

anywhere on the form and choose the command for Form Properties.
The Form Properties window will appear.

3. In the Where to store results section of the Form Properties window, click
the Send to option, delete any information that may be in the File name field,
and enter your e-mail address in the E-mail address field:

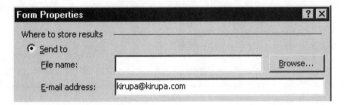

4. Click OK to close the Form Properties window.

5. Save your page and preview it in your Web browser. Type your name into
the Name text box and **I think the form works**!!! into the Comments text
area and click the Submit button. After a few seconds, you will see a Form
Confirmation page just like the following:

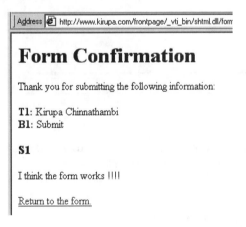

10

6. After a few seconds, you will receive an e-mail with the information
you submitted:

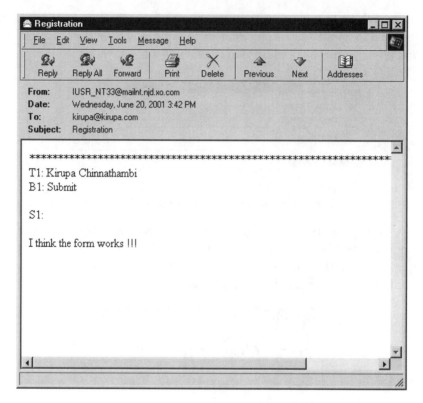

Note

For the forms that we will create in this module to work, your Web server must
have the FrontPage Server Extensions installed.

Creating Forms

A form is comprised of the actual form area; the form objects, which are various
elements that are inside the form area, such as a Name field and a Comments
field; and the buttons, which enable the visitor to submit the information.

Follow these instructions to create a form and customize it to send information through e-mail:

1. Create a new document in your FrontPage Web.

2. Select Insert | Form from the Form submenu (see Table 10-1). A basic form will appear in FrontPage with a Submit and a Reset button.

3. As you can see, the form itself is rather small, making it hard to add form objects to it. To remedy this, place the mouse pointer directly before the Submit button and press ENTER a few times. (Make sure you place the mouse pointer before the Submit button instead of highlighting or selecting the Submit button.) The following image shows what your form should look like:

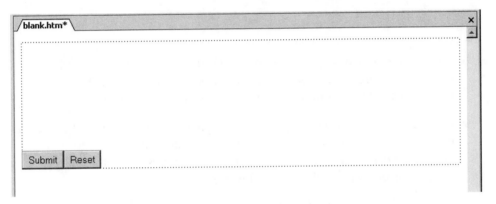

4. Place the mouse cursor in the upper-left corner of the form area and choose Insert | Form | Textbox (see Table 10-1). A text box will appear inside your form.

5. Place the mouse pointer directly in front of the text box and type **Location:**; the text box will shift to the right to accommodate the word. Increase the font size of **Location:** so that it matches the height of your text box.

6. Place the mouse pointer on the line after the text box. If the mouse pointer cannot be seen because of its proximity to the text box and Submit button, manually skip a line by pressing ENTER or SHIFT-ENTER. When the mouse

10

pointer is where you want it, select Insert | Form | Text Area (see Table 10-1). A text area allowing multiple lines of information appears in your form.

7. Because the text area is too small, click the text area, and small resize boxes will appear along the edges of the text area. Select and drag the boxes until the text area is the size you want:

8. To label the text area, place the mouse pointer on the first line after the text box and press RETURN to create a line space between the text box and the text area. Type **Comments:** in the line space you created.

9. I modified the font size and style to make the page look better and to match the size of the form objects. Please refer to Module 3 for formatting text. To remove blank space, press BACKSPACE several times above the buttons. Your form should look like the following image:

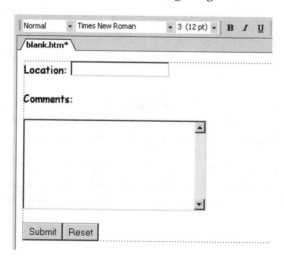

10. Now that we have the actual form designed, we will send the information via e-mail by right-clicking anywhere on the form and choosing Form Properties. In the Form Properties window, delete the information in the File name field and enter your e-mail address in the E-mail address field.

12. Save this file and preview it in your Web browser.

You can view and test out my version of this exercise by going to http://www.kirupa.com/frontpage/blank.htm. You can also see it in FrontPage by opening the file *blank.htm*.

Using Form Objects

Up until this point, we have been using two form objects: the text box and text area. As you see in Table 10-1, there are many more objects that can be added. While I will not discuss how to use every single form object, I will explain how to use the more common objects such as checkboxes, option buttons, and drop-down boxes.

Creating and Using Checkboxes

Checkboxes are boxes that you place a check mark in to select or deselect options. Unlike option buttons, which you will learn about later, you can check many checkboxes at one time.

Follow these directions to create and use a checkbox:

1. Open the file *formobjects.htm* in your FrontPage Web.

2. Right-click anywhere in the form and choose Form Properties. In the Form Properties window, delete the information in the File name field and enter your e-mail address in the E-mail address field.

3. Enter a few line spaces after the text area by placing the mouse pointer after the text area and pressing ENTER twice.

4. Select Insert | Form | Checkbox (see Table 10-1). A checkbox will appear in the space you created below the text area.

10

5. Add some text directly to the right of the checkbox. Type in **Sign me up for the free newsletter**.

6. Press ENTER, and place a checkbox on that line. Add **Contact us about the free offer**. Your form should look similar to that of the following:

7. Save the file and preview it in your browser.

8. Fill out the form by typing information in the text boxes, adding a small comment in the Service Comments text area, and checking the checkboxes. Click the Submit button after you have filled out the form.

9. The Form Confirmation page will appear, which displays whether checkboxes are checked: the checkboxes that have been checked receive a value of On, and the checkboxes that are not checked receive a blank value:

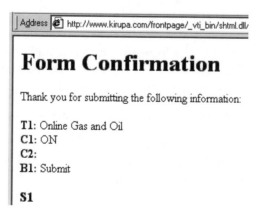

Creating and Using Option Buttons

Just like checkboxes, option buttons provide a set of choices for the user to choose from. Unlike checkboxes, only one option button at one time can be selected.

Follow these directions to create and use an option button:

1. Using the *formobjects.htm* file we were working on in the last section, place the mouse pointer after the first text box and press ENTER once.

2. In the space that was just created, type **Please rate our service**.

3. Press the ENTER key again, and select Insert | Form | Option (see Table 10-1). An option button will be placed in the form.

4. After the option button has been placed, type **Excellent** directly after the option button. Add a few spaces (horizontal spaces, not line spaces) after the word "Excellent" by pressing the SPACEBAR twice. Insert another option button after the spaces, and add **Fair** directly after it. Add a two more spaces after "Fair" and insert another option button. Add **Poor** after the third option button. You will now have three options buttons and their captions on a single line.

5. Save your file and preview it in your browser.

6. Select an option and notice that you are able to select only one choice at a time. When you click the submit button, you will see the confirmation page. Notice that the option button that was selected is displayed by its series number V2.

Creating and Using Drop-Down Boxes

Creating drop-down boxes is a little more involved than the other objects that you have created, placed, and used so far: you have to add the text that is displayed in the list and specify whether it will be selected by default.

To create and use a drop-down box, follow these directions.

1. Using the *formobjects.htm* file we were working on in the last section, add a line space after the text area by pressing the ENTER key. In that blank space, type **Store Location**.

2. Create another line space by pressing ENTER. In the blank space you created, select Insert | Form | Drop-Down Box (see Table 10-1). After you have

10

inserted the drop-down box, you will only a see the drop-down box's basic structure. No choices will be listed: you will have to add in the choices.

3. To add the choices, right-click the drop-down box and select the command for Form Field Properties. Once you have selected that command, the Drop-Down Box Properties window will appear:

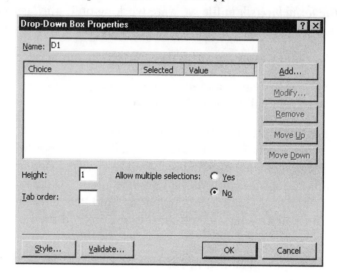

4. In the Drop-Down Box Properties window, click the Add button. When you click the Add button, the Add Choice window will appear. In the Choice field, type **Online**. Below the Choice field, you will see the Initial State section. Click the Selected option in the Initial State section: clicking the selected option makes Online the first choice displayed in the drop-down box when the form is displayed.

5. Click OK to close the Add Choice window.

6. In the Drop-Down Box Properties window, click the Add button, and the Add Choice window will appear. Enter **Japan** into the Choice box. In the Initial State section, click Not Selected because we already made Online the default. Click OK to close the Add Choice window.

7. To add more choices to the drop-down box, click the Add button and type **New Zealand** into the Choice box in the Add Choice window. Click OK to close the Add Choice window. In the Drop-Down Properties window, you can see that each choice you add gets displayed in the order in which it was entered.

8. Add the following choices to the Drop-Down Properties window: **India**, **Russia**, and **Antarctica**. Your Drop-Down Properties window should look like the following:

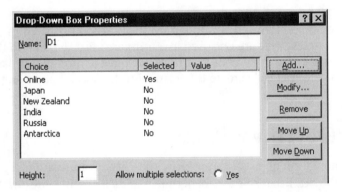

9. Click OK to close the Drop-Down Properties window. The drop-down box will display the word "Online." The word "Online" is displayed first because you selected the Selected option in step 4.

10. Save the page and preview it in your browser.

10

11. Fill out the information and click the Submit button. The following is an image of the Form Confirmation page. The choice from the drop-down box that you selected in the form is displayed in the Form Confirmation page with the word "D1:"

Form Confirmation

Thank you for submitting the following information:

T1: buywater.com
R1: V3
D1: India
C1:
C2: ON
B1: Submit

Note

We have been adding form objects to a form that already exists. Form objects cannot appear unless they are enclosed in a form area first. If you add the form object to an area in the document that does not have a form already laid out, FrontPage will automatically create the form with the Submit and Reset buttons.

About Form Values

As you add more form objects to your form, the Form Confirmation page becomes cluttered with text. Because each form object adds its own values in the Form Confirmation page, having many form objects can make it difficult to track the

Ask the Expert

Question: I have used online forms that enabled me to navigate between each form object by pressing TAB. Is there a way that I can add this capability?

Answer: FrontPage automatically takes you to the next form object when you press TAB. Although sometimes, when form objects are aligned horizontally, pressing TAB will not always select every form object. When option buttons are selected, you will have to use the arrow keys to navigate from one option button to another. Pressing TAB will jump to the next form object instead of selecting the next option button.

To solve that problem, FrontPage provides the Tab order box in the Form Field Properties window. When you right-click any form object and select the command for Form Field Properties, you will see the Tab order box displayed in the Form Field Properties window. In the Tab order box, enter a number for the order in which the Tab key will jump to each form object. You will always start the first form object with a value of 1, the second form object that you want the TAB key to jump to with a value of 2, and so on.

information to the form object. You can make reading the Form Confirmation page much easier by assigning short one-word descriptive form values to the form objects. Instead of seeing cryptic numbers and text, you can use plain-English to describe your form objects in the Form Confirmation page.

Assigning Form Values

To assign form values, follow these instructions:

1. Open *formvalues.htm* in your FrontPage Web. This form should look familiar because this is the same form that you used earlier in the module.

2. Right-click on the form and choose Form Properties. In the e-mail address box, enter your e-mail address. Make sure you delete any information that is found in the File name field.

3. To assign a custom value to first text box. Right-click the text box and select the command for Form Field Properties. The Text Box Properties window will appear.

10

4. On the first line of the Text Box Properties window, you can see the Name field contains T1, meaning that T1 is the name that has been assigned to the text box.:

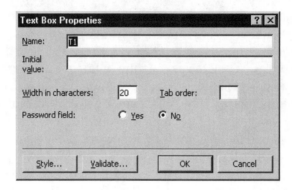

5. In the Name field of the Text Properties box, type **RetailerName**.

┤*Tip*

Make sure that the name you assign to the form object does not have any spaces. If you try to use spaces, FrontPage will display an error message asking you to change the value you entered.

6. Click OK to close the Text Box Properties window.

7. Save the *formvalues.htm* page and preview it in your browser. When you fill out the information and click Submit, you will notice that the Form Confirmation page looks different. Instead of the cryptic value of T1 for the text box, you will see the descriptive word "RetailerName:"

8. Right-click on the Excellent option button and choose Form Field Properties. The Option Button Properties window will appear. In the

Value field, enter **Excellent**. Click OK to close the Option Button Properties window.

9. Repeat the instructions in step 8 to change the value for the Fair and Poor option buttons. The Fair option buttons should have a value of Fair, and the Poor option button should have a value of Poor.

10. Right-click on the Service Comments text are and choose Form Field Properties. The TextArea Box Properties window will appear. In the Name field, enter **ServiceComments**. Click OK.

11. Right-click on the Store Location drop-down box and choose Form Field Properties. The Drop-Down Box Properties window will appear. In the Name field, enter **StoreLocation**. Click OK.

12. Right-click on the Sign me up for the free newsletter checkbox and choose Form Field Properties. The Check Box Properties window will appear. In the Name field, enter **Newsletter**. Click OK.

13. Repeat Step 12 for the second checkbox. Right-click on the Contact us about the free offer checkbox and choose Form Field Properties. The Check Box Properties window will appear. In the Name field, enter **FreeOffer**. Click OK.

Your Form Confirmation page should look like the following image once you have completed assigning the values for all the form objects:

Form Confirmation

Thank you for submitting the following information:

RetailerName: Musical Palace
ServiceRating: Excellent
StoreLocation: Japan
Newsletter: ON
FreeOffer: ON
Submit: Submit

ServiceComments

The recommendation by your staff for the latest Bee Gees' CD was great. I love that album.

Return to the form.

10

1-Minute Drill

- Are forms on Web pages single objects?
- If you have five checkboxes, how many checkboxes can be selected at one time?

Customizing Forms

Forms in FrontPage can be customized in numerous ways. In the last section, you learned to assign values to form objects, and in the next few sections, you will learn to modify still other properties of forms that will improve the form's layout and functionality.

Form Layout

Just like text in a Web page, forms can be organized to make it easier to read. It is best not to clutter form objects around in a form because it makes it difficult for the visitor to fill out all the information. By using tables and cells, you can effectively organize all the form objects in your form.

To add a table inside your form, follow these directions:

1. Create a new page in your FrontPage Web, and open it in FrontPage.

2. Select Insert | Form | Form to insert a form.

- No. Forms use various form objects such as text boxes, buttons, drop-down boxes, and more to work.
- Five. There is no limit to the number of checkboxes selected at one time.

3. Once your form is inserted, you will see the form outline and two buttons. Place the mouse pointer before the Submit button and press ENTER once to create one line space in your form.

4. Insert your mouse pointer in the top row of your form and create a 4 × 2 table by using the Insert Table icon from the Standard toolbar. Merge the cells in the last row and set the table's border to zero. (Please refer to Module 6 if you need a refresher on how to create and format a table.) Your form should look like the following image:

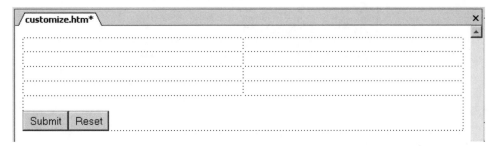

5. In the left cell on the top row, type **First Name**. In the right cell on the first row, insert a text box using the Form submenu.

6. In the left cell on the second row, type **Last Name**. In the right cell on the second row, insert another text box.

7. In the left cell on the third row, type **City**. In the right cell in the third row, insert another text box. The form will now contain one column of words and one column of text boxes, with an empty, merged cell at the bottom.

8. In the merged cell on the bottom, type **Additional Information**. With the cursor after the word "Information," press ENTER, and on the next line, insert a text area. Increase the size of the text area till it takes up the whole cell.

10

You should decrease the extra space separating the columns by right-clicking in the table and choosing Table Properties. The Table Properties window will appear. Decrease the values for Cell Spacing and Cell Padding. Your form should look like the following image:

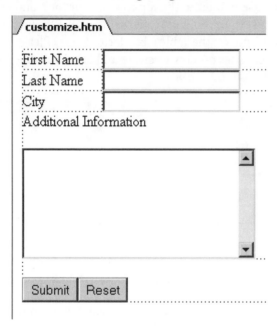

9. At this point, you should increase the cell padding, add some cell background color, and change the font styles, making the form colorful and lively.

10. Name your form objects by entering in a custom value. To name a form object you right-click on the form object and choose Form Field Properties. The form object's Properties window will appear. In the Name field, enter the value that you want your form to have.

11. Type your e-mail address into the E-mail address field of the Form Properties window.

12. Save the current page and preview it in your browser. You can see that your form looks much better.

To see and use my form, go to http://www.kirupa.com/frontpage/customize.htm.

Creating a Form Confirmation Page

The Form Confirmation page you see once a form has been submitted is the default form used by FrontPage. The default Form Confirmation page is functional, but it doesn't have much style. Because I am certain that your site has a unique style of its own, we will learn how to create our own confirmation page.

To create our own confirmation page, follow these directions:

1. Import the file *customize.htm* into your FrontPage Web. Once the file has been imported, open it in FrontPage. If you went to my site to look at my version of the previous section's work, you will see that *customize.htm* is very similar to the one on my site.

2. Make sure you enter an e-mail address in the Send to box in the Form Properties window for the form. Keep this file open because we will be modifying it later.

3. Inside your FrontPage Web, create a new page. Save the new page as *confirmation.htm*. Once you have saved the page as *confirmation.htm*, open it in FrontPage. Type **Information Received** in large, bold letters. Save the page.

4. Display the page *customize.htm* in FrontPage. Right-click the form and choose the Form Properties command. In the Form Properties window, click the Options button, and the Saving Results window will appear. In the Saving Results window, select the Confirmation Page tab:

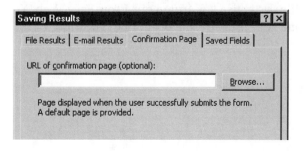

5. In the URL of confirmation page field, type **confirmation.htm**. If you are not sure where the file is located, click the Browse button to find and select it. Click OK to close the Saved Results window. Click OK to close the Form Properties window.

6. Save the *customize.htm* page and preview it in your browser. Fill in the information and click the Submit button. The confirmation page you created will be displayed.

Tip

You can create elaborate confirmation pages. You can even add your site's navigation links, images, and more. Think of your confirmation page as another page that you create in FrontPage with hyperlinks, tables, images, and so on.

Enhancing the Confirmation Page

When you do not specify a confirmation page, you will see the default confirmation page instead. While the default confirmation page does not look nice, it does display information from the form objects that you submitted. Information contained in a text box, drop-down menu, and other form objects is displayed in the confirmation page.

Yet in the confirmation page we created in the previous section, information from the form objects was not displayed. The following instructions will explain how to display information from the form objects in the confirmation page:

1. Import the file *field.htm* into your FrontPage Web. Open the page, and you will see that it looks similar to the confirmation page you created in the previous section.

2. Open the file *customize.htm* from your FrontPage Web. You will now have both *field.htm* and *customize.htm* open. In the upper-left of your screen, below the Formatting toolbar, you will see tabs with each page's name on it. When you click a tab, FrontPage will display that page. This feature is quite useful when you are working on two pages at the same time.

3. Click the tab for *field.htm*. We want to display the name of the person who submitted the form directly after the words "Thank You."

4. Go to the *customize.htm* file page by selecting the *customize.htm* tab. Because we want to display the first name, right-click the First Name field and select the Form Field Properties command. As you can see, FirstName has been assigned to the Name field:

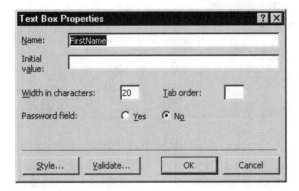

5. Write down the value, FirstName, for the name of the first name Text box so you do not forget it. Click OK to close the Text Box Properties window

6. Click the *field.htm* tab. Place the mouse pointer after the word "You" and before the word "for." Press the SPACEBAR to add a space so the mouse pointer will be evenly centered between both words. While your mouse pointer is in between the words, select Insert | Web Component. The Insert Web Component window will appear. Select the Advanced Controls component

10

type. The Choose a control menu box displays the Advanced Controls components. In the Choose a control menu box, select Confirmation Field:

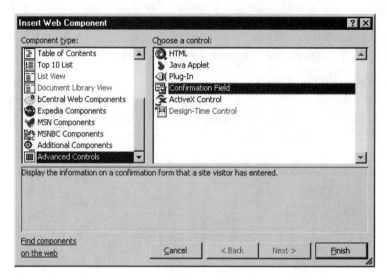

7. After you have selected Confirmation Field, click the Finish button, and the Confirmation Field Properties window will appear. In the Confirmation Field Properties window, enter the value of the field that you would like to display, which, in this case, is **FirstName** (because I named my version of the text box "FirstName").

8. After you have entered **FirstName**, click OK to close the Confirmation Field Properties window. You will see the Text box name FirstName you entered appears in brackets in between the words "You" and "for."

9. Save this file.

10. We will need to edit the *customize.htm* page. You will need to modify the form in that page so that it displays the *field.htm* confirmation page. So, enter

field.htm in the Confirmation field. If you are not sure how to add a confirmation page, please refer to the previous section.

11. Once the confirmation page, *field.htm*, has been set in the form found in *customize.htm*, save this page and preview it in your browser.

When you submit the form, notice that the confirmation page displays the name entered in the First Name field. To see how the form works, go to http://www.kirupa.com/frontpage/firstname.htm.

Validating Form Objects

When you fill out a form online and click the Submit button, you may receive a message telling you to fill in a certain box, use correct numbering, and more. Those messages appear because the developer added validation points to the form and form objects. Validation points ensure that the data that is being sent is correctly formatted, filled out, and so on.

Validating Text

Let's say your form has a field for a state abbreviation. Because U. S. state abbreviations do not contain numbers, the state abbreviation field should not allow numbers to be submitted. You can use validation points to ensure that data entered does not include numbers.

To validate text, follow these directions:

1. Import the file *validating.htm* to your FrontPage Web. Once you have it imported, open the page in FrontPage. You will see three text boxes and a text area.

2. Make sure that the form will save the results to your e-mail address. Right-click on the form and choose Form Field Properties. The Form

10

Field Properties window will appear. In the Send to field, enter your e-mail address.

3. To make sure that the person who fills out this form does not enter any numbers in the text box to the right of the word "Planet," we need to make sure that the information he types in is only letters. To do this, right-click the "Planet" text box and select the command for Form Field Properties. From the Form Field Properties window, click the Validate button. The Text Box Validation window will appear:

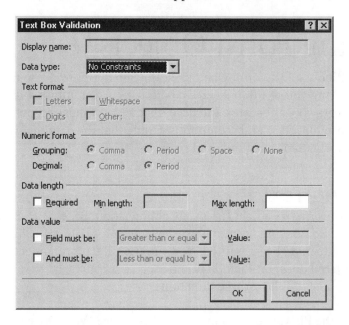

4. In the Text Box Validation window, click the arrow in the Data type field to activate the Data type drop-down menu. Because we only want the user to enter text, select the Text command from the Data type drop-down menu.

5. After you have selected the Text command, you will see that the boxes in the Text format section (right below Data type) are now active. Check the Letters checkbox.

6. Going back to the top of the Text Box Validation window, enter **Planet** in the Display name field. Click OK to close the Text Box Validation window.

7. Save this file and preview it in your Web browser. Type a number (or a combination of letters and numbers) in the Planet text box and click the Submit button. You will get a message asking you to only enter letters:

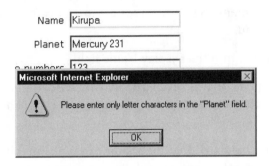

8. Now try typing a word, pressing the SPACEBAR, and clicking the Submit button: you will receive the error message again because spaces are not considered to be letter characters.

9. To enable spaces, you need to go back to the Text Box Validation window and check the Whitespace checkbox. If you do not check the Whitespace checkbox, you can type one word composed entirely of text without any spaces to submit the form.

Please keep this file open, as we will be using it in the next section as well.

Controlling Character Length

You may have noticed that some online forms have a specified limit as to how much you can type. Some of the forms ask you to type in less than five-hundred characters, one-thousand characters, five characters, or other amount.

To control the character length in your form, follow these directions:

1. Using the *validating.htm* page from the previous lesson, right-click the text area and select the Form Field Properties command. In the Form Field Properties window that appears, click the Validate button, and the Text Box Validation window will appear.

2. For this exercise, we do not want the visitor to type in anything that will take more than ten characters. In real life you would use a higher number, but for this exercise we will use a smaller number to save time. In the Text Box Validation window, click the arrow in the Data type field to activate the drop-down menu. Select the Text command from the Data type drop-down menu.

3. Enter **Comments** into the Display Name field.

4. Because comments that people write may include numbers, spaces, and letters, check the Letters, Digits, and Whitespace checkboxes in the Text format section.

5. So far, we have validated that the visitor can type anything in the text area and it will be accepted, but we still need to control the character length to ten characters.

6. In the Data length area, enter **10** in the Max length field.

7. Click OK to close the Text Box Validation window. Click OK to close the Form Field Properties window.

8. Save this page and test it in your Web browser. Notice that when you enter anything longer than ten characters in the Comments text area, FrontPage displays an error message.

Please keep this page open, as you will be using it in the next section as well.

Validating Numbers

Just like validating text, you can validate numbers. While you can use validation points to ensure that information entered does not contain text, you can make sure that the information submitted falls within a certain number range, contains the right number of digits, and more.

In this lesson, you will learn how to make sure that the entered number is greater than a certain value:

1. In the *validating.htm* page, we want the visitor to type a number greater than 1000 in the Enter number greater than 1000 text box. Because there is no set limit as to how high the number can go; we will use a method that is effective for validating numbers entered are greater than 1000.

2. Right-click the Enter a number greater than 1000 text box and select the Form Field Properties command. In the Form Field Properties window, select the Validate button to display the Text Box Validation window.

3. In the Text Box Validation window, select the arrow in the Data type field and select Number from the drop-down menu. Type **Enter Number** in the Display name field.

4. In the Numeric format section, select Comma in the Grouping area. Select the Period option in the Decimal area.

5. Now, we need to make sure that the number entered is greater than 1000. In the Data value area, check the Field must be checkbox. After you check the Field must be checkbox, the drop-down menu to the right of it becomes active. From that drop-down menu, select Greater than. Enter **1000** in the Value field:

6. A great way to check to see if the selections you made will work is by reading the Data value section. Our selections make the Data value read, "Field must be Greater than 1000," which is what we want.

7. Click OK to close the Text Box Validation window. Click OK to close the Form Fields Properties window.

8. Save this page and test it in your Web browser. In the third text box, enter a number less than 1000. Click the Submit button, and your browser will display that the following message: Please enter a value greater than 1000 in the Enter Number field.

10

To see how my version of the *validating.htm* file works, go to http://www.kirupa.com/frontpage/validating.htm.

Tip

Just as you were able to create a custom confirmation page for your form, you can create a custom validation form. To do this, you simply go to the Saving Results window as you would for specifying the confirmation page, but you enter the address of the validation page in the URL of validation failure page field.

Saving Results

In this entire module, you saved all the form information by having your Web server send it to your e-mail address, but you can actually save the form information submitted in many formats beside e-mail. You can tell FrontPage to save your form results in a text file, html page, and even in a database. In the next few sections you will learn how to save your form results in various formats.

Saving Form Results as a File

In this lesson, you will learn how to save the form information as a file:

1. Import the file *contactform.htm* into your FrontPage Web. Once you have that file imported, open it in FrontPage. This form will look somewhat familiar because we used a similar form in a previous section.

2. Before we set up the form to save the results as a file, make sure all the form objects have a name specified. Please refer to the Assigning Form Values section if you do not remember how to name form objects. That will ensure that the various portions of your results will be clearly labeled.

3. Once you have specified the name values for the form objects, right-click the form and choose the command for Form Properties. From the Form Properties window, click the Options button.

4. After you click the Options button, the Saving Results window will appear. In the Saving Results window, select the File Results tab

5. In the File name field of the File Results tab, type **store**. Because we want the form object names to displayed in the results, make sure the Include field names checkbox is checked.

6. In the File format drop-down menu, select HTML (FrontPage will automatically assign the appropriate extension to the name you entered).

7. As an option, you may want to store your form results in another file by filling out the information in the File name field in the Optional second file section. Saving form information in another location is useful if you want to save your results in different file formats or have a backup of the form results in a single file.

8. Click OK to close the Saving Results window. Click OK to close the Form Properties window.

9. Save the file and test it in your browser. You will see the confirmation page after the information has been submitted.

10. To view your form results, go to View | Folders from the menu bar. Look in the list of files to find *store.htm*. Right-click *store.htm* and select the Preview in browser command.

Tip
You may also save the information submitted in the form by entering the filename into the File Name section of the Form Properties window.

10

Keeping Form Information Private

When your form results are being saved, your visitors may be able to see the location where your files are being saved. They can also view the information other people have submitted. To prevent visitors from having access to the form results, FrontPage creates a private folder called _private in your FrontPage Web. Because we do not want unauthorized users to have access to the saved results, we need to make sure that FrontPage writes the form information to a file in the _private folder.

To keep form information private, follow these directions:

1. From the Folders View (View | Folders), copy the file *store.htm* into the _private folder.

2. After the *store.htm* has been copied into the _private folder, open the *contactform.htm* file. Right-click on the form and select the Form Properties command. Click the Options button in the Form Properties window, and the Saving Results window will appear. The File Results tab should be selected in the Saving Results window. In the box where it has your file name *store.htm* entered, click the Browse button and browse to the _private folder and select the *store.htm* file. Click the OK button, and the location of the file will be displayed in the File name field:

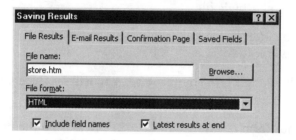

3. Save and test the form in your browser. The form results will be written to the *store.htm* file in the _private folder. You will see the Confirmation page once the information has been submitted.

4. Try to open the *store.htm* file stored in the _private folder in your browser, and your browser will display an error message stating that file access is forbidden. So how will you access the results in this file? You can open the stored results in FrontPage by opening that file from the Folders View.

Note

The _private folder is automatically created by FrontPage when your FrontPage Web is created. If your FrontPage Web did include a _private folder, you can create a new folder that disables browsers from viewing its contents. To create a new folder that keeps contents private, create a new folder and give it a name you want.; it does not have to be _private. Once you have created that folder, right-click it and select the Properties command. Uncheck the Allow files to be browsed box. When form results are stored in the folder you just created, your visitors will be unable to see the information contained in it.

Saving Form Results Using E-mail

Even though you should already be familiar with the basics of sending your form information through e-mail, there is another method of saving form information by using e-mail.

To use another method of saving form results through e-mail, follow these directions:

1. Import the file *e-mail.htm* into your FrontPage Web and open it in FrontPage Right-click the form and select the Form Properties command. From the Form Properties window, click the Options button.

2. After clicking the Options button, the Saving Results window will appear. Select the E-mail Results tab. In the E-mail address to receive results field, you will see a generic e-mail address that I entered. Enter your e-mail address into the E-mail address to receive results field.

3. From the Saving Results window, you can customize how your form results will be formatted when displayed in your e-mail program. In the E-mail message header section, enter the text Form Results. The text Form Results

10

will be displayed as the Subject of your message and the Reply-to line of your message.

4. Save and preview the page in your browser. Complete the form and click the Submit button. Shortly you will receive your form results in your e-mail box:

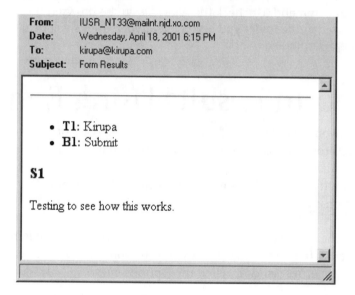

Note

Many e-mail programs do not support HTML-formatted messages. Before you use the HTML format option, you need to make sure your e-mail program supports it. The latest versions of Outlook Express support HTML formatted e-mail messages.

Saving Additional Information

In FrontPage, you can save additional information about the person submitting the form. Besides the form information, you can save information such as the user's time, their browser, and more. Saving such information is useful because it allows Web developers to customize their site for a certain group of browsers, and so on.

To save additional information, follow these directions:

1. Import the file *additional.htm* into your FrontPage Web. Once you have imported the file, open it in FrontPage. You will see that this file is similar to many of the forms you created in the previous sections.

2. Specify an e-mail address to which the form results will be saved. To specify an e-mail address, right-click on the form and choose Form Properties. The Form Properties window will appear. In the E-mail address field, enter your e-mail address.

3. From the Form Properties window, click the Options button, and the Saving Results window will appear. From that window, select the Saved Fields tab.

4. In the Saved Fields tab, you will see the Form Fields to save menu box and other commands:

5. If you would like to know when visitors submitted information to your Form, you can set the style of that information in the Date and time area. Click the Date format drop-down menu and select the third selection from the list. Click the Time format drop-down menu and choose the first time command. If you do not want to display the time when the form is submitted, select the commands for (none) in both the Date format and Time format drop-down menus.

6. In the Additional information to save section, there are options for you to get additional information about your visitor. Checking or unchecking these boxes allows you to get the remote computer name, the username, and the browser type your visitor is using. Make sure you check the three checkboxes found in the Additional information to save text area.

7. After you have selected your Saved Fields options, save the page and test it in your browser. Once the form information has been submitted, check to see how the form results look in your mailbox. You will see that the form results will display your computer's name on the Internet, the operating system you use, the type of browser you use, the date, and more.

10

1-Minute Drill

● Can all e-mail programs display HTML-formatted messages?
● What are characters?

Saving Form Information to a Database

An alternative to saving form results in a file or through e-mail is a database. There are many advantages to saving form information in a database: you can retrieve the information easily, you can use the data in other programs such as Microsoft Access, and the information is organized. To use the database functions of FrontPage, you do not need to have any database software.

Best of all, you can view the database information easily from a Web browser. To save form information to a database, follow these directions:

1. Import the file *database.htm* into your Web server. After the file has been imported, open the file in FrontPage.

2. After you have opened the file *database.htm* in FrontPage, right click the form and select the Form Properties command. The Form Properties window will appear.

3. In the Form Properties window, delete the information in the e-mail address field (because we will be saving the information to a database) and select the Send to database option. Now, click the Options button.

4. After you have clicked the Options button, the Options for Saving Results to Database window will appear. From this window, you will customize the properties of the database.

● No
● Characters can be letters, numbers, or spaces.

5. In the Options for Saving Results to Database window, select the Database Results tab, shown next. Click the Create Database button in the Connection area to tell FrontPage to create a new database for our form. After a few seconds, FrontPage will display a message telling you of the name and the location of the database it has created for you in your Web. Click OK to close the message.

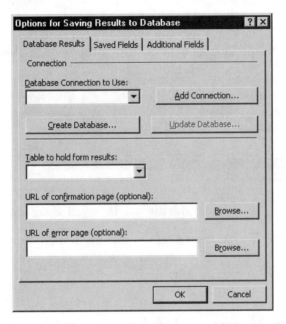

6. Now, to make sure that the form information will get transferred to the database. To do this, click the Saved Fields tab in the Options for Saving Results Database window.

7. In the Saved Fields tab, there are three form fields listed. Double click each form field and click OK in the Modify Field window.

8. Select the Additional Fields tab and remove all the fields found there by selecting each item and clicking the Remove button. Click the Database Results tab and enter **confirmation.htm**. (If you do not enter an address for a confirmation page, FrontPage will provide you with the default confirmation page.)

10

Note

In the Modify Field window, you can modify where the form results will be saved in the database.

9. Once you close all the windows open in FrontPage by clicking the OK button, FrontPage will prompt you with a message stating that this HTML file will have to be saved with the Active Server Pages (ASP) extension. To do this, select File | Save As from the menu bar, and the Save As window will appear. In the Save As window, using the Save As Type drop-down menu, select the Active Server Pages option:

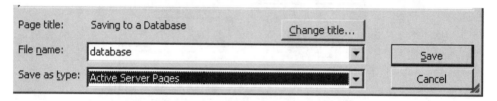

10. Click the Save button, and the file will be saved as *database.asp*.

11. Now that your file has been saved in the ASP format, preview the page in your browser. Fill out the form and press the Submit button. You will see the Confirmation page appear.

Retrieving Form Information from a Database

Now that you have saved the form information to a database, we need to find a method of displaying the form data. The easy method of viewing the form information would be go to the directory in which the database is located and open the database itself. While that method would work, what if you did not know how to navigate through a database, and what if you did not have the right database programs to view the program? To overcome these problems, FrontPage provides a way in which the database information can be displayed on any Web browser.

The following instructions teach you to create a new document and to set it up to display database results:

1. From the Folders view (View | Folders) in FrontPage, create a new document and save it as *results.htm*.

2. Once you have created that file, open it in FrontPage. Select Insert | Database | Results from the menu bar, and the Database Results Wizard window will appear.

3. Because we already created a database, select the Use an existing database connection option and select the database that you created in the previous section by using the drop-down menu:

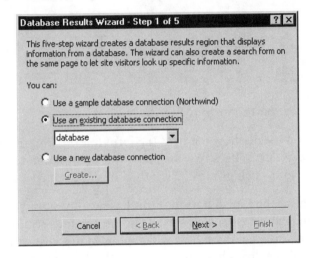

4. Click the Next button to go to Step 2 of the Database Results Wizard.

5. In Step 2, you will see the option to select the source from which the database information will be retrieved. FrontPage automatically selects the Record source option and specifies the database name from which results will be retrieved from. You should accept the selections that FrontPage has made by clicking the Next button to go to Step 3.

6. In Step 3, if you are familiar with databases, you may explore the More Options and Edit List buttons. If not, click the Next button to go to Step 4.

10

7. In Step 4, you can customize how you want the database results to be displayed. Using the drop-down menu, select Table – one record per row if it is not already selected.

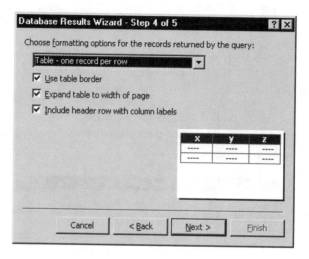

8. Click the Next button to go to Step 5.

9. In Step 5 you specify how many of the form information records will be displayed at a time. The way to display form information records is to split the records into small groups. Click the Finish button.

10. After you click the Finish button, FrontPage will prompt you to save this file with an ASP file extension. Just as in the previous section, select File | Save As, and the Save As window will appear. In the Save As window, using the Save As Type drop-down menu, select the Active Server Pages option and click the Save button.

11. After you saved your file with the ASP extension, preview this page in your browser. You will see the form results from the form you submitted in the previous section in a tabular format:

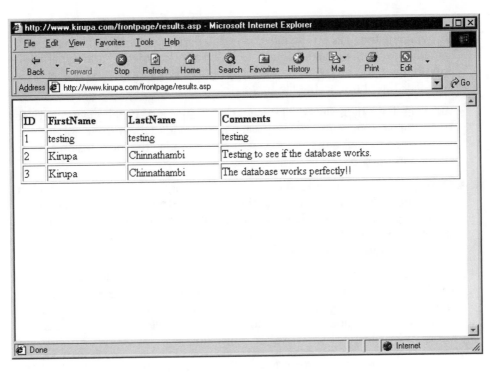

index.htm

Project 10-1: Using Forms

The following are the goals for this project:

- Modify a form
- Add additional items to form objects
- Hyperlink pages

Step by Step

1. Upload the entire Project folder into your FrontPage web. Please refer to Module 9 for information on publishing and uploading files and folders to a Web server.

10

2. Once the Project folder has been uploaded, open the file *index.htm*. We want to hyperlink the links on the left side of the page. The first link, Home, has already been hyperlinked. Highlight "Post Your Comments" and hyperlink the phrase to the file *comments.htm*. Highlight "Tech Support Contact" and hyperlink the phrase to the file *contact.htm*.

3. After you have hyperlinked all the links on the left side of the *index.htm* page, open the file *comments.htm*. You will have to modify the form to submit the information to your e-mail address. Before we modify the form, assign a name to the form objects.

4. Once you assigned a name to the form objects, right-click the form and select the Form Properties command. In the Where to store results section of the Form Properties window, delete any text in the File name field and enter your e-mail address in the E-mail address field. After you entered your e-mail address, click the OK button to close the Form Properties window.

5. Before you save the *comments.htm* file, make sure you hyperlinked the links on the left side of that page. You can tell whether the links are hyperlinked or not by seeing if they are underlined. Links that are underlined are hyperlinked. Links that are not underlined are not hyperlinked. (Please refer to step 2 to verify which file gets hyperlinked to which link.)

6. Save the *comments.htm* file and open the file *contact.htm*. Once the file has been opened, assign a name to the individual form objects. Right-click on each form object and choose Form Field Properties. From the form object's property window that appears, enter a value in the Name field.

7. After you assigned a name for the values, add an extra item to the drop-down box object by right clicking the drop-down box and selecting the command for Form Field Properties. The Drop-Down Box Properties window will appear. From the Drop-Down Box Properties window, click the Add button. From the Add Choice window, enter **Other** in the Add Choice field. Click OK to close the Drop-Down Box Properties window.

8. In the Drop-Down Properties window, make sure that the word "Other" is in the last choice. If it is not, select Other and click the Move Down button until it becomes the last choice. Click the OK button to accept the changes and close the Drop-Down Properties window.

9. We now need to make the form save the information. For the *contact.htm* page, let's make the form save all the information to a HTML page in our FrontPage Web. To do this, right-click the form on this page and select the Form Properties command. From the Form Properties window, click the Options button.

10. In the File Results tab of the Saving Results window, use the default filename FrontPage assigns and select the HTML bulleted list command in the File format drop-down menu. FrontPage will automatically change the extension of the filename listed in the File name box. You should notice the location where it saves this file. FrontPage does not always save the form results in the current Project folder. Click OK to close all the windows displayed. You should hyperlink the links found on the left of the page.

11. Save the *contact.htm* file and preview the site. Test all the forms to see how they work. You should remember that if you saved the form results for the *contact.htm* into the _private folder, you will not be able to see the results using your Web browser.

To see and test my version of this project, go to http://www.kirupa.com/ frontpage/project/index.htm.

Summary

Forms are a great way to receive input and feedback from your site's visitors. You can create forms and format them easily in FrontPage. Often times, you may want to validate form objects to make sure that your visitors are entering information correctly. Another advantage of forms is that they can be saved in various formats. From e-mail to files to databases, with FrontPage you can customize how the form information is stored and viewed.

10

☑ Mastery Check

1. Why is it recommended that you assign name values to form objects?

2. How will you change the order of an item listed in a drop-down menu?

3. What can you use to help organize form objects in a form?

4. Can custom confirmation pages be created?

5. What Web component is used to enter form content on a confirmation page?

6. Is it possible to limit the number of characters a person can enter into a text box or text area?

7. How do you make a folder private so that Web browsers cannot view HTML pages contained within it?

Module 11

Animating Your Site

The Goals of This Module

- Animate page elements
- Create transitions between pages
- Create hover buttons
- Use marquees

W hen the Hypertext Markup Language (HTML) was first created, there was very little in the language structure that supported special effects such as animation, transitions, and more. As HTML evolved, a subset of HTML, Dynamic HTML (DHTML) was introduced.

One of DHTML's strong points is its ability to animate various page elements such as text, tables, and buttons. In FrontPage, you can animate page elements, add page transitions, create sophisticated hover buttons, create marquees, and more. Best of all, you can simply point and click your way to animating your pages without having to write a single line of code.

For the directions in this module, please download the various images and sample source files for Module 11 from http://www.kirupa.com/frontpage or http://www.Osborne.com.

Animating Page Elements

One of the best ways to get your Web site visitor's attention is to use short animation sequences. In FrontPage, you can animate text from form buttons to tables. FrontPage also enables you to customize animations so that they play when the visitor clicks or hovers their mouse pointer over a location on the page, during page load, and more. There are numerous animations you can apply to page elements, and the following four sections will help you to understand and use the animation features available in FrontPage.

The DHTML Effects Toolbar

You will use the DHTML Effects toolbar for animating in FrontPage. To access the DHTML Effects toolbar, go to View | Toolbars | DHTML Effects. The following illustration displays the DHTML Effects toolbar:

Table 11-1 lists the drop-down menu and gives its function.

Name	Function
On	Specifies the criteria under which the animation will play.
Apply	Enables you to select the animation effect that will be applied to the text, images, and more.
< Choose Settings >	Further formats the animation effect selected. Not all animation effects will enable this menu.

Table 11-1   The DHTML Effects Toolbar

Note

You need to make sure your browser supports DHTML animations. If you are using any browser older than Netscape 4 or Internet Explorer 4, your browser does not support DHTML.

Animating Objects to Play When a Page Loads

To animate an object to play when the page loads, follow these instructions:

1. Open the file *objects.htm* page (this file is included in the source files you should have downloaded for this module). You will see two elements: an image of a walking knight and some text. We will animate the text in this lesson. The walking knight image will be animated in the next section.

2. From the menu bar, go to View | Toolbars | DHTML Effects to display the DHTML Effects toolbar. Please refer to Table 11-1 for information regarding the menus in DHTML Effects toolbar.

3. Click anywhere on the text with the mouse pointer. Notice that in the DHTML Effects toolbar, the drop-down menu for On becomes active.

4. Click the On drop-down menu on the DHTML Effects toolbar, and you will see four commands that specify when the animation will play. We want the animation to play when the page loads in a browser, so choose the Page load command.

5. After you select the Page load command, the drop-down menu for Apply will become active. Click the Apply drop-down menu and select the Elastic command.

11

6. After you have selected the Elastic command, the Choose Settings drop-down menu will become active. Click the Choose Settings drop-down menu, and select the From right command. At this time, the DHTML toolbar should look like this:

7. Save this page and preview it in FrontPage.

8. As you preview the page, you will see that the text flies in from the right and slowly stops.

Keep the *objects.htm* page open, as we will be adding to it in the next section.

Animating Objects to Play in Response to the Mouse Pointer

To modify animations so that they react to the mouse pointer, follow these directions:

1. Using the *objects.htm* page from the last section, select the image of the walking knight with the mouse pointer. On the DHTML toolbar, click the On drop-down menu and select the Mouse over command.

2. Click the Apply drop-down menu and select the Swap Picture command.

3. After you select the Swap Picture command, the Choose Settings drop-down menu will appear. Click the Choose Settings drop-down menu and select the Choose picture command. From the Picture window, select the image file *swap.gif* from the source files you downloaded.

4. After you have selected *swap.gif*, click the OK button to close the Picture window.

5. Save the page and preview it in FrontPage. As the page loads, the text will come in from the right. After the text comes in from the right, place the mouse pointer over the walking knight image on the left, and it will be replaced by the *swap.gif* image, which is a knight on horseback. The following illustration shows both images:

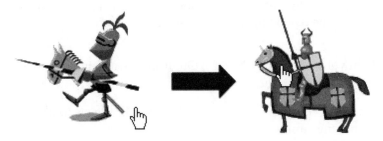

Tip

Each command in the On drop-down menu on the DHTML toolbar comes with its own set of animations that you can customize to suit your site.

Keep the *objects.htm* page open, as we will be adding to it in the next section.

Note

When swapping images using the Swap Picture command, the images should have the same pixel size. When one image is smaller than another image, the smaller image will be scaled to the size of the larger image. When smaller images are scaled to the size of a larger image, the smaller images look blurry and jagged.

Animating Text Formatting

When animating objects such as text or tables, you are not limited to making the objects fly or zoom in with some special effect. You may have seen sites where the text changes color, fonts, and more when the mouse pointer is moved over the text. While most of those text effects were created using Cascading Style Sheets (CSS), we will create a basic text effect using the DHTML toolbar. (You will learn about CSS in Module 15.)

To animate text to change its text style in response to the mouse pointer, follow these directions:

1. Using the *objects.htm* page from the previous section, type your name below the table. Indent your name so it appears near the middle of your page.

11

Note

Make sure the font style for your name is set to default. Changing the font and/or font style will cause the formatting not to work properly. For the animation to work, the font has to be the default font used by FrontPage.

2. Highlight your name and click the On drop-down menu on the DHTML Effects toolbar. From the On drop-down menu, select the Click command.

3. Click the Apply drop-down menu on the DHTML Effects toolbar and select the Formatting command.

4. Click the Choose Settings drop-down menu and select the Choose Font command. The Font window will appear.

5. In the Font window, select any number of options that you wish to apply to your name. After making your selections, click the OK button to close the Font window. The font style will be visible only when the animation is clicked.

6. Save the page and preview it. As you preview the page, click your name, and the various options you applied to your name will be visible. Your name will have the font style you selected applied until you click it again.

The following image shows how my name looks after it is clicked. I applied both the Underline and Overline effects from the Font window:

<u>Kirupa Chinnathambi</u>

Changing Font Styles for Text Formatting

To overcome the nuisance of being unable to format text before animating its formatting, there is a solution.

To change the font style for text before animating its formatting, follow these directions:

1. Open the *objects.htm* file.

2. Right-click anywhere on your page and select the Page Properties command. In the General area of the Page Properties window, select the Style button.

3. After you select the Style button, the Modify Style window will appear. In the Modify Style window, click the Format button and select the Font command from the drop-down menu.

4. In the Font window, select the font and any other options that you want as the default font. After you have selected the font and font style, click the OK button to close the Font window.

5. Click OK to close the Font window. Click OK to close the Modify Style window. Click OK to close the Page Properties window.

6. The font style for your name (from the previous section) will be updated to the font styles you selected in the Modify Style window.

Page Transitions

Navigating from page to page is a simple procedure: you click a link, and the page loads. You can make the transition between pages a little more exciting by adding page transitions. Page transitions are short animations that transition you from one page to another page.

―|*Note*

Page transitions will not work in Netscape browsers. Newer versions of Netscape will show the page without the transition. Older versions of Netscape will display error messages when a page transition tries to play.

11

Creating Page Transitions

To learn how to create page transitions, you will apply the transition effect to two pages that are hyperlinked to each other.

The following instructions will guide you to create page transitions for your pages:

1. Open the file *transition.htm* in FrontPage. You will see a hyperlink in the center of the page. Press CTRL and click the link using the mouse pointer and another page called *transition2.htm* will open.

2. Look at the upper-left corner, below the Formatting toolbar, and you will see two tabs representing the two open pages. You can switch between the pages by clicking the tabs:

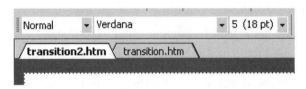

3. Select the *transition.htm* tab. From the menu bar, choose Format | Page Transition. After you have selected the Page Transition command, the Page Transitions window will appear.

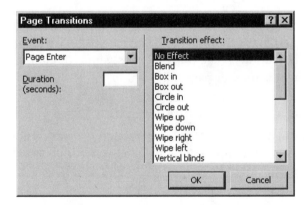

Table 11-2 lists the options in the Event drop-down menu of the Page Transitions window and other options in the Page Transitions window, with a brief description of each.

Item	Description
Page Enter	Plays a transition effect when a visitor enters a page
Page Exit	Plays a transition effect when a visitor leaves a page
Site Enter	Plays a transition effect when a visitor enters your site from another site
Site Exit	Plays a transition effect when a visitor leaves your site to go to another site
Duration (seconds)	Specifies, in seconds, how long the transition effect will play
Transition effect	Selects the transition effect

Table 11-2   Page Transitions Window

1. In the Event drop-down menu of the Page Transitions window, select the Page Enter command.

2. In the Duration field, enter 3. By entering **3** in the Duration field, you are telling the animation to play for three seconds.

3. In the Transition effect menu box, select the Wipe left command.

4. Click OK to close the Page Transitions window.

5. Save this page.

6. Open the *transition2.htm* page by clicking the *transition2.htm* tab. Preview this page in your browser. Once the page has loaded in your browser, click the hyperlink.

7. Your transition should look similar to Figure 11-1.

8. Let's add another transition. Click the *transition2.htm* tab to display the *transition2.htm* page in FrontPage and choose Format | Page Transition.

9. In the Page Transitions window, select the Site Exit command in the Event drop-down menu. Enter **5** in the Duration box. Finally, select Circle out in the Transition effect menu box.

11

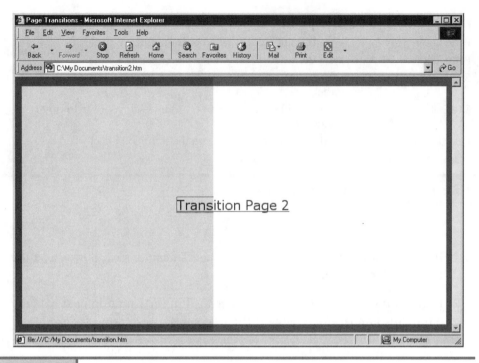

Figure 11-1 A Wipe left page transition

Ask the Expert

Question: The page transitions that I apply are not being displayed in my browser. What should I do to make the transitions work?

Answer: Almost all versions of Netscape browsers do not support page transitions. You need to use Internet Explorer to view the transitions. If you are using Internet Explorer 4 or higher and are still not seeing page transitions, the transitions are disabled in your browser. In Internet Explorer, choose Tools | Internet Options. You should see the Internet Options window. Click the Advanced tab, and you will be presented with numerous settings regarding your Internet Explorer browser configuration. Check the Enable page transitions checkbox.

10. Click OK to close the Page Transitions window and then preview the *transition2.htm* page in your browser.

11. While viewing the page, enter **http://www.yahoo.com** into the address (or Uniform Resource Identifier [URL]) box.

12. As your browser leaves your page to go to Yahoo, you will see the Circle out transition effect play, as shown in Figure 11-2.

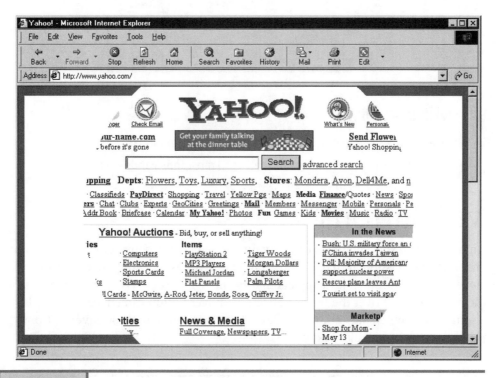

Figure 11-2 The Circle out transition effect playing

11

Check the Enable page transitions box and retest your page transitions pages. The following illustration displays the Enable page transitions box in Internet Explorer 5.*x*:

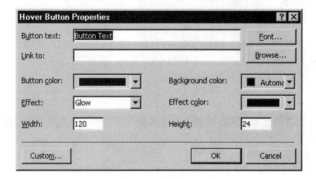

1-Minute Drill

- Are all browsers capable of displaying DHTML animations?
- What does the Duration field in the Page Transitions window specify?

Hover Buttons

Animation and special effects can be valuable navigation tools. One method of enabling your visitors to navigate through your site is by using hover buttons. Hover buttons are small Java applets that FrontPage creates. When a user moves the mouse pointer over the hover button, the hover button can change color, play a sound, or even display an image. Best of all, you can hyperlink hover buttons just as you would regular text or images.

- No
- The number of seconds the transition effect will play

Creating Hover Buttons

The following instructions will guide you to creating a hover button:

1. Create a new page in FrontPage.

2. Select Insert | Web Component. In the Web Component window, select the Hover Button command from the Dynamic Effects selection found in the Component type menu:

3. After you have selected the Hover Button command, press the Finish button to close the Web Component window. After you click Finish in the Web Component window, the Hover Button Properties window will appear.

4. In the Hover Button Properties window, type **Weather** into the Button text field (the word you type in the Button text field is the word that will be displayed on your button).

5. In the Link to field, enter **http://www.weather.com**.

6. The Button color option determines the color your button will have before the mouse pointer hovers over the button; select Green from the Button color drop-down menu.

7. The Background color option determines the background color that your hover button will have; select Green from the Background color drop-down menu.

8. The Effect options determines what effect the button will display; select Glow from the Effect drop-down menu.

11

9. The Effect color option determines the color that your button will transform to when the mouse is hovered over it; select Blue from the Effect color drop-down menu.

10. In the Width field, enter 120. In the Height field, enter 30.

11. Click OK to close the Hover Button Properties window.

12. Save the page as *hover.htm* and preview it in your browser.

Note

The hover button will not work unless you save the file because only after you save the file will FrontPage will create and add the Java applets needed to make the hover button work.

Please keep this page open, as you will use it in the next section as well.

Modifying Hover Buttons

We will modify the button you created in the last section by adding a small sound clip that plays when a mouse pointer is placed over the hover button and by making the button's image change when a mouse pointer is placed over the hover button.

Follow these instructions to modify the hover button:

1. With the page that you created from the previous section open, right-click the hover button and select the Hover Button Properties command. The Hover Button Properties window will appear.

2. In the Hover Button Properties window, select the Custom button. After you click the Custom button, the Custom window will appear.

3. To add a sound file to the hover button, in the Play sound section of the Custom window, select the On hover field.

4. To select a sound file, click the Browse button to the right of the On hover field. Browse for and then select the *seagull.au* file that is included with the files you downloaded for this module (you may have to select the All

Files command from the Files of type drop-down menu to select the
seagull.au file):

5. To place an image as the button, in the Custom window enter the path
   to the image *park.jpg* in the Button text field. Use the Browse button to
   browse for the image if you do not know where the button is located. In
   the On hover field, enter the path to the image *night.jpg*. Use the Browse
   button to locate the image you if you do not know where it is.

6. Click OK to close both the Custom window. Click OK to close the Hover
   Button Properties window.

7. If the image is too small to fit inside the button, you should resize the button
   to fit the image size. To resize the button, select the button with the mouse
   pointer and use the resize handles to adjust the hover button size.

Note

Because hover buttons are Java applets, they take up more system resources than
other effects. The more Java applets loaded on a site, the slower the site becomes.
A page with numerous hover buttons will crash a browser running on a slower
computer, so try not to have too many hover buttons on one page.

8. Save the page and preview it in your browser. When you hover the mouse
   pointer over the button, the image will change and a sound file will play.
   If you cannot hear the sound, make sure you have a program installed
   for interpreting sound files ending with the extension, *.au.* You can
   download the free Windows Media Player for hearing sound files with
   the *.au* extension and other popular sound formats from the following
   site: http://www.microsoft.com/windows/windowsmedia/.

Note

For sounds to work in hover buttons created in FrontPage, they have to be in
the *.au* format. If the sound is in any other sound format, such as *.wav* or *.mp3*,
the button's sound will not be heard.

Marquees

Have you ever visited a site that had text scrolling horizontally? If you have, you saw a *marquee*. If you have never seen a marquee, view the file *marquee.htm* in your browser. A marquee is text that can scroll continuously in one direction or scroll continuously in alternating directions.

Creating Marquees

Follow these directions to learn how to create a marquee:

1. Create a new document in FrontPage. Select Insert | Web Component. The Insert Web Component window will appear. Select Dynamic Effects from the Component type menu box and select Marquee. Click the Finish button to display the Marquee Properties window:

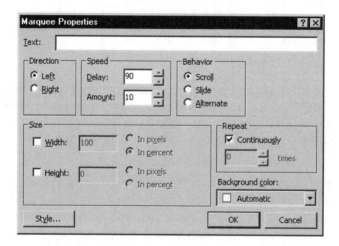

2. In the Text field of the Marquee Properties window, type **This is an example of text that scrolls in a marquee**.

3. Click the OK button to close the Marquee Properties window.

4. Save this page and preview it in a browser to see the marquee.

Keep this page open, as we will learn how to format the marquee in the next section.

Formatting Marquees

The Marquee Properties window has numerous marquee properties that can be modified. To format the marquee, follow these directions:

1. Right-click the marquee and select the command for Marquee Properties. Table 11-3 identifies each option in the Marquee Properties window and describes what it does.

2. By default, a marquee moves left to right. Select the Right option to change the direction the marquee moves.

3. Select the Alternate option to vary the direction the marquee scrolls.

Item	Description
Left	Sets the marquee to scroll in from the left; this is the default.
Right	Sets the marquee to scroll in from the right.
Delay	Sets the number of milliseconds that you want the marquee to wait before scrolling onto the screen again.
Amount	Controls how fast the marquee scrolls; the higher the number, the faster the marquee will scroll.
Scroll	The basic marquee action: the marquee simply scrolls across the page.
Slide	Sets the marquee to scroll once and stop at the edge of the marquee area; this is very similar to the Fly Left or Fly Right animation on the DHTML Effects toolbar.
Alternate	Sets the marquee to scroll in both directions. Once the marquee reaches the edge of the marquee area, the text will scroll in the opposite direction.
Width	Sets the width of the marquee.
Height	Sets the height of the marquee.
Repeat	Specifies the number of the times the marquee will repeat. If the Continuously box is checked the marquee will repeat indefinitely. To enter the number of the times the marquee should repeat, uncheck the Continuously box. Enter a value for the number of times in the times field.
Background Color	Sets the background color of the marquee.

11

Table 11-3   The Marquee Properties Window Settings

4. Check the Width checkbox and enter 75 in the Width field. Make sure the In Percent option button to the right of the Width field is checked.

5. Because we want the marquee to loop only 10 times, uncheck the Continuously checkbox. Enter **10** in the times field.

Note

You can adjust the font of a marquee in one of two ways: you can click the Style button from the Marque Properties window and select the Font command from the Format button, or you can use the Formatting toolbar.

6. Let's change the background color of the marquee. Click the Background Color drop-down menu and select the Yellow color.

Note

Most versions of Netscape do not support marquees.

1-Minute Drill

- Can hover buttons be images?
- How can you increase your marquee's speed?

- Yes
- You can increase your marquee's speed by entering a larger value in the Amount field in the Marquee Properties window.

index.htm

Project 11-1: Applying and Modifying Animation

The following are the goals for this project:

● Animate text and images

● Add page transitions

● Hyperlink text links

Step by Step

1. Open the file *index.htm* and display the DHTML Effects toolbar.

2. Highlight the words "Architect FX" and, using the DHTML Effects toolbar, select the Page load command from the On drop-down menu; select the Fly in command from the Apply drop-down menu; and select the Along corner command from the Choose Settings drop-down menu.

3. To add a page transition, select Format I Page Transitions. In the Page Transitions window, select Page Enter in the Event field; set the duration to **2**; and select Random bars vertical in the Transition effect menu box.

4. Save the *index.htm* page and open the *about.htm* page.

5. In the *about.htm* page, highlight the words "Architect FX." Using the DHTML toolbar, select the Page load command from the On drop-down menu and select the Drop in by word command from the Event drop-down menu.

6. Hyperlink the words "Return Home" to the *index.htm* file.

7. Launch the Page Transitions window by choosing Format I Page Transition. In the Page Transitions window, set the Event to Page Enter, set the Duration

11

to **2**, and set the Transition effect to Random. Click OK to close the Page Transitions window.

8. Save this file and open the *cities.htm* page.

9. In the *cities.htm* page, select the image of the bus. Using the DHTML toolbar, select the Page load command in the On drop-down menu, select the Fly in command in the Apply drop-down menu; and select the From bottom corner command in the Choose Settings drop-down menu.

10. Add a page transition that plays a random effect for 2 seconds when the page is entered. This page transition is the same as the transition you created in step 4.

11. Hyperlink the words "Return Home" to the *index.htm* page.

12. To add a marquee to the *cities.htm* page, insert your mouse pointer in the empty space below the words "New York" and above the words "Return Home." Choose Insert | Web Component and select the Marquee command from the Dynamic Effects component type. In the Text field, type **We are currently building a new city called "Sydney."** Click OK to close the Marquee Properties window.

13. Select the marquee using your mouse pointer. In the Formatting toolbar set the font to be Verdana, the font size to 10, and the font color to dark blue.

14. Save this page and open the *links.htm* page.

15. In the *links.htm* page, highlight all the words between the word "Links" and the bulleted list. In the DHTML Effects toolbar, select the Page load command in the On drop-down menu, select the Elastic command in the Apply drop-down menu, and select the From right command in the Choose Settings drop-down menu.

16. To add a page transition, go to the Page Transitions window and select the Site Exit command for in the Event drop-down menu, select the Random command in the Transition effect menu box, and enter **3** in the Duration field.

17. Hyperlink the words "Return Home" to the page *index.htm* and save this page.

18. Make sure all pages that are currently open are saved. Open the *index.htm* page and preview it in your browser to see how the various animations that you added display in the various pages. Go to the Links page. Click a URL link and watch the Site Exit transition play.

To see my version of this exercise, open the file *index.htm*, which is in the Answers folder.

Summary

By using DHTML and other languages such as JavaScript and Java, Web sites can become more lively and animated. FrontPage easily handles the animation features of a Web site from text effects to page transitions. Best of all, animations in FrontPage can be set to play in response to user actions such as hovering the mouse, clicking an object, and more.

11

✓ Mastery Check

1. What does the acronym DHTML stand for?

   _____

   _____

2. When do page transitions play?

   _____

   _____

3. Are hover buttons

   ● DHTML scripts?
   ● CSS tags?
   ● Java applets?
   ● DirectX?

4. What extension format should the sound added to a hover button be in?

   _____

   _____

5. What is a marquee?

   _____

   _____

6. When swapping an image using the Swap Picture command in the DHTML toolbar, how many images are involved?

   _____

   _____

Module 12

Using FrontPage Web Components

The Goals of This Module

- Learn to incorporate Web components
- Modify Web components
- Create a navigation method using link bars

To help you create an interactive site, FrontPage comes with a set of software tools called *Web components*. These components help you to create search forms, hit counters, navigation bars, and more.

Using Web Components

To access all of the FrontPage Web components, from the menu bar, select Insert | Web Component. After you have selected Web Component, the Web Component window will appear.

Table 12-1 lists the icons found in the Insert Web Component window, as well as their name and function.

Icon	Name of Component	Function
	Dynamic Effects	Adds a hover button, marquee, or banner ad manager
	Web Search	Provides your visitors with a method of searching your site
	Spreadsheets and Charts	Incorporates charts and spreadsheets
	Hit Counter	Keeps track of the number of visitors to your site
	Photo Gallery	Creates a photo gallery with several templates
	Included Content	Includes and customizes content from other pages
	Link Bars	Creates navigational links customized for your site
	Table of Contents	Creates a table of contents
	Top 10 List	Provides a list of useful information such as visited pages, referring domains, browsers, and more

Table 12-1 FrontPage Web Components

Icon	Name of Component	Function
	bCentral Web Components	Promotes your site on Microsoft's bCentral site
	Expedia Components	Provides your visitors with a customized map from Expedia
	MSN Components	Allows your visitors to search the Web and receive stock quote information directly from Microsoft Network (MSN)
	MSNBC Components	Provides a list that automatically updates itself with information from MSNBC
	Additional Components	Adds additional components to your Web page
	Advanced Controls	Adds and modifies Hypertext Markup Language (HTML), Java applets, ActiveX controls, and more

Table 12-1   FrontPage Web Components (*continued*)

As you go through the instructions in this module, if you forget which icon is which, you can refer back to Table 12-1.

Because the Web components reside on your FrontPage Web, you will need to ensure that your Web server is configured with the latest version of the FrontPage Server Extensions software.

Note

You may have noticed that Table 12-1 does not include the List View and Document Library View components. Because those two components require SharePoint Server software to be installed and are intended for use on corporate intranets, we will not cover these two components in this book.

12

For the directions in this module, please download the various images and sample source files for Module 12 from http://www.kirupa.com/frontpage or http://www.Osborne.com.

Dynamic Effects

Dynamic effects are used in FrontPage to create special effects in hover buttons, marquees, and banners. You learned how to create hover buttons and marquees in Module 11, so, in this module, we will create banners with transitioning images.

Creating a Banner Ad

To create banners, follow these directions:

1. Create a blank document in your FrontPage Web.

2. Open that page in FrontPage and select Insert | Web Component. The Insert Web Component window will appear.

3. In the Insert Web Component window, select the Dynamic Effects icon. The Choose an effect menu box will display the components related to Dynamic Effects. From the choices listed in the Choose an effect menu box, select the Banner Ad Manager option and click the Finish button. The Banner Ad Manager Properties window will appear, as here:

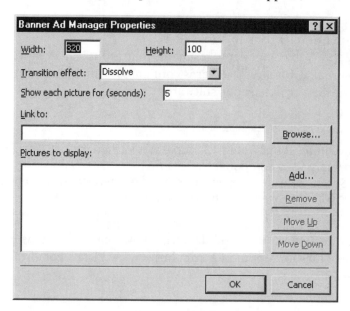

The following is a list of the options in the Banner Ad Properties window and what each option does:

- **Width** Adjusts the width of your banner; make sure that the width of the banner is the same as the width of your images.

- **Height** Adjusts the height of your banner; make sure that the height of the banner is the same as the height of your images.

- **Transition Effect** Selects the transition effect that will be played when the banner ad changes images.

- **Show each picture for (seconds)** Adjusts the number of seconds each image in the banner ad will be shown before the next image is displayed.

- **Pictures to display** Adds the images that will be displayed in the banner ad. You can use the Move Up and Move Down buttons to adjust the order in which the images will display.

4. Before we specify the banner images, let's change the size of the banner ad. In the Width and Height fields of the Banner Ad Manager Properties window, enter **320** and **60**, respectively.

5. In the Link to field, enter **http://www.kirupa.com/frontpage**. You can adjust the hyperlink properties such as opening a new window, frame targets, and others by clicking the Browse button.

6. Now comes the part in which you specify the images that will be displayed in the banner ad. Click the Add button to launch the Add Picture for Banner Ad window. Browse for the image *banner1.jpg*. (That file is included with the source files you should have downloaded for this module.)

7. Repeat step 6 and add the images *banner2.jpg* and *banner3.jpg*. After you have inserted these three images, the Pictures to display box in the Banner Ad Properties window will display the three image files and their locations:

12

Pictures to display:

images/banner1.jpg
images/banner2.jpg
images/banner3.jpg

8. Click OK to close the Banner Ad Manager Properties window, and you will see a banner ad containing the images we specified.

9. Save this file and preview it in your browser. The banner will transition between the three images we selected.

You can view the banner ad that I completed by visiting http://www.kirupa.com/frontpage/bannerad.htm.

Modifying the Banner Ad

To modify a banner ad, follow these instructions:

1. Right-click on the banner ad and select Banner Ad Manager Properties.

2. In the Link to field, enter **http://www/yahoo.com**.

3. Enter 3 in the Show each picture for (seconds) field.

4. Click the Transition effect drop-down menu and select Box Out.

5. Save the file and preview it in your browser.

The banner ad will rotate images every three seconds. The images will use the Box Out transition effect, and clicking the banner ad will take you Yahoo!'s Web site.

Note

You should have all your images the same width and height as your banner ad. Images of different sizes will cause the banner ad to resize the differently sized images to the banner ad size, and when images are scaled, they lose their quality.

Web Search

No matter how easy your navigation system is, the easiest way for visitors to find information on your site is to search using keywords. FrontPage provides the Web Search component for you to create a search page.

Creating a Search Page

1. Create a blank document in your FrontPage Web.

2. Open that page in FrontPage and select Insert | Web Component; the Insert Web Component window will appear.

3. In the Web Component window, select the Web Search icon and double-click the Current Web selection in the list on the right. The Search Form Properties window will appear.

4. Click the OK button in the Search Form Properties window. You will see the search form in your document. Save this file and preview it in your browser.

5. Now that you are previewing the page, enter a keyword to search for in the Search for box and click the Start Search button. When you click the Start Search button, the pages that contain the keyword will be displayed in the Search Page, see Figure 12-1.

6. Save this page.

Keep this page open because we will be using it in the next section.

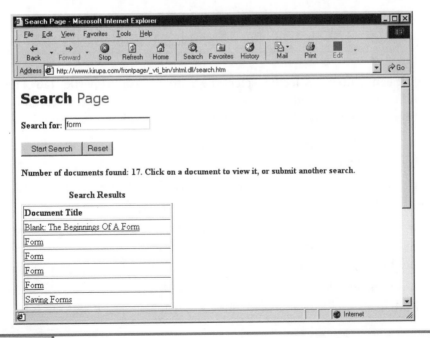

12

Figure 12-1   When you search the pages that contain that keyword will be displayed.

Modifying the Search Page

1. Using the Search Page from the last section, right click the Search Page and select the Search Form Properties command. The Search Form Properties window will display:

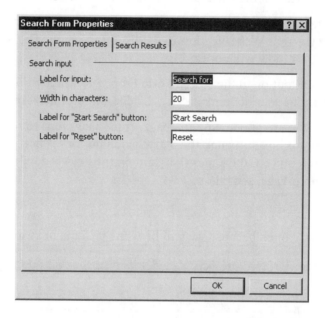

2. If it is not already selected, select the Search Form Properties tab. The following is a list and brief description of the options in the Search Form Properties tab of the Search Form Properties window:

- **Label for input** Adjusts the text that is displayed before the search box in your document.

- **Width in characters** Adjusts the width of the search box in your search form.

- **Label for "Start Search" button** Changes the text that is displayed for the Start Search button.

- **Label for "Reset" button** Changes the text that is displayed for the Reset button.

3. In the Label for "Start Search" button, delete the "Here" in Search Here.

4. Enter **30** in the Width in characters field. That will allow more characters to be entered in the Search for box when previewed.

5. To modify how the search results are displayed, click the Search Results tab. The following is a list and brief description of the options in the Search Results tab of the Search Form Properties window:

- **Word list to search**   Specifies the locations where the search results will be generated from. When you see search results, the results are generated from all nonhidden files in your FrontPage Web. You should use the keyword "All" to search your entire Web. The only time you would change the keyword from "All" is if you are using a guest book. You will learn about guest books in Module 13.

- **Date format**   Displays the date when each page in the search results was last modified. You need to check the Display file date check box in the current window to activate the Date format drop-down list.

- **Time format**   Selects a time format for your search results. You need to check the Display file date check box to activate the Time format drop-down list.

- **Display Score**   Chooses whether you want to display a score that measures how accurate the results are in the search results.

- **Display file date**   Selects the last date the files found in the search results page were modified. You use the Date format and Time format drop-down menus to modify how the date will be displayed.

- **Display file size**   Displays the file size of each file found in the search results page.

6. Check the Display Score, Display file date, and Display file size checkboxes and click OK.

7. The Date format and Time format drop-down menus will be enabled. Click the Time format drop-down menu and select the first choice below the (none) choice.

8. Click OK to close the Search Form Properties window. Save and preview the page in your browser to see the changes made to the search form.

12

Spreadsheets and Charts

You may have seen sites that enable you to input information, calculate data, and more. You can use FrontPage to create a spreadsheet that can be used from a browser to display and modify information such as data, graphs, and more. Because modifying these components requires knowledge in areas such as database management and Microsoft Excel, I will only explain how to incorporate and use basic functions of the components found in the Spreadsheets and Charts type.

Creating a Spreadsheet

The Office Spreadsheet component is a smaller version of Microsoft Excel that can be used in a Web page. Using the Spreadsheet component, you can view data from an existing Excel data source, and you can input your own data and export it to Microsoft Excel. Best of all, you can add your own formulas, adjust the data style, and more from the confines of your browser.

Follow these directions to create a spreadsheet:

1. Launch the Insert Web Component window by selecting Insert | Web Component from the menu bar.

2. From the Insert Web Component window, select the Spreadsheets and charts icon. The Choose a control menu box will change to display the components for the Spreadsheets and charts icon. Double-click the Office Spreadsheet command on the Choose a control menu box on the right. A spreadsheet will be inserted into your document.

3. Save the page and preview it in your browser. You will see that you can easily enter data and format the data in your browser just as you can in Microsoft Excel.

4. To modify how the data looks, right-click the spreadsheet and select the Commands and Options command. You can modify the font, border, numbering style, formulas, and more in the Commands and Options window.

5. To export the data for use in Microsoft Excel, click the Export to Microsoft Excel icon. The Export to Microsoft Excel icon is the third icon from the right.

The following image shows an example of a spreadsheet that I created and formatted in my browser:

Office Spreadsheet

	A	B	C	D	E
1		Running Speed	Endurance		
2	Cheetahs	58 mph	High		
3	Elephants	4 mph -20 mph	High		
4	Turtles	.3 mph	Moderate		
5	Rabbits	45 mph	Moderate		
6	Kirupa Chinnathambi	75 mph -80 mph	High		

Sheet1

Ask the Expert

Question: Instead of having my visitors fill out all the information in the spreadsheet, is it possible for me to display a spreadsheet with some information already filled out for my visitors?

Answer: Yes. To display data in the spreadsheet for your visitors, you will need to add information to the Office Spreadsheet component in FrontPage. When you click the spreadsheet in FrontPage, you will see that you can edit and add data to the spreadsheet, just as you would in your browser. In the spreadsheet, fill in any information in FrontPage and preview the page in your browser. Make sure you save the page first. The information you entered into the spreadsheet in FrontPage will be saved along with the HTML page; therefore, when your visitors visit your page in a browser, they will be able to see the information you entered in the spreadsheet and then add their information.

12

Creating a Chart

You are not limited to inserting a spreadsheet in FrontPage; you can insert charts as well. The Office Chart component enables you to create a chart by entering your own data values or importing the data values from another file. You can also combine the Office Chart component to work with the data values from the spreadsheet created using the Office Spreadsheet component.

1. To create a chart, follow these directions: Launch the Insert Web Component window by selecting Insert | Web Component from the menu bar.

2. From the Insert Web Component window, select the Spreadsheets and charts icon. The Choose a control type menu box will display the components for the Spreadsheets and charts icon. Double-click the Office Chart command from the Choose a control type menu box. Your document will look like Figure 12-2.

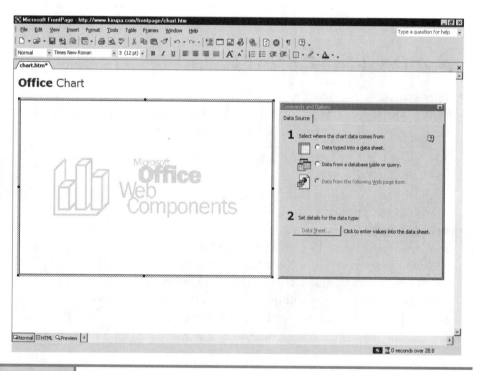

Figure 12-2　The Office Chart component in a FrontPage document

3. In the Commands and Options window, you will specify whether you want the chart to receive data from a data sheet, database table, query, or open Web page item such as an Excel document or a worksheet. (the latter two methods of receiving data require some knowledge of using a database or modifying existing worksheets). We will create a chart from a data sheet.

4. In the Commands and Options window, select the Data typed into a data sheet option. After you select that option, click the Data Sheet button.

5. After you click the Data Sheet button, you will see a miniature worksheet in which you will be able to enter values:

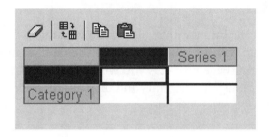

6. In the first box next to Category 1, enter **Rainfall**. To the right of the word "Rainfall", enter **57**. In the box to the right of Category 2, enter **Temperature**. To the right of the word "Temperature", enter **75**.

7. A chart will be created to accommodate the information you entered:

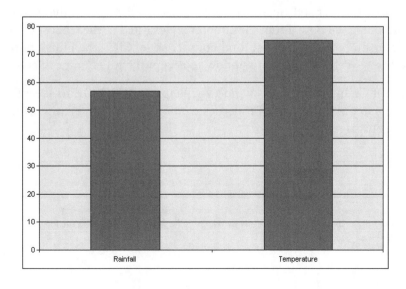

12

8. You can adjust the color, chart type, data values, and other chart features just as you would in Microsoft Excel by selecting the various chart objects such as the lines, workspace, labels and more in the chart itself.

1-Minute Drill

● Can transitions be added to images in banners?

● Why is the Web Search component useful?

Hit Counter

Ask any Web developer if they want to know how many visitors visit their site, and almost all of them will say yes. To measure the number of visitors visiting pages in your site, FrontPage provides you with the Hit Counter component. A hit counter is a small image that counts and displays the number of visitors who have come to your page.

Creating a Hit Counter

1. Create a new page in FrontPage. Launch the Insert Web Component window by selecting Insert | Web Component from the menu bar.

2. From the Insert Web Component window, select the Hit Counter icon. The Choose a counter style menu box will appear on the right of the Insert Web Component window. From the counter styles listed in the Choose a counter style menu box, select the second counter style. Click the Finish button in the Insert Web Component window to accept the hit counter selection.

3. The Hit Counter Properties window will appear. Click OK to accept the choices in the Hit Counter Properties window. A hit counter will be inserted into your page.

● Yes

● It helps your visitors find information quickly by searching for keyword(s) related to the information they are looking for.

4. Save the page and preview it in your browser. Click the Refresh or Reload button on your browser five times and notice that your hit counter increases sequentially each time the page gets reloaded:

Modifying the Hit Counter

Just like other FrontPage components, you can modify hit counters. Not only can you change the counter style, you can also reset the counter and adjust the fixed number of digits.

Follow these directions to modify a hit counter:

1. Right-click the hit counter and select the FrontPage Component Properties command from the menu that appears.

2. The Hit Counter Properties window will appear after you select the FrontPage Component Properties command:

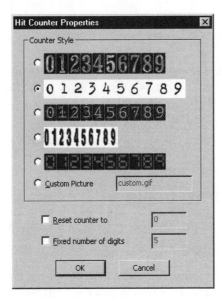

12

The following is a list and brief description of the options in the Hit Counter Properties window:

- **Counter Style**   Selects the counter style for your hit counter. You can use one of FrontPage's counter styles, or you can create your own counter style from an image.

- **Reset counter to**   Changes the initial value for your counter. By default, your counter will start with the default initial value of 0, but you can override the default value and enter any number you wish.

- **Fixed number of digits**   Specifies the number of digits your counter will count up to. When a value of 4 is entered, the hit counter will display up to 4 digits. A number that passes the 4-digit mark will have its first digit removed so that only 4 digits are visible in the counter.

3. Check the Reset counter to checkbox. The text field to the right of the Reset counter to check box will be enabled. Enter **5,000** in the Reset counter to field.

4. Check the Fixed number of digits checkbox. Enter **6** in the Fixed number of digits field that becomes enabled.

5. Click OK to accept the changes made and to close the Hit Counter Properties window.

Photo Gallery

A great way to let others know more about the subject of your site is to include a photo gallery about the subject. A photo gallery is simply a page primarily filled with pictures. While creating photo galleries is usually considered to be a long and arduous process, FrontPage automates the process of creating photo galleries and enables you to create custom galleries such as slide shows, vertical lists, and more.

Creating a Photo Gallery

1. Create a new page in FrontPage. Launch the Insert Web Component window by selecting Insert | Web Component from the menu bar.

2. In the Insert Web Component window, select the Photo Gallery icon. The Choose a Photo Gallery Option menu box will appear on the right of the Insert Web Component window. From the Choose a Photo Gallery Option

menu box, select the second photo gallery option and click the Finish button.

3. After you click the Finish button, the Photo Gallery Properties window will appear. In the Photo Gallery Properties window, click the Add button and select the Pictures from Files command from the menu that appears.

4. After you select the Pictures from File option, the File Open window will appear. In the File Open window, browse to the Photo Gallery folder (this folder is included in the source files you downloaded for this module).

5. In the Photo Gallery folder, you will see seven images. Select all seven of the images and click the Open button. Click OK to close the Photo Gallery Properties window.

6. Save the page and preview it in your browser. Notice that when you click an image, a larger version of the image is displayed. Your page should look similar to Figure 12-3.

Keep this page open, as we will use it in the next section.

Figure 12-3   The Photo Gallery page previewed in a browser

Modifying the Photo Gallery

You may remember that the Insert Web Component window offered several formats of photo galleries for you to choose from. I will show you how to change the photo gallery layout, edit some photo settings, and more:

1. Using the file from the previous section, right-click the photo gallery and select the Photo Gallery Properties command. The Photo Gallery Properties window will appear.

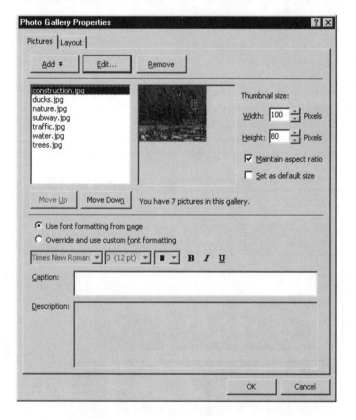

2. To change the photo gallery layout, select the Layout tab in the Photo Gallery Properties window. In the Choose a layout box, select the Vertical Layout photo gallery style. The Preview box will show you an example of how images are arranged in a vertical layout. Click OK to close the Photo Gallery Properties window.

3. After you have closed the Photo Gallery Properties window, you will see your photo gallery change to match the vertical layout you selected.

4. To add some text labels to the photo gallery, right-click the photo gallery and select the Photo Gallery Properties command. If it isn't already selected, select the Pictures tab.

5. In the Pictures tab, select the image *construction.jpg*.

6. In the Caption field, enter **Construction**. In the Description field, enter **This image represents a construction site**.

7. Select Override and use custom font formatting option. After you have selected the Override and use custom font formatting option, the drop-down menus for the font and point size will become active. Select Verdana for the font and select 2 (10 pt) for the point-size. Select the word "Construction" in the Caption field and select Arial for the font, select 3 (12 pt) for the point-size:

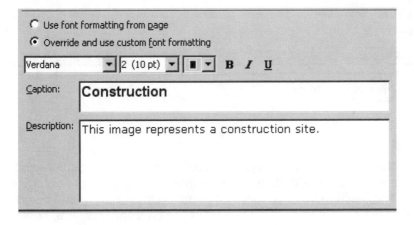

8. To add a caption and description to other images, select them from the list and edit the caption and description as you did for the *construction.jpg* image.

9. After you have finished giving the images captions and descriptions, click OK to close the Photo Gallery Properties window.

10. Your photo gallery should look something like Figure 12-4.

12

Figure 12-4   My photo gallery

Note

You can change between photo gallery layouts, even after the captions and descriptions have been added. Because the montage layout does not have text captions and descriptions, if you select that option, the captions and descriptions you added will not be displayed. If you select the horizontal, vertical, or slide-show layouts, the caption and description text will appear again. The slide-show layout is unique because it enables you to navigate between each image with a navigation bar custom tailored to the images in your photo gallery. You can view a photo gallery in the slide-show layout by going to http://www.kirupa.com/frontpage/ photogallery.htm.

Included Content

To help maintain your site and update it easily, FrontPage includes several useful tools to insert content from one page onto another page, display pages and images on a certain date, and more. You can also include information in your page such as the current page's Uniform Resource Identifier (URL), the author's name, the name of the person who last modified the current page, and/or the page's description. This information is not for your visitors, but is for other people who will work on your Web site, so they know who created the site, modified it last, and so on.

Substituting Content

To substitute your name, follow these directions:

1. Create a new page in FrontPage. Launch the Insert Web Component window by selecting Insert | Web Component from the menu bar.

2. In the Insert Web Component window, select the Included Content icon. The Choose a type of content menu box will appear on the right of the Insert Web Component window. From the Choose a type of content menu box, select the Substitution option. Click the Finish button to close the Insert Web Component window.

3. After you close the Insert Web Component window, the Substitution Properties window will appear.

4. Click the Substitute with drop-down menu and select the Author command. The name of the author (you) will be displayed in FrontPage.

5. Save this file as *substitution.htm* because you will use this file in the next section.

Note

The author name is the user name you use to log in to your Web server.

Entering Descriptions

In the previous section, you selected Author from the Substitute with drop-down menu in the Substitution Properties window. When you select the Description command from the Substitute with drop-down menu, you will see that no information gets displayed when you preview the page in your browser. The reason you do not see any information using the Description command is because you haven't specified a description anywhere for this page.

To add a description, follow these instructions:

1. Go to the FrontPage Folder View by selecting View | Folders from the menu bar. In the Folders View, right-click the current page you are editing (*substitution.htm*) and select the command for Properties. Because our filename is *substitution.htm*, the window that appears is titled substitution.htm Properties:

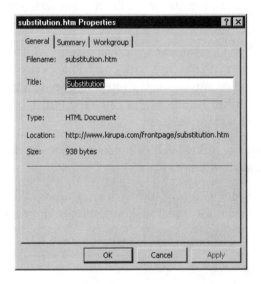

2. In the substitution.htm Properties window, select the Summary tab. In the Summary tab, type **This is an example of the description** into the Comments text box.

3. After you have typed that in, click the OK button to close the substitution.htm Properties window.

4. Click View | Page from the menu bar to go back to the *substitution.htm* file you were working on and preview the page in your browser.

5. When you preview your page, you will see that the description, "This is an example of the description," that you entered in the Comments text box is displayed in your browser.

Inserting Repeated Content

A very useful component that I use often in my site is the Page component. When you enter information that needs to be repeated on different pages, you can enter the information in two ways: you can copy and paste the information on each page or use the Page component.

While it may seem easier to use the first method of repeating information on other pages, what if you made a mistake in entering the information that is being copied? Will you go back and manually adjust each page you pasted the information to, or, would you like to simply edit one page and have the information updated on all the pages at the same time? More than likely, you will choose the latter option.

Inserting Content from One Page into Another Page

1. Import the files *page.htm* and *page2.htm* into your FrontPage Web. After the files have been imported, create a new page in FrontPage.

2. In the new page you have just created, type your first and last name. Do not add any formatting to the text you just entered. We will format the text later.

3. Save this page as *name.htm*.

4. Open the file *page.htm* in FrontPage. In the table in the center of the page, we will insert the page you created with your first and last name.

5. Select Insert | Web Component from the menu bar. In the Include Web Component window, select the Included Content icon. The Choose a type of component menu box will display the Included Content components. Select the Page option from the Choose a type of component menu box and click the Finish button.

6. After you click the Finish button, the Include Page Properties window will appear.

12

7. In the Page to include field in the Include Page Properties window, enter the path to the *name.htm* page you just created. You can also use the Browse button to browse for the file.

8. After the file path *name.htm* has been entered in the Page to include text field, click OK to close the Include Page Properties window. The *name.htm* page that contains only your name will be displayed in the *page.htm* page.

9. Keep the *page.htm* page open and open the page *page2.htm*. Insert the *name.htm* page in the table in the *page2.htm* page just like you did for the *page.htm* page. Save the *page2.htm* page and the *page.htm* page and preview the *page.htm* page in your browser.

10. When the *page.htm* page is previewed in your browser, click the Next page link, and you will see that the *name.htm* page is displayed on both the *page.htm* and *page2.htm* pages.

11. The real advantage that the Page component has over copy and paste is the capability to update and display the information across all the pages easily at the same time. To do this, open the *name.htm* page in FrontPage.

12. After you have opened the *name.htm* page, increase the font size, add some color, change the font, and more to your name. Be creative!

13. After you modified the font style for your name, save the *name.htm* page. Because the *name.htm* page has been updated, the *page.htm* and the *page2.htm* pages will display the updated *name.htm* page.

14. Now, open the *page.htm* page and preview it in your browser. Click the Next Page link that hyperlinks to *page2.htm*, and you will see that when the pages display, your name has been updated with the font style you applied to the *name.htm* page.

Note

Because we only used the *name.htm* page on two pages, it might have seemed easier to simply copy and paste the information. But imagine if your name was used on over one hundred pages in your site. Would you rather modify them manually by opening all one hundred pages and editing the font style, or would you use the Page component to modify the *name.htm* page and have your name be updated on all one hundred pages at the same time?

Automatically Changing Content

Just like the Page component, the Page Based on Schedule component enables you to merge one page with another page. The only difference is that the Page Based on Schedule Component enables you to change the pages automatically on a certain date. For example, using the Page Based on Schedule component, you can set an included page with the text Welcome to automatically change to Merry Christmas on December 31.

To change content automatically, follow these instructions:

1. Create a new document and open it in FrontPage.

2. Select Insert | Web Component from the menu bar. From the Include Web Component window, select the Included Content icon. Select the Page Based On Schedule component from the Choose a type of component menu box at the right side of the window and click the Finish button.

3. The Scheduled Include Page Properties window will appear:

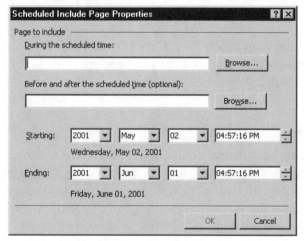

The following is a list of the options in the Scheduled Include Page Properties window:

● **During the scheduled time** Specifies the page that will be displayed during the time you schedule the page to be displayed.

● **Before and after the scheduled time** Specifies the page that will be displayed before and after the scheduled time. (During the scheduled time, the page mentioned in the During the schedule time field will be displayed.)

- **Starting**   The starting date in which the page in the During the scheduled time box will be displayed.

- **Ending**   The ending date in which the page in the During the scheduled time box will no longer be displayed. (The page mentioned in the Before and after the scheduled time will be displayed after the ending date.)

4. In the During the scheduled time field, type the path or browse for a file to be displayed between the times you will specify.

5. In the Before and after the scheduled time field, enter the path or browse for a file that will be displayed before and after the time you specify.

6. In the Starting drop-down menus, specify the year, the month, the day, and the minute that you want the page you specified in the During the scheduled time field to display.

7. In the Ending drop-down menus, specify the year, the month, the day, and the minute that you want the page you specified in the Before and after the scheduled time field to display.

Automatically Changing Images

The Picture Based on Schedule component enables you to schedule the display of a picture instead of a page during a set period of time. For example, you can automatically change an image to a Halloween pumpkin throughout the month of October by using the Picture Based on Schedule Component.

To change an image automatically, follow these instructions:

1. Select Insert | Web Component from the menu bar. From the Include Web Component window, select the Included Content icon. Select the Picture Based On Schedule component from the Choose a type of component menu box at right side of the window and click the Finish button. The Scheduled Picture Properties window will appear.

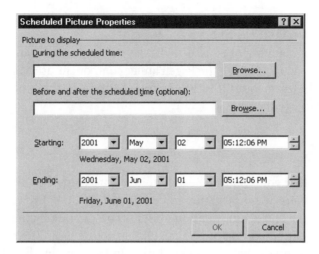

The following is a list of the options in the Scheduled Picture Properties window:

● **During the scheduled time**   Specifies the image that will be displayed during the times you specify.

● **Before and after the scheduled time**   Specifies the image that will be displayed before and after the scheduled time.

● **Starting**   The starting date in which the image in the During the scheduled time box will be displayed.

● **Ending**   The ending date in which the image in the During the scheduled time box will no longer be displayed. (You will see the image mentioned in the Before and after the scheduled time after the Ending date.)

2. In the During the scheduled time field, type the path or browse for a image to be displayed between the times you will specify.

3. In the Before and after the scheduled time field, enter the path or browse for an image that will be displayed before and after the time you specify.

4. In the Starting drop-down menus, specify the year, the month, the day, and the minute that you want the image you specified in the During the scheduled time field to display.

5. In the Ending drop-down menus, specify the year, the month, the day, and the minute that you want the image you specified in the Before and after the scheduled time field to display.

12

Displaying Banners

The Page Banner component is used to display a custom page banner for the page that it is being used in. Because the Page Banner component uses FrontPage themes to work, we will learn about how to use page banners in the Module 13, which discusses FrontPage themes.

Link Bars

It is important that your visitors be able to navigate your Web site easily. While you can create your own navigation system by using links, FrontPage provides tools to aid you to create a navigation system. The Link Bars components help you to create a bar based on your navigation structure, a link bar of custom hyperlinks for your site, back and next links, and a changing link bar.

Creating a Navigation Structure

You should be familiar with creating a basic Navigation view from Module 9, and we will extend upon that knowledge in this module. A navigation structure is the layout of all your Web's pages in the FrontPage Web. FrontPage uses the way the pages are organized to customize the Link Bars components.

The following instructions will guide you to create a navigation structure that will be used for the rest of this module:

1. Open a FrontPage Web. Select File | Open Web and open the linkbars Web from files you downloaded for this module.

2. After you have opened the linkbars Web, select View | Navigation to go to the Navigation view. You will see your home page (*index.htm*) displayed as an icon in the center of the Navigation view.

3. Drag the files *help.htm* and *services.htm* from the Folder List pane on the left of the Navigation view to the home page icon. After moving the *search.htm* and *services.htm* files, drag the *search.htm* file to the Help file icon. Your navigation structure should look like the following image:

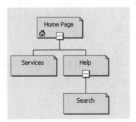

4. Save this page.

Keep this page open, as we will be use it in the next section.

Creating a Link Bar

1. Open the file *index.htm* from the linkbars FrontPage Web you opened in the previous section.

2. From the *index.htm page*, place the mouse cursor in the cell directly below the blue cell with the title.

3. Select Insert | Web Component. From the Web Component window, select the Link Bars icon. The Choose a bar type menu box will appear. Select the Bar with custom links option from the list on the right. Click the Finish button to accept the selection.

4. After you click the Finish button, the Create New Link Bar window appear. In the name field, enter **Links**. Links is now the name for the link bar that we will create. Click OK to close the Create New Link Bar window. The Link Bar Properties window will appear:

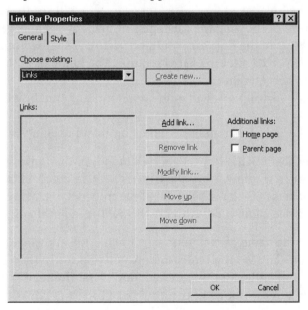

5. In the Link Bar Properties window, click the Add link button and the Add to Link Bar window will appear.

6. In the Add to Link Bar window, select the file *help.htm* and click the OK button. You will see the file *help.htm* appear in the links box in the Link Bar Properties window. Click the Add Link button again and add the files *index.htm*, *search.htm*, and *services.htm*. The Links box in the Link Bar Properties window should look like the following image:

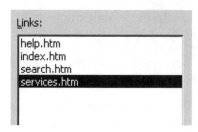

7. Save this page.

Keep this page open, as we will use it in the next section.

Modifying the Link Bar

If you look at the link bar in the *index.htm* page, you will see that it can be improved. Instead of showing the filenames of the individual pages, a word describing the page in the link bar would be useful. Also, the home page link (*index.htm*) is displayed after the *help.htm* link. The home page link should come before the *help.htm* link.

The following instructions will guide you to modify the link bar:

1. Right-click the link bar and select the command for Link Bar Properties.

2. To reorder the links, select the *index.htm* link in the Links box of the Link Bar Properties window. After the file has been selected, click the Move up button. Next, select the *services.htm* link and click the Move up button until the *services.htm* link is directly below the *index.htm* link.

3. To change the name of the links, select *index.htm* and click the Modify Link button. The Modify Link window will appear. In the Text to display box at the top of the Modify Link window, type **Home**. Click OK to close the Modify Link window. In the Link Bar Properties window, you will see that the link *index.htm* is now listed as "Home" in the Links box.

4. To change the name for the remaining links, follow the same procedure that is given in step 2 and change the link *services.htm* to **Services**, the link *help.htm* to **Help**, and the link *search.htm* to **Search**. Your Links bar should look like the following image:

5. Click OK to accept the changes and to close the Link Bar Properties window.

6. Save and preview the *index.htm* page. You will see that the link bar looks much better. The link names are known by their names instead of their filenames with the *.htm* extension. You will also see that when you click a link from the link bar, that page does not have a link bar. You will have to add a link bar to each page individually.

7. To add a link bar to each page, open the files *index.htm*, *services.htm*, *help.htm*, and *search.htm* in FrontPage.

8. Display the *index.htm* page first. (Remember from Module 11 that you can change from page to page by clicking the page's filename tab below the Formatting toolbar.) Right-click the link bar and select the Copy command.

9. Display the *services.htm* file and right-click the empty cell below the blue cell. Select the Paste command for from the menu that appears. You have now pasted the link bar in the *services.htm* file.

10. Paste the link bar in the *help.htm* and *search.htm* pages in the same location (the empty cell below the blue cell).

11. Save the files (a quick method of saving multiple files that are open is to go to the File menu and select the Save All command) and preview them in your browser. You will see that every page linked to the original link bar will have its own link bar.

12

Keep the *index.htm*, *services.htm*, *help.htm* and *search.htm* files open because we will use them in the next section.

Creating Back and Next Links

A simpler navigation method for your site is the use of back and next links.

1. In the *index.htm* page, place your mouse cursor below the entire table.

2. Select to Insert | Web Component. From the Web Component window, select the Link Bars icon. The Choose a bar type menu box will appear. Select the Bar with back and next links option from the Choose a bar type menu box. Click the Finish button to accept the selection.

3. The Link Bar Properties window will appear with the same files and settings from the previous section.

4. To modify the style of the back and next links, click the Style tab in the Link Bar Properties window, and select the style below the Use Page's Theme: Arcs. (This is the same style that you selected in the "Creating a Link Bar" section in this module.) Also check the Use Active Graphics check box. Click OK to accept the changes and to close the Link Bar Properties window.

5. Your back and next links in the *index.htm* page should look like the following image. Because you are viewing the home page (*index.htm*), there is no back link because you can only move forward through the site from the home page:

6. Copy the back and next links to the empty space below the table in the *services.htm*, *help.htm* and *search.htm* files.

7. Save all the pages and preview the pages in your browser, and you will see that the back and next links follow in the same order as the link bar. The order of the pages in the Links box of the Link Bar Properties window also specifies the order in which the back and next links will link.

Note

Did you notice that when you move the mouse over the back and next links, the arrow in the image highlights? That is because you checked the Use Active Graphics check box in the Style tab of the Link Bar Properties window in number 4 of this section.

Keep the *index.htm, services.htm, help.htm,* and *search.htm* files open because we will use them in the next section.

Creating a Changing Link Bar

The Bar Based on Navigation Structure component is used to create a changing link bar. A changing link bar is useful for sites with numerous pages listed in their navigational structure. Having hundreds of links display horizontally or vertically on a single page is not practical. To display only a certain portion of link bars, you will use create a changing link bar. The links in this bar are dependent upon the navigation structure, so the links displayed will change as you go from page to page.

To create a changing link bar, follow these instructions:

1. Display the *index.htm* file in FrontPage. Select the left cell with your mouse cursor and select Insert | Web Component. The Insert Web Component window will appear.

2. In the Web Component window, select the Link Bars icon. The Choose a bar type menu box will appear toward the right of the Insert Web Component window. Select the Bar based on navigation structure option from the list on the right. Click the Finish button to accept the selection. The Link Bar Properties window will appear:

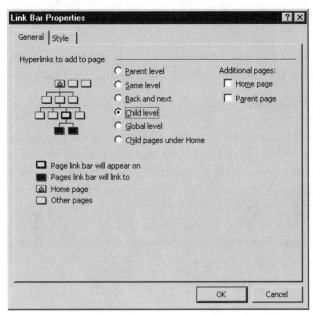

3. In the Link Bar Properties window, you will see a graphical representation of a page structure. If you select the various options in the Hyperlinks to add to page area, the page structure image will change to display the files that correspond to that section of the navigation structure.

4. For the *index.htm* page that you are working on right now, select the Child pages under Home command.

5. Click the Style tab to change the bar style. Select any theme other than the second theme you have been using for the previous two lessons. After you have selected a theme, select the Vertical option in the Orientation and appearance area; this will make the navigation bar vertical instead of horizontal.

6. Click OK to accept the changes and to close the Link Bar Properties window. You will see the link bar based on your navigation structure displayed in the left cell in the *index.htm* page.

7. Copy the link bar that you just created and paste it in the left cell of the *services.htm*, *help.htm*, and *search.htm* files.

8. Because the *help.htm* page has the *search.htm* page linked to it in the navigation structure, we can modify the link bar you just created to show only the *search.htm* page. To do that, display the *help.htm* page. Right click the link bar that is based on the navigation structure and select the Link Bar Properties command.

9. From the Link Bar Properties window, select the Child level option. Click OK to accept the change and to close the Link Bar Properties window.

10. Save all the files and preview them in your browser.

While previewing, you will see that all the pages except the *help.htm* page display the Home, Services, and Help link, and that the Search link is not displayed. That is because in our navigation structure, the Search page was not connected to the home page, it was connected to the Help page only. When you click the Help page, you will only see the Home and Search links because we selected the Child level option from the Link Bar Properties for the link bar on the *help.htm* file. You cannot add the child level option for the other files because they had no files linked to them.

Table of Contents

Besides the option to search your site, you can provide your visitors with a table of contents page. A table of contents is useful because it provides links to pages contained in the Web. Not only can you display links to pages contained in your Web, you can also display pages grouped by categories.

Creating a Table of Contents

To create a table of contents page, we will use the For This Web Site component:

1. Create a new document in FrontPage. Select Insert | Web Component. The Insert Web Component window will appear.

2. In the Insert Web Component window, select the Table of Contents icon. The Choose a table of contents menu box will appear. From the Choose a table of contents menu box, select the For This Web Site option and click the Finish button. The Table of Contents Properties window will appear:

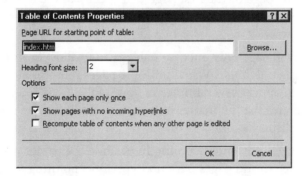

3. Click OK to accept the choices and to close the Table of Contents Properties window. After you close the Table of Contents Properties window, you will see a basic outline of the table of contents in your document.

4. Save the file and preview it in your browser. If your Web contains pages that link to each other, you will see a listing of those pages.

Keep the file open because you will learn how to customize the table of contents in the next section.

12

Customizing the Table of Contents

We will use the Table of Contents Properties window to customize the table of contents:

1. Using the file from the previous section, right-click the table of contents and select the Table of Contents Properties command. The following is a list of each of the options in the Table of Contents Properties window:

   - **Page URL for starting point of table**   Specifies the URL from which the table of contents will collect its information. You can specify the name of a page in a folder, but the table of contents will only index and display the pages contained in that folder. To index the entire FrontPage Web, you need to enter the address of your site's home page.

   - **Heading font size**   Adjusts the size of the heading. The smaller the heading number, the larger the text; the larger the heading number, the smaller the text. When you change the heading number, the phrase "Table of Contents Heading Page" will change its text size in FrontPage. The home page or the first page you specify to the index will replace the Table of Contents Heading Page text when the page is previewed in a browser.

   - **Show each page only once**   Enables you to allow FrontPage to display each page only once. When multiple pages refer to one page, that one page will appear several times in your table of contents. Checking this box ensures that no matter how many sites link to one page, the pages will be displayed only once.

   - **Show pages with no incoming hyperlinks**   Enables you to allow FrontPage to add pages with no hyperlinks pointing to them from the home page to be indexed.

   - **Recompute table of contents when any other page is edited**   Enables you to recreate the table of contents if a file is added or created. Because recreating the table of contents for a large site will take a long time, the best option is to keep this box unchecked and manually open the table of contents page to recreate all the links.

2. Click the Heading font size drop-down menu and select 1 (largest).

3. Click OK to close the Table of Contents Properties window. Preview the page in your browser. The heading font size will be larger.

Creating a Table Of Contents Based on Page Category

In FrontPage, you can categorize pages from the Folders view. When you categorize pages, FrontPage keeps track of all the files that belong to the same category. By using the Table of Contents component's Based on Page Category selection, you can display pages of like categories in a table of contents.

Follow these directions to create a table of contents based on page category:

1. Before we actually add the table of contents, we need to categorize some pages. To categorize the pages, go to your Folders view by selecting View | Folders. Right-click the *test.htm* page and select the Properties command. In the Properties window, click the Workgroup tab:

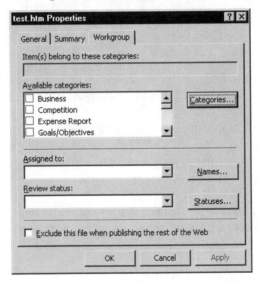

2. Check the Competition box in the Available categories menu box. After you have made your selection, click the Apply button.

3. If you have more files in your Web, you may want to categorize them in the Competition category as you did in step 2. Adding a page in a category does not affect the contents of the page.

4. After you have categorized a few pages, we can create the table of contents. To create the table of contents, create and open a new document in FrontPage. From the new document, select Insert | Web Component. The Insert Web Component window will appear.

12

5. In the Insert Web Component window, select the Table of Contents icon. The Choose a table of contents menu box will appear. Select the Based on Page Category option from the Choose a table of contents menu box and click the Finish button. The Categories Properties window will appear:

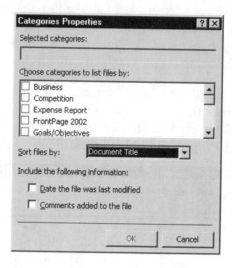

6. In the Category Properties window, select the Competition category you assigned to the pages from the Folders view in steps 2 and 3. Once you have the categories selected, click the OK button to accept the categories and to close the Category Properties window.

7. Save the page and preview it in your browser. The pages you assigned the Competition category to from the Category Properties window will be displayed.

1-Minute Drill

● How do you access a FrontPage Web's Navigation view?

● If I select larger heading numbers for the table of contents heading size, will I get larger text or smaller text?

● By selecting View | Navigation from the menu bar
● Smaller text

Top 10 List

To help you to manage your site better, FrontPage has the Top 10 list, which provides information such as the most popular browsers visiting your site, sites referring to your site, number of visitors, and more. This information can help you to design your site for various browsers, to promote popular pages, and more. To use the Top 10 List Component, you must have the SharePoint Extensions installed and the Site Usage enabled in the SharePoint Extensions.

Adding a Top 10 List

The following instructions will guide you to add a Top 10 List Component to your site:

1. Create and open a new document in FrontPage. Select Insert | Web Component. The Insert Web Component window will appear.

2. In the Insert Web Component window, select the Top 10 List icon. The Choose a usage list menu box will appear on the right. You can select any option from the Choose a usage list menu box. For this lesson, select the Referring URLs option. Click the Finish button. The Top 10 List Properties window will appear:

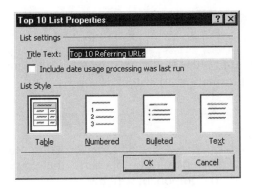

3. In the Top 10 List Properties window, select the Bulleted list style. Click OK to close the Top 10 List Properties window.

4. Save the page and preview it in your browser.

12

Automatic Content

The automatic content components are the bCentral Web, Expedia, MSN, and MSNBC components. What sets these components apart from the other components you have used is that these components automatically update themselves with the latest information. If you add MSNBC's Business Headlines component, visitors visiting your site will see the latest MSNBC business news without your having to update your site at all.

Following these instructions to add an automatic content component:

1. Create and open a new document in FrontPage. Select Insert | Web Component. The Insert Web Component window will appear.

2. In the Insert Web Component window, select the MSN Components icon and select the Stock quote option on the right. Click the Finish button. You will see a table with the MSN Stock quote option displayed:

MoneyCentral Stock Quote
Enter Symbol(s) [   ] [Go]

3. Save the page and preview it in your browser. Enter the symbol for a stock, and the information on a stock is shown.

Note

To insert other bCentral, Expedia, MSN, and MSNBC components, you will follow the same steps. The only difference will be, of course, that you will select a different option from the Insert Web Component window.

index.htm,
help.htm,
photo.htm,
search.htm,
services.htm

Project 12-1: Using FrontPage Web Components

The following are the goals for this project:

● Use the Page option

● Implement a link bar

● Create a photo gallery

● Add a search page

Step by Step

1. Open the FrontPage Web for this project by selecting File I Open Web. Browse to the directory where the source files for this module are and open the Project Web folder.

2. Once the FrontPage Web has been opened, make sure you are in the Folders View (View I Folders). Open the *index.htm*, *help.htm*, *photo.htm*, *search.htm*, and *services.htm* pages in FrontPage.

3. To add a copyright statement at the bottom of each page, display the *index.htm* page. Place your mouse cursor in the white space below the entire table. Launch the Insert Web Component window and select the Included Content component type. From the list on the right, double-click the Page component. You will see the Include Page Properties window. In the Page to include box, browse for the file *copyright.htm*. Click OK after you have selected the file.

4. The file *copyright.htm* will be displayed at the bottom of the *index.htm* page. Right-click the page you just inserted and select the Copy command. Paste this file below each table in the *help.htm*, *photo.htm*, *services.htm*, and *search.htm* pages.

5. To add a Search component, display the file *search.htm*. Once the Search page is displayed, insert your mouse pointer below the last line of text in the table. Launch the Insert Web Component window and select the Web search component type. Double-click the Current Web command from the list on the right. The Search Form Properties window will appear. Click OK

12

to accept the choices made by the Search Form Properties window. After the Search component has been inserted, save this file.

6. To add a photo gallery to the *photo.htm* page, display the *photo.htm* page in FrontPage. Insert your mouse cursor below the text inside the cell. Launch the Insert Web Component window and select the Photo Gallery component type. On the right of the Insert Web Component window, there should be several photo gallery layouts visible. Double-click the third photo gallery layout.

7. In the Photo Gallery Properties window, add the images contained in the photo gallery folder of your source files by clicking the Add button. The following images should be listed:

8. Click OK to close the Photo Gallery Properties window. The slide show photo gallery should be visible in the *photo.htm* page.

9. The last component we will be adding for this project is the Link Bars component. Because I have already created the navigation structure, all you have to do is insert the link bar. To do this, display the *index.htm* page. Place your mouse pointer in the empty cell below the blue-colored cell. Once your mouse pointer is in the empty cell, launch the Insert Web Component window. Select the Link Bars icon and double-click the Bar with custom links selection from the Choose bar type menu box on the right side of the Insert Web Component window.

10. In the Create a New Link Bar window, give your link bar a name and click the OK button. The Link Bar Properties window will appear. In the Link Bar Properties window, click the Add link button. In the Add to Link bar window, add the following files: *index.htm, help.htm, photo.htm, search.htm,* and *services.htm*.

11. Make sure your links are organized like the links in the following image. If they are not, use the Move up and Move down buttons to adjust the links in this order:

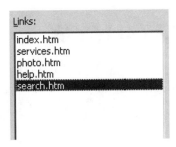

12. We need to modify the link text so that it does not show the link's filename to the visitor. To do this, select the *index.htm* link and click the Modify link button. The Modify Link window will appear. At the top of the Modify Link box, change the *index.htm* to **Home**. Click OK to go back to the Link Bar Properties window.

13. Repeat step 12 for the remaining links in the Links box. Change *services.htm* to **Services**, change *photo.htm* to **Photos**, change *help.htm* to **Help**, and change *search.htm* page to **Search**.

14. The last step in completing the link bar is to adjust the style. Select the Style tab in the Link Bar Properties window. Select the fourth style with the description A graphical theme based on the Axis theme. In the Style tab, select the check boxes for Active Graphics and Use Vivid Colors. Click OK to accept the changes and close the Link Bar Properties window.

15. The link bar will be inserted in the empty cell below the blue-colored cell. Right-click the link bar and select the Copy command. Paste the link bar in the same location on the *help.htm*, *photo.htm*, *search.htm*, and *services.htm* files. Save all the files currently open and preview the *index.htm* page in your browser.

Summary

FrontPage Web components help to simplify complex tasks. Without FrontPage Web components, creating a search page, inserting a picture gallery that acts as slide show, displaying an image on a certain date, and more would take much longer and require a greater understanding of programming languages. With the use of automatic content such as a weather ticker, news banner, and more, you can provide your visitors with automatically updated information each time they visit.

12

✓ *Mastery Check*

1. Can you customize the amount of time that an image in a Banner Ad Manager component will appear?

_____

_____

2. What is the difference between the Page based on schedule component and the Page component?

_____

_____

3. What does a hit counter do?

_____

_____

4. Does the slide-show layout of the Photo Gallery component automatically create the necessary links to display the photo?

_____

_____

5. What are some advantages of using the automatic content components?

_____

_____

6. What is the easiest way to edit a page that has been inserted using the Page component?

_____

_____

Module 13

Using Themes and Templates

The Goals of This Module

- Learn to use FrontPage themes
- Create a page banner and apply document styles
- Build a guest book
- Construct a discussion Web

One way to attract visitors to and keep them interested in your site is to use interesting and creative combinations of color and design. Besides simple text and background color, we have not ventured into the styles, text, and images that FrontPage provides to make your site look stunningly artistic. FrontPage themes enable you to select a style and color scheme and apply it to your entire site.

In Module 10, you learned how to create forms that enabled the visitor to write messages to you. In this module you will learn how to create two forms, a guest book and a discussion Web, that enable visitors to leave comments and to have discussions with one another, respectively, and all of these will be viewable by anyone who visits your site.

For the directions in this module, please download the various images and sample source files for Module 13 from http://www.kirupa.com/frontpage or http://www.Osborne.com.

About FrontPage Themes

FrontPage themes are a set of styles that you can use to liven up your Web site. Themes make it easy for anyone who is not artistically talented or short on time to create a beautiful site. By using themes, you can focus more on the site content and not have to worry about the intricacies of site design such as color, consistency, images, legibility, and more.

Using FrontPage Themes

To get your feet wet using themes, we will apply a theme to a single Web page:

1. Open the file *themes.htm*. You will see a black-and white document containing only text.

2. From the menu bar, select Format | Theme. The Themes window will appear.

3. In the list on the left of the Themes window, select the Axis theme.

4. Click OK to apply the Axis theme and to close the Themes window. You will see that the original *themes.htm* page looks improved with the Axis

theme applied. The text is formatted differently, the bulleted list uses images, and there is a background image:

Themes

You see themes in places such as books, movies, plays, and more. I bet you never knew that the program you use for Web development, FrontPage, supports themes. Themes are great ways to enhance your site.

- Themes improve your site in the following ways:
    - Themes make your pages more colorful
    - Themes help you to have a consistent design throughout your site.

Contact:

Kirupa Chinnathambi
kirupa@kirupa.com

5. Save the *themes.htm* page.

Keep this page open because we will customize it in the next section.

Customizing Themes

The Themes window provides numerous options that can be modified to customize your theme:

1. While in the *themes.htm* page, select Format | Theme. The Themes window, as shown in Figure 13-1, will appear. The following list provides brief descriptions of each option in the Themes window:

- **All pages**   Applies the current theme to all pages in the FrontPage Web.
- **Selected page(s)**   Applies the current theme to the pages open or selected in FrontPage.
- **Vivid colors**   Uses livelier, brighter colors in the place of darker colors in the theme.
- **Active graphics**   Enables small animation effects such as image rollovers.
- **Background picture**   Applies a background picture to the current theme.

13

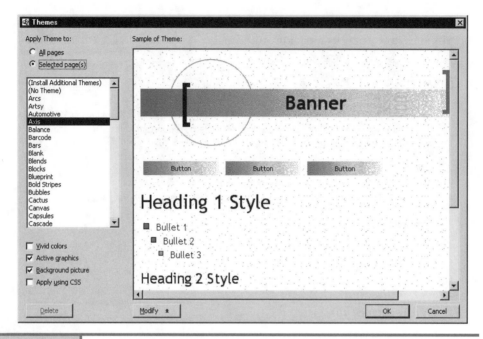

Figure 13-1 The numerous options of the Themes window

- **Apply using CSS** Enables you to use Cascading Style Sheets (CSS) to apply the theme's color and graphic scheme. You will not notice any changes to your theme when you uncheck this box because the theme is still being applied—it is just being applied using CSS.

2. Check the box for Vivid colors. Click OK to close the Themes window.

Note

When themes are used, the Background tab in the Page Properties window will be disabled. Only by removing the theme will you be able to enable the Background tab. When using themes, you will not have to use the Background tab because all of the background properties such as color, images, and hyperlink colors can be accessed from the Modify Theme window.

Modifying Theme Elements

FrontPage comes with numerous preformatted themes. A theme is simply a set of colors, graphics, and text, and you can modify those elements in a few easy steps.

Modifying Colors

1. Launch the Themes window by selecting Format | Theme.

2. In the Themes window, click the Modify button. After you click the Modify button, the Colors button will appear directly above the Modify button. Click the Colors button, and the Modify Theme window for colors will appear, as shown in Figure 13-2.

The following sections will explain how to modify the color schemes, the color wheel, and custom color combinations.

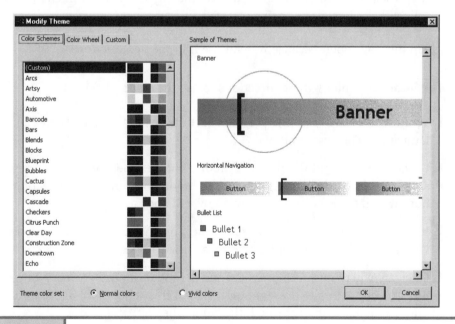

Figure 13-2   Modify colors using the Themes window.

13

Keep the Modify Theme window open because we will use it in the next section.

Color Schemes   Follow these directions to adjust the colors in your current theme:

1. While in the page from the previous section, select Format | Theme to launch the Themes window.

2. In the Themes window, click the Modify button. The Colors, Graphics, and Text buttons will appear above the Modify button. Click the Colors button, and the Modify Theme window will appear.

3. On the right side of the Modify Theme window, you will see a sample of your current theme. On the left side of the Modify Theme window, you will see a list of the FrontPage themes installed and their color schemes. If you select a theme in the list, the sample of your theme will change to reflect the colors of the theme selected.

Keep this page open because we will use it in the next section.

Color Wheel   Follow these directions to use the color wheel:

1. While in the page from the previous section, select Format | Theme to launch the Themes window.

2. In the Themes window, click the Modify button. The Colors, Graphics, and Text buttons will appear above the Modify button. Click the Colors button, and the Modify Theme window will appear.

3. In the Modify Theme window, select the Color Wheel tab. A color wheel with a partially transparent circle inside it will appear.

4. Click anywhere in the color wheel and drag your mouse cursor. Notice how the five colors to the right of Colors in this scheme change as you drag the mouse cursor through the color wheel:

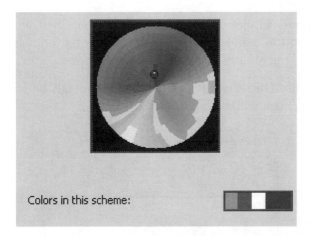

5. As you change the colors from the color wheel by dragging the mouse through the color wheel, you will see that your theme in the Sample of theme box will change to reflect the color change.

6. Drag the mouse through the color wheel until you find a color you like. You must choose a color that enables the text to be visible in the Sample of theme menu box. Choosing colors that are too bright or too dull will make reading text more difficult.

7. To adjust the brightness of the colors you have selected, slide the Brightness indicator. As you adjust the brightness of the colors, you will see that your theme in the Sample of theme box will change to reflect the color change.

8. Drag the brightness indicator until you get the darkness or brightness of the color you want.

9. After you have made your selections, click OK to close the Modify Theme window. Click OK to close the Themes window.

Keep this page open because we will use it in the next section.

Custom   Instead of changing the color to the overall theme, you can choose to adjust only the individual theme elements such as text, bulleted headings, banner text, and more:

1. While in the page from the previous section, select Format | Theme to launch the Themes window.

13

2. In the Themes window, click the Modify button. The Colors, Graphics, and Text buttons will appear above the Modify button. Click the Colors button, and the Modify Theme window will appear.

3. In the Modify Theme window, click the Custom tab, which has two drop-down menus: Item and Color:

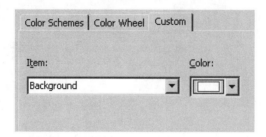

4. Click the Item drop-down menu and select the Body theme element. The sample of your theme will display the text that will be affected when you modify the Body theme element.

5. Click the Color drop-down menu and select the color for Navy. When you select a color from the color menu, notice that the sample of your theme on the right of the Modify Theme window changes to reflect the selection you made.

6. Click OK or Cancel to close the Modify Theme window.

7. Click OK to close the Themes window.

8. Save this page and preview it in your browser. The changes you made to the theme's colors will be visible in the Body text.

Tip

The Body text is referred to as *Regular Text Sample* in the sample area of the Modify Theme window.

Keep this page open because we will use it in the next section.

Modifying Graphics

The themes you apply to your pages have numerous images and small graphics in them. The bullets in the bulleted lists are individual graphics. When you apply a theme to a banner (which you will get to do later in this module), you are working with graphics. Just like theme colors, you can extensively modify each graphical element of your theme:

1. While in the page from the previous section, select Format | Theme to launch the Themes window.

2. In the Themes window, click the Modify button. After you click the Modify button, you will see the Graphics button appear above the Modify button along with the Colors and Text buttons. Click the Graphics button, and the Modify Theme window for graphics will appear, as shown in Figure 13-3.

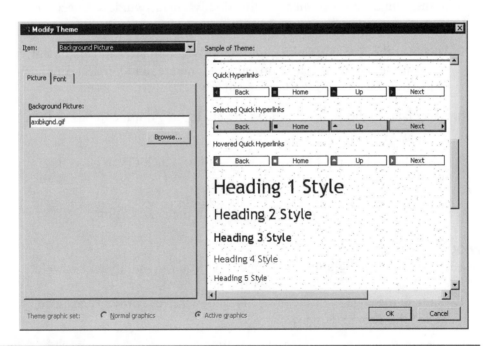

Figure 13-3   Modify theme graphics using the Modify Theme window.

13

3. At the top of the Modify Theme window, you will see the Item drop-down menu. Each element that uses graphics in your theme is listed in the Item drop-down menu. Select to the Background Picture item from the Item drop-down menu. In the Background Picture field, enter the path to the *background.jpg* image file.

4. As you may have noticed, theme elements such as banners, navigation buttons, and more contain text. To adjust the font style of graphics, click the Font tab in the Modify Theme window.

5. Select an item from the Item drop-down menu. In the Item drop-down menu, graphics that do not contain text will have the Style options grayed out. Items that do contain text such as the Banner item will have the Style options enabled.

6. In the Item drop-down menu of the Modify Theme window, select the Banner item.

7. To adjust the Banner graphic's font, font style, font size, and alignment, you will use the Style, Size, Horizontal Alignment, and Vertical Alignment drop-down menus and the Font menu box.

8. Select Bold in the Style drop-down menu. In the Font menu box, select Book Antiqua.

9. Click OK to close the Modify Theme window. Click OK to close the Themes window.

Keep this page open because we will use it in the next section.

Modifying Text

Just as with colors and graphics in your theme, you can modify text as well:

1. While in the page from the previous section, select Format | Theme to launch the Themes window.

2. In the Themes window, click the Modify button. After you click the Modify button, you will see the Text button appear above the Modify button. Click the Text button, and the Modify Theme window for text will appear.

3. To modify text characteristics of a theme, click the Item drop-down menu and select Heading 1

4. After you select Heading 1, select Times New Roman in the Font list on the left of the Modify Style window.

5. Click OK to accept the font selection and to close the Modify Theme window.

1-Minute Drill

● What are themes?

● Can individual elements of a theme such as text, graphics, and color be modified?

Page Banner Component

You may remember that the Page Banner component was introduced in Module 12, and there you were told that we would cover it in this module, where we discuss themes. The reason we are covering the Page Banner component in this module is because the Page Banner component requires that a theme be applied in order for the banner to display properly. What the Page Banner component does is enable you to enter text and display it either as a theme graphic or as plain text.

Creating a Page Banner

1. Open the Banner FrontPage Web from the files downloaded for this module.

2. After the Banner Web has loaded, open the *index.htm* file.

3. Insert your mouse pointer in the top cell of the *index.htm* file.

4. Open the Insert Web Component window by selecting Insert | Web Component.

13

● Themes are preformatted styles of colors, graphics, and text that can be applied to Web pages.

● Yes.

5. In the Insert Web Component window, select the Included Content
   component type. Select the Page Banner component on the right side
   of the Insert Web Component window and click the Finish button. The
   Page Banner Properties window will appear:

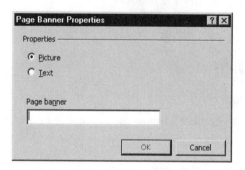

Tip

You can also insert the Page Banner component by selecting the Page Banner
command from the Insert menu.

---

6. Select the Picture option. In the Page banner text box, enter **Package
   International**. Click the OK button to close the Page Banner Properties
   window. The words you entered will appear in the first row.

7. Now, you need to apply a theme to this page to display the Page banner
   component the way it should be viewed: with custom colors and graphics.
   To apply a theme, select Format | Theme and select the Axis theme. While
   in the Themes window, uncheck the Background picture box.

8. Click OK to accept the theme selection. The page banner will look like
   the following:

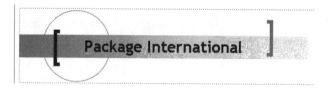

Note

The Page Banner component will not display if the page you are inserting the banner to is not part of a navigation structure. If you try to insert a page banner to a page that is not part of the navigation structure, you will be unable to enter the text to display in the Page Banner Properties window. Please refer to Module 12 for more information on page banners.

Document Styles

When you apply a theme to text of which you have already modified the font style, you will notice that the theme does not get applied to the text. There are two ways to format text in FrontPage: You can directly modify it by using the various font menus in the Formatting toolbar, or you can refer to the file using CSS. You will learn more about CSS in Module 14, but in a nutshell, CSS uses document styles to modify characteristics of objects such as text and images. Themes do not apply their unique font style to text that has been formatted using the Formatting toolbar's font menus. Document styles can be used to overcome this problem.

The following instructions will guide you in applying document styles to text:

1. Create a new document in FrontPage.

2. In the Formatting toolbar, select Style | Heading 1. Place your mouse cursor anywhere on the document and type **Heading 1**.

3. Press ENTER and select Style | Heading 2. Type **Heading 2**.

4. Press ENTER and select Style | Heading 3. Type **Heading 3**.

5. Repeat this step for **Heading 4**, **Heading 5**, and **Heading 6**.

6. Place your mouse pointer in the line after Heading 6, and select Style | Menu List. Type **Menu** after the bullet that appears.

7. Press ENTER and select Style | Normal. Type **Normal text**.

13

8. Press the ENTER and select Style | Numbered List. Type **Numbered list**. Your document should look like the following:

Heading 1

Heading 2

Heading 3

Heading 4

Heading 5

Heading 6

- Menu

Normal text

1. Numbered list

9. To apply a theme to the current document, select Format | Theme from the menu bar. In the Themes window, select a theme that you like. After you have selected a theme, click the OK button to close the Themes window. Because themes have preset font formatting for the document styles you applied, the text you typed will change to reflect the text styles of that theme.

Ask the Expert

Question: I am using FrontPage themes in my site, and I notice that many other sites are using the same theme on their sites. What should I do?

Answer: You could change your site's theme to something else, but that is not the most practical solution. The best solution is eventually to shy away from using themes. As you become more experienced in Web design, you should try to experiment with different designs. A good site to visit for discovering sites with different, professional designs is CoolHomepages (http://www.coolhomepages.com).

Guest Books

A guest book enables visitors to leave comments on your Web site. When information is submitted to a guest book, the information is not sent to you directly. The information submitted through a guest book is displayed on the guest book page. Any questions or comments your visitors make will be displayed for everyone who visits your site to see.

Because anyone who visits your site can view guest book, you should tell your visitors to communicate anything of a personal or urgent manner to you via e-mail.

Creating a Guest Book

The following instructions will guide you in creating a guest book for your Web site:

1. Make sure you are currently in your FrontPage Web. From the menu bar, navigate to File | New | Page or Web. The New Page or Web pane will appear to the right of the FrontPage window.

2. From the New Page or Web pane, select the Page templates command. The Page Templates window will appear. From the Page Templates window, select the Guest Book template and click the OK button.

3. You will see a new document with a guest book form already created for you. Save this file and preview it in your browser.

4. Test your guest book by typing **Testing to see if the guest book works** in the text area in your browser. Click the Submit Comments button to submit the information you typed. You will see the confirmation page if the information was submitted successfully.

13

5. Now go back to the previous page and click the Refresh button on your browser. The sentence you entered will be visible directly below the guest book form and will look similar to this:

Date:
    5/7/01
Time:
    7:10:48 PM
Remote User:

Comments

    Testing to see if the guestbook works.

Tip

Because the guest book is a form, you can modify the form properties for the guest book. Just as with forms you created in Module 10, you can create a custom confirmation page, have the information be e-mailed, save the data to a database, and more. Please refer to Module 10 for information on using and modifying forms.

Discussion Web

Have you posted messages on a message board? The discussion Web is very similar to a message board because it enables you to post messages and view replies to messages. Unlike guest books, the comments and responses submitted by visitors appear in an organized method.

Best of all, FrontPage makes it easy for you to create and maintain a discussion Web. You can perform complicated tasks such as setting up a search form, enabling your visitors to register, creating an automatic table of contents, and more.

Creating a Discussion Web

Unlike previous tools we have used for complicated tasks, FrontPage provides an interactive wizard for creating a discussion Web.

Note

To create a discussion Web, your Web server needs to be running the latest version of the FrontPage Server Extensions. You will need to contact your Web server host or administrator to ensure that your server is using the FrontPage 2000 version of the FrontPage Server Extensions or higher.

To create a discussion Web, follow these instructions:

1. In a new document in FrontPage, select File | New | Page or Web. In the New Page or Web pane that appears on the right of the FrontPage window, select the Web Site Templates command. From the Web Site Templates window, select the Discussion Web Wizard template and click the OK button. After a few moments, you will see the Discussion Web Wizard window.

Tip

You do not have to go through each step of the Discussion Web Wizard. You can click the Finish button and accept the default settings FrontPage provides for your discussion Web.

2. The Discussion Web Wizard provides you with a series of questions and options related to your discussion Web. Click the Next button to be presented with the first set of options regarding your discussion Web, as shown in Figure 13-4. The following is a list of the options with a brief description of each:

   - **Submission Form**   Enables your visitors to submit information to your discussion Web. You cannot disable this feature because it is required for your visitors to be able to post comments.

   - **Table of Contents**   Enables you to decide whether you want to provide your visitors with a table of contents that categorizes all posted information.

   - **Search Form**   Searches for words in the discussion Web (not the whole site).

   - **Threaded Replies**   Enables you to allow your visitors to post replies to specific articles in your discussions.

13

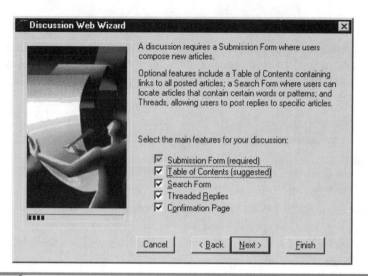

Figure 13-4 Selecting the main features for your discussion in the Discussion Web Wizard

- **Confirmation Page** Enables you to provide your visitors with a confirmation page that lets them know that the comments submitted were received.

3. Make sure all the options are checked and click the Next button.

4. The Discussion Web Wizard will then provide you with options regarding the name of your discussion Web and where the submitted articles will be stored. In the Enter a descriptive title for this discussion field, type **My Discussion**. The title, My Discussion, will be displayed on every page of your discussion Web.

5. The Discussion Web Wizard will then display choices regarding the form fields that will be displayed when your visitor submits information to your discussion Web. The form fields that you select will be filled out by your visitor before submitting the information to be posted to the discussion Web. The information your visitor enters in the form field will be visible to other users as well. Select the Subject, Comments option and click the Next button, see Figure 13-5.

6. The Discussion Web Wizard will then display choices that enable you to decide whether registered users will be allowed to post in your discussion

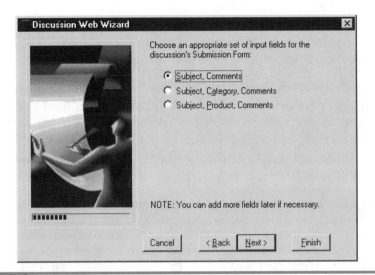

Figure 13-5 | Enabling registered visitors to post to your discussion

Web or if anybody can post in your discussion Web. Select the second choice, No, anyone can post articles.

Note

In order to enable only registered users to browse and post in your discussion Web, you need to modify your FrontPage Web's Web Permissions, and you need a UNIX-based server to support the FrontPage Server Extensions. Because this is a rather advanced task, I will not be covering that topic in this book.

7. Click the Next button to be presented with more choices regarding your discussion Web.

8. The two choices you will now see are regarding the discussion Web's table of contents and the order the posted articles will appear in the table of contents. When you select the first choice for Oldest to newest, the articles that were submitted most recently will appear at the bottom of the table of contents. When you select the second choice, Newest to oldest, the opposite will be true, and the most-recently submitted articles will appear at the top of the table of contents. Select Oldest to newest and click the Next button.

13

9. The Discussion Web Wizard now enables you make the table of contents page your discussion Web's home page. If you select Yes, the current home page will be overwritten with the table of contents. Select Yes and click Next.

10. Here the Discussion Web Wizard provides choices regarding the search form's results of your discussion Web. You might remember from Module 12 that you can customize the results of a search form. The same choices that were available in the Search Form Property window are also available in this step of the Discussion Web Wizard. Select the Subject, Size, Date option, as shown in Figure 13-6.

11. Click Next to see the next step of the Discussion Web Wizard, which is one of my favorite steps because you get to select a Web Theme for your entire discussion Web.

12. In this step, click the Choose Web Theme button and select a theme from the Choose Theme window. To make your discussion Web lively, check the boxes for Vivid Colors, Active Graphics, and Background picture.

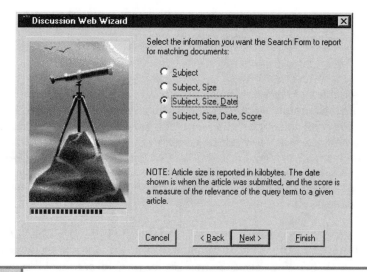

Figure 13-6 Use the Discussion Web Wizard or the Search Form Property window to customize your search form.

Click the OK button to close the Choose Theme window and to accept the theme you have chosen and press the Next button.

13. Here the Discussion Web Wizard window enables you to select the layout of the pages in your discussion Web. When you select a layout choice, you will notice that the layout image on the left of the Discussion Web Wizard window changes to reflect how the layout will look. You should understand that the last two choices will only work on browsers capable of viewing frames. Select the option for No frames and click Next.

14. After clicking the Next button you'll see a confirmation screen stating that you completed all the steps for creating your discussion Web. You will also see a brief summary of the options you selected in the previous screens.

15. Click the Finish button to enable FrontPage to create your discussion Web based on the choices you selected.

16. When back in your document, select View | Folders and open the *index.htm* page or another page you specified.

17. Preview the page in your browser and test your discussion Web by clicking the Post link and typing your message. You will see that the changes you specified in the Discussion Web Wizard are displayed throughout your Web. If you click a message that you posted, you will see the message and you will get the option to reply to only that message.

1-Minute Drill

● Do themes apply their font styles to text that has already been formatted?

● What is the name of the wizard that guides you through the process of creating a customized discussion Web?

● No
● The Discussion Web Wizard

Project 13-1: Using FrontPage Web Components

The following are the goals for this project:

● Apply themes

● Modify document styles

● Create a discussion Web

Step by Step

1. From the Project Web folder that you downloaded for this module, open the file *index.htm* by selecting View I Folders and double-clicking the *index.htm* file.

2. Highlight the word "Welcome" and change its document style to Heading 2. Use the Style drop-down menu from the Formatting toolbar to change the selected text's document style.

3. Let's apply a theme to this entire FrontPage Web. In the *index.htm* file currently open, select Format I Theme. In the Themes window, select the Postmodern theme. Select the check boxes for Vivid Colors, Active Graphics, and Background Picture.

4. Because we want to apply the theme to all pages in the current Web, select the option for All Pages at the top of the Themes window. Click OK to accept the theme selections. Click the OK button in the warning box that says changes will be made to the entire Web.

5. The next step is for you to create a discussion Web. Because you are currently working in the Project Web, which is on your hard drive, make sure you open a FrontPage Web that has the FrontPage Server Extensions installed. You should see another FrontPage window appear with your new FrontPage Web loaded.

6. From the FrontPage Web on your Web Server, choose File I New I Page or Web. In the New Page or Web pane, select the Web Site Templates command. The Web Site Templates window will appear.

7. Select the Discussion Web Wizard template and change the location your discussion Web will be created in. Click OK to accept the discussion Web template and any changes you may have made.

8. The Discussion Web Wizard window will appear. Click the Next button and make any customizations you feel are necessary for your discussion Web. Make sure that the descriptive title for your discussion Web is Puzzle Club and that the theme you select is Postmodern. This is so that the discussion Web and your Project Web look similar.

9. After you have completed all the steps in the Discussion Web Wizard and clicked the Finish button, your discussion Web will be created. Now, go back to the Project Web and open the *index.htm* file from the Project Web.

10. In the table where it says "Join the popular Puzzle Club...", highlight the last word, "here." Right-click "here" and select the Hyperlink command. From the Insert Hyperlink window that appears, enter the address of your discussion Web. After you enter the address of your discussion Web make sure you modify the hyperlink so that it opens in another browser window.

11. Save the *index.htm* file and preview it in your browser.

Summary

FrontPage includes great features to help improve your site, and it also saves you time by designing the colors, graphics, and more of your site. FrontPage themes simplify the design of your site by enabling you to apply preformatted styles onto your Web pages. You also learned how to use document styles to format the text in your site, and to use page banners. If you combine themes with a guest book and a discussion board, your visitors will enjoy visiting your site and will actively participate in it.

13

✓ *Mastery Check*

1. What do themes do?

_____

_____

2. What does the Active Graphics checkbox in the Themes window perform?

_____

_____

3. What the one key requirement for making a Page Banner component work?

_____

_____

4. What makes guest books unique compared to e-mail and regular forms?

_____

_____

5. Can themes be applied to a discussion Web?

_____

_____

6. What is a submission form in a discussion Web?

_____

_____

Module 14

Plug-Ins, ActiveX Controls, and Java Applets

The Goals of This Module

- Incorporate plug-ins
- Use ActiveX controls
- Explore Java applets

Web sites today are more interactive than ever before. With more powerful computers, visitors can engage themselves in navigating through a virtual reality gallery, browsing around a 360-degree panoramic image, using an online calendar to figure out what day their birthday will occur 20 years from now, and more. While Hypertext Markup Language (HTML) and related Web-programming languages can handle some of the basic functions of multimedia and interactivity, this module will introduce you to three technologies that can make your site more interactive: plug-ins, ActiveX controls, and Java applets.

For the directions in this module, please download the various images and sample source files for Module 14 from http://www.kirupa.com/frontpage or http://www.Osborne.com.

Plug-Ins

Plug-ins are pieces of software that display information on your Web page. While plug-ins can be used to display information such as text, they are often used to perform tasks that interact with the user by, for example, enabling them to navigate through a virtual reality gallery, modify the colors of a cell phone, and more. There are numerous plug-ins that can be downloaded for free or for a nominal fee. Popular plug-ins include Adobe's Acrobat Reader, RealNetworks' RealPlayer, Macromedia's Flash and Shockwave players, and many more.

Even though many plug-ins are installed along with your Web browser, not all visitors will have the required plug-in that you use. While some Web pages automatically install plug-ins on the visitor's computer, many Web pages simply display error messages when the visitor does not have the required plug-in installed.

Because plug-ins are separate pieces of software, FrontPage cannot edit plug-ins directly. FrontPage can only modify the HTML to call up the plug-in to display the file and any plug-in properties that the author of the plug-in allows.

Incorporating Plug-Ins

In this section, you will learn how to incorporate a Macromedia Flash file by using FrontPage's Plug-In Properties window. Before we start the lesson, make sure you have the latest version of the Macromedia Flash player installed. To install a free Macromedia Flash Player, go to the following address: http://www.macromedia.com/downloads/.

Follow these instructions to add a plug-in:

1. Create a blank document in FrontPage. Make sure the blank page you just created is displayed.

2. Select Insert | Web Component. In the Web Component window that appears, select Advanced Controls and then the Plug-In Command. Click the Finish button to display the Plug-In Properties window:

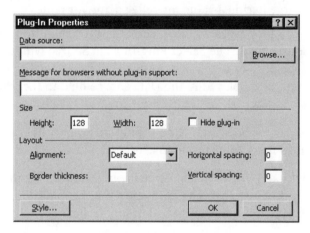

The following is a list of the various fields and commands of the Plug-In Properties window with a description of each:

● **Data Source**   Specifies the file that the plug-in will use. You can also use a Uniform Resource Identifier (URL) to link to the file.

● **Message for browsers without plug-in support**   Displays text that appears if a browser does not support plug-ins.

● **Height**   Specifies the height of the plug-in in pixels.

● **Width**   Specifies the width of the plug-in in pixels.

● **Hide plug-in**   Enables you to keep the plug-in hidden. When the plug-in is hidden, it will not be visible in the browser. You may check this box when displaying files such as sound clips that do not need to be visible to the visitor.

● **Alignment**   Specifies the alignment of the plug-in. This is similar to aligning text.

14

- **Border thickness** Enables you to specify the thickness of a black border that surrounds the plug-in.

- **Horizontal spacing** Enables you to set the horizontal spacing between the plug-in and the nearest object. This is similar to entering a value for cell spacing for tables.

- **Vertical spacing** Enables you to set the vertical spacing between the plug-in and the nearest object above and below the plug-in. This is similar to entering a value for cell spacing for tables.

3. In the Plug-In Properties window, click the Browse button to the right of the Data source field. The Select Plug-In Data Source window will appear. Browse to the plug-in folder and double click the *frontpage* file. The path to the file will be displayed in the Data source field in the Plug-In Properties window.

4. In the Message for browsers without plug-in support field, type **Your browser does not support plug-ins.**

5. In the Height and Width fields, enter the pixel values **40** and **300**, respectively. Because this is an animation that people should see, the box for Hide plug-in should be left unchecked.

6. In the Alignment drop-down menu, select the Left command. In the boxes for Horizontal spacing and Vertical spacing, enter the values **5** and **10**, respectively.

7. Click OK to close the Plug-In Properties window.

8. Save this page and preview it in your browser. The Flash animation will be displayed in your browser:

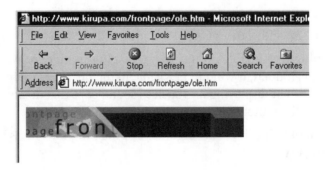

While you just learned to incorporate plug-ins by using a Macromedia Flash file, you would follow a similar path for incorporating plug-ins of any file type. You are not restricted to using only certain file formats to incorporate plug-ins. As long as there is a program capable of interpreting the plug-in information, you can use it. You should make sure you provide a link for your visitors so they can download any software necessary to view the plug-in.

ActiveX

ActiveX is a technology pioneered by Microsoft that can be added to Web pages to extend HTML's capabilities. Unlike plug-ins, ActiveX objects (called "controls") enable developers to unite Windows programming with the World Wide Web without the user having to download additional software. Your computer probably has numerous ActiveX controls installed. Many ActiveX files are installed by Windows, by third-party programs, from Web sites, and from other installation sources. When browsing through your hard drive, you may have noticed files ending with the *.ocx* filename extension. Files ending in the *.ocx* extension are ActiveX controls files.

When you visit a Web site that uses an ActiveX control that is not installed on your system, the necessary ActiveX control will be downloaded to your computer from that Web site. While downloading the control sounds easy and simple, there are security threats posed by enabling an ActiveX control to be downloaded. Developers may force you to download ActiveX controls that could potentially damage your system. To prevent malicious developers from damaging computer systems by using ActiveX, a digital signature is displayed with valid information regarding the developer of the control.

Note

Most versions of Netscape browsers do not support ActiveX controls in Web pages.

Incorporating ActiveX Controls

Incorporating ActiveX controls is almost as simple as inserting plug-ins:

1. Create a new document in FrontPage.

2. Select Insert | Web Component to display the Insert Web Component window.

14

3. In the Insert Web Component window, select the Advanced Controls component type and select ActiveX Control from the Choose a control menu box. Click the Next button, and you will see a list of ActiveX controls found in your system:

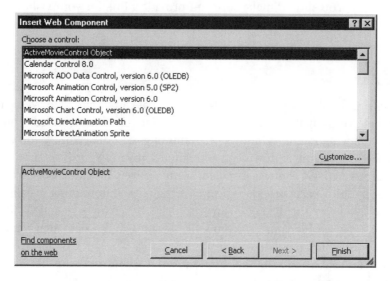

4. After you have made those selections, click the Next button.

5. In the Insert Web Component window, select Calendar Control 8.0, and click the Finish button.

6. You will see a calendar displayed in your document.

7. Save the file and preview it. You will see that the calendar not only displays today's date, but it also enables you to select a specific date between the years 1900 and 2100!

Save this page as *activex.htm,* and keep it open because we will use it in the next section.

Ask the Expert

Question: I downloaded and installed some ActiveX controls from a Web site. When I try to insert that ActiveX control into my Web page, that specific ActiveX control is not listed among the choices from the Insert Web Component window. How can I select a specific ActiveX control that I know is installed on my system yet cannot be found by FrontPage?

Answer: Follow these instructions to see all the ActiveX controls that you can incorporate into your Web pages:

1. Go the Insert Web Component window (Insert | Web Component) and select the Advanced Controls selection.

2. Select ActiveX Control from the right side of the Insert Web Component window and click the Next button. You will see a brief list of ActiveX controls displayed in the Insert Web Component window.

3. Press the Customize button to see the Customize ActiveX Control List window.

4. Check any controls that you would like to use and click OK. The ActiveX Control can now be selected from the Insert Web Component window.

Customizing ActiveX Controls

Because ActiveX controls were not created in FrontPage, they cannot be edited directly. Even though the actual ActiveX control cannot be edited, you can modify the ActiveX control's HTML that it requires to work in a browser.

To modify an ActiveX control, follow these directions:

1. If is it not already open, open the *activex.htm* page with the calendar ActiveX control. Right-click the calendar ActiveX control and select the ActiveX Control Properties command.

14

2. The ActiveX Properties window will appear. Because one ActiveX control is different from another ActiveX control, each ActiveX control has its own unique properties, and, because of that, you will see more tabs or fewer tabs in your ActiveX Control Properties window. The two tabs that will appear for all ActiveX controls are the Object Tag tabs and Parameters tabs. Select the Object Tag tab in the ActiveX Control Properties window:

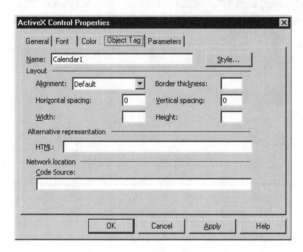

The following is a list of the commands and fields in the Object Tag tab with a description of each:

● **Name**   Specifies the ActiveX control's name.

● **Alignment**   Specifies the alignment of the ActiveX control. This is similar to aligning text or contents in a cell.

● **Border thickness**   Enables you to enter a value for the thickness of the border. The border will surround the ActiveX control.

● **Horizontal spacing**   Enables you to set the horizontal spacing between the ActiveX control and the nearest object. This is similar to entering a value for cell spacing for tables.

● **Vertical spacing**   Enables you to set the vertical spacing between the ActiveX control and the nearest object above and below the plug-in. This is similar to entering a value for cell spacing for tables.

- **Width**   Enables you to enter a value for the width of the ActiveX control.

- **Height**   Enables you to enter a value for the height of the ActiveX control.

- **HTML**   Enables you to write a message for visitors using browsers that do not support ActiveX. The message can be either plain text or HTML tags.

- **Code Source**   Enables you to add the location of the ActiveX control. When visitors do not have the required ActiveX control, browsers such as Internet Explorer refer the user to a location you specify to download and install the ActiveX control.

3. Click the Parameters tab to see all the settings for your ActiveX control:

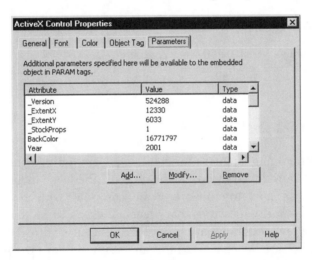

Note

For most users, the settings in the Parameters tab will seem cryptic. Unless you understand the ActiveX control's various settings, you should either refer to the documentation that comes with the ActiveX control or use the various tabs contained in the ActiveX Control Properties window. (For the Calendar 8.0 ActiveX control currently selected, most of the settings from the Parameters tab can be modified by changing settings in the General, Font, Color, and Object tag tabs.)

14

4. To modify any settings in the Parameters tab, select the ActiveX control attribute and click the Modify button. The Edit Object Parameter window will appear.

5. From the ActiveX Control Properties window, select the BackColor attribute and click the Modify button. The Edit Object Parameter window will appear.

6. Select the Data option (if it is not already selected), and delete any numbers that you might find in the Data field. Once all the numbers have been deleted, enter the following number into the Data field: **45252352**.

7. Click the OK button to close the Edit Object Parameter window and click OK to close the ActiveX Control Properties window. Your Calendar's background color will now be powder blue instead of dull gray.

1-Minute Drill

● How are plug-ins installed in your computer?

● What file extension do all ActiveX controls share?

Java Applets

A popular programming language for creating programming content for the Internet is Java. Introduced by Sun Microsystems, the Java language is popular for two reasons: its capability to work on any computer with the Java virtual machine and its security measures that prevent a user's computer from being damaged from a Java program. Java programs do not use your processor or system settings to run. When a Java program is run, the Java program creates a virtual space in your computer to run the Java program. The virtual space is known as a *virtual machine*, and any computer that is equipped with a Java virtual machine can run small Java programs called *applets*.

Unlike plug-ins or ActiveX controls, Java programs are very restricted on what they can and cannot do in your computer. Java applets pose less of a security threat than plug-ins and ActiveX controls because they cannot change any settings such as hardware and software in the local computer. Programmers,

---

● Plug-ins are usually preinstalled with your Web browser or downloaded and installed from a Web site.
● .ocx

always coming up with interesting phrases for complicated topics, call the restrictions posed on a Java applet the "Java sandbox." It is called the Java sandbox because Java applets cannot go beyond the restrictions imposed by the virtual sandbox. You can consider the sandbox to be the virtual machine and the area around the sandbox to be your computer. Because the Java applet cannot go beyond the sandbox, the Java applet cannot harm your system.

Note

The Java applet that will be used for the following lessons is called "Wave" and was created by Radu Vissarion. The applet can be found at http://javaboutique.internet.com/Wave/. The required Java applet is also included with the source files you downloaded for this module.

Incorporating Java Applets

Incorporating Java applets is as simple as incorporating ActiveX controls or plug-ins. The main difference in incorporating Java applets is that they usually require some customization to work in your browser.

The following instructions will guide you to add a Java applet in FrontPage:

1. Open the *java.htm* file from the Java folder contained in the source files for this module.

2. Launch the Insert Web Component window by selecting Insert | Web Component. Select Advanced Controls from the component type list. Select the Java applet selection from the right side of the Insert Web Component window. Click the Finish button.

3. The Java Applet Properties window will appear. Type the source name, **Wave.class**, in the Applet source field. Make sure the word "Wave" in *Wave.class* is capitalized; the Java language differentiates between lowercase filenames and uppercase filenames. Click the OK button to close the Java Applet Properties window.

4. In your document, you will see that FrontPage displays a square-shaped box with the letter *J* in it. When you preview the page in your browser, you will see that nothing is displayed. We will fill in the missing pieces of the Java applet in the next section.

Keep the *wave.htm* file open for the next section.

14

Modifying Java Applets

The following instructions will guide you to make the *wave.class* Java applet from the previous section work:

1. If not already open, open the *java.htm* file. Right-click the Java applet and select the Java Applet Properties command. The Java Applet Properties window will appear:

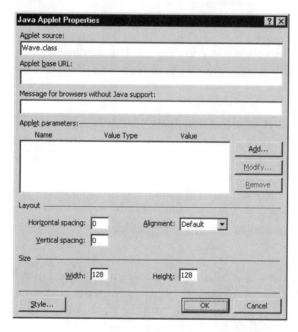

The following is a list of each field in the Java Applet Properties window with a brief description of each:

● **Applet source**   Enables you to enter the name of the Java applet. Most Java applets end with the *.class* file extension.

● **Applet base URL**   Enables you to add the URL path to the applet file. Make sure you do not use *http://* to display the Java applet's file path. If your Java applet is in a folder called "classes," you would enter **/classes** instead of the full path.

● **Message for browsers without Java support**   Enables you to enter a message that will display for users who use browsers that do not support the Java technology.

- **Applet parameters** Enables you to add, modify, and remove settings for the Java applet to work. The parameters of a Java applet specify what the applet should do, which file to display, and more. The parameters for Java applets vary, depending on the applet's function.
- **Horizontal spacing** Enables you to set the horizontal spacing between the Java applet and the nearest object.
- **Vertical spacing** Enables you to set the vertical spacing between the Java applet and the nearest object above and below the plug-in.
- **Alignment** Enables you to select the alignment of the Java applet in your Web page.
- **Width** Specifies the horizontal size of the applet.
- **Height** Specifies the vertical size of the applet.

2. In the Java Applet Properties window, the words "Wave.class" should be displayed in the Applet source field. If not, enter **Wave.class** in the Applet source field. Make sure you capitalize "Wave" in "Wave.class."

3. We will leave the Applet base URL field blank because the *Wave.class* applet file is in the same directory as the *java.htm* file.

4. In the Message for browsers without Java support field, type **Your browser does not support Java applets. Please upgrade your browser.**

5. The tricky part is adding the *Wave.class* applet's parameters. Click the Add button in the Applet Parameters field, and you will see the Set Attribute Value window:

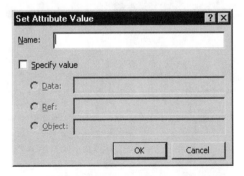

6. In the Set Attribute Value window, type **image** in the Name field. Select the Specify value check box, and the Data option will be enabled.

14

7. In the Data field, type the image filename, **kirupa.jpg**. The Java applet will manipulate this image file in creating the wave effect. Click OK to accept the data.

8. You will see the information you just entered displayed in the Applet parameters field of the Java Applet Properties window.

9. Click the Add button again. The Set Attribute Value window will appear. In the Name field, type **horizMotion**; make sure you type the word with this exact capitalization. Select the Specify value checkbox, and enter the following value into the Data field: **0.03**. Click OK to accept the information entered.

10. Let's leave the Layout properties of this applet at the default settings as specified by FrontPage, but let's modify the size of the Java applet as seen in the browser. In the Width box, enter **199**. In the Height box, enter **55**. Your Java Applet properties window should look like the following illustration:

11. Click OK to accept the changes made to the Java applet's settings and to close the Java Applet Properties window.

12. Save the *java.htm* file and preview it in your browser. You will see that the *kirupa.jpg* image file is animated with the wave effect. You should understand that not all Java applets are used for special effects such as the wave effect. Java applets can be anything from simple word processors to complex navigation systems to online games.

index.htm

Project 14-1: Incorporating Plug-Ins, ActiveX Controls, and Java Applets

The following are the goals for this project:

- Use plug-ins
- Use ActiveX Controls
- Modify a Java applet's parameters

Step by Step

1. From the project folder, open the file *index.htm*. In the *index.htm* file, press CTRL and click the Calendar hyperlink. The *calendar.htm* file will be displayed. We will add the Calendar 8.0 ActiveX control to this file.

2. Insert your mouse pointer below the "Computer Magic" title. Launch the Insert Web Component window by selecting Insert | Web Component. From the Insert Web Component window, select the Advanced Controls component type. Select the ActiveX control from the right side of the Insert Web Component window and click the Next button.

3. From the Insert Web Component window, select the Calendar Control 8.0 ActiveX control and press the Finish button. You will see the calendar control displayed in your Web page. Save the *calendar.htm* and close it.

4. The *index.htm* file should be displayed. Open the *circle.htm* page by pressing CTRL and clicking the Rotating 3-D Circle hyperlink.

5. Go back to the Insert Web Component window (Insert | Web Component). Select Advanced Controls from the component type box. Select the Plug-In control from the right side of the Insert Web Component window and click the Finish button.

6. The Plug-In Properties window will appear. In the Data source field, browse for the file *3d.swf* by using the Browse button. Type the following sentence into the Message for browsers without plug-in support field: **Your browser does not support plug-ins.**

7. In the Height and Width fields, enter **300**. Click OK to accept the plug-in settings. Save the *circle.htm* file and go back to the *index.htm* file.

8. In the *index.htm* file, open the *water.htm* file by pressing CTRL and clicking the Water Effect hyperlink. In the *water.htm* file, you will modify the Java applet's properties.

9. Right-click the Java applet and select the Java Applet Properties command. The Java Applet Properties window will appear. You will need to add a parameter to make the Java Applet work. Click the Add button to display the Set Attribute Value window. In the Set Attribute Value window, type **image** in the Name field. Check the Specify value check box. In the Data field, enter the image filename **computer.jpg**.

10. Click OK to close the Set Attribute Value window. Click OK again to close the Java Applet Properties window. Save the *water.htm* file and open the *index.htm* file.

11. Preview the *index.htm* file. Navigate through the hyperlinks to see the plug-in, ActiveX control, and Java applet work.

Summary

Plug-ins, ActiveX controls, and Java applets are great for making your site interactive and more functional. Plug-ins provide your visitors with a media experience in a compact file. ActiveX controls enable the power of Windows applications to be used within the Web browser. The versatility and security of Java applets make them an ideal choice for uses varying from Web-based applications to simple effects.

✓ *Mastery Check*

1. What is a plug-in?

_____

_____

2. Who developed the Java language?

_____

_____

3. Do ActiveX controls work in all browsers?

_____

_____

4. What window will you use to access a plug-in file's properties?

_____

_____

5. What are a Java applet's parameters?

_____

_____

6. What are files that end with the *.class* extension?

_____

_____

14

Part IV

Doing More with FrontPage

Module 15

Web Programming Languages

The Goals of This Module

- Learn to use HTML in FrontPage
- Explore Cascading Style Sheets (CSS)

There are numerous Web technologies available for you to use to create your Web site. Using FrontPage, you don't have to learn various Web languages, such as Hypertext Markup Language (HTML), Dynamic HTML (DHTML), CSS, and others, because FrontPage takes care of the programming for you. But FrontPage does provide you with tools to modify or add HTML code, adjust CSS properties, and more. This module will not teach you HTML, but it will explain how to use the HTML features of FrontPage. Any HTML code that you will need to know and use will be provided in this module.

For the directions in this module, please download the various images and sample source files for Module 15 from http://www.kirupa.com/frontpage or http://www.Osborne.com.

HTML in FrontPage

FrontPage uses HTML extensively when creating your Web pages. Even though you do not directly modify the HTML, every action you make in FrontPage, such as typing text, inserting images, splitting frames, adding a background color, and others, get written in HTML by FrontPage. I displayed some HTML code examples in the first few modules of this book.

Looking at HTML in FrontPage

Before FrontPage, HTML was written in text editors such as Notepad. The HTML code written in Notepad could not be tested for accuracy without actually previewing the page in your Web browser. The introduction of FrontPage changed the writing and testing of HTML. While many people use FrontPage to avoid learning HTML, there are people who use FrontPage exclusively for its HTML features.

Figure 15-1 displays how HTML is displayed in FrontPage. In the HTML view in FrontPage, notice that portions of the code are color coded for easier reading. The color coding makes it easier for developers to read HTML and to find and fix errors.

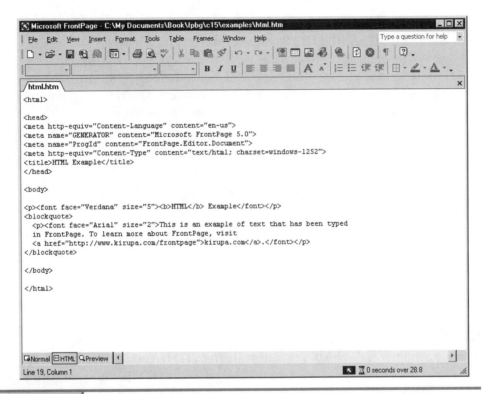

Figure 15-1   The HTML view in FrontPage

Writing HTML in FrontPage

To write HTML in FrontPage, follow these instructions:

1. Create a new document and select the HTML command to go to the HTML view.

2. Insert your mouse cursor between the <BODY> and </BODY> tags and type the following line of code:

```
<p><a href="http://www.kirupa.com/frontpage">Visit kirupa.com</a></p>
```

3. The code you typed will be color coded for easier reading. When you type text in FrontPage, the HTML code for the text is displayed in the HTML view. The opposite holds true as well. When you type HTML code in FrontPage, the resulting text or HTML equivalent, such images, tables, and more, is displayed in Normal view. Choose the Normal command to see how the HTML code you typed looks in Normal view:

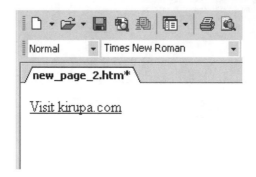

Inserting HTML

There are numerous Web sites that provide free HTML code that you can copy and paste into FrontPage. You can copy and paste the HTML, but what if you need to paste the HTML code in an exact location on a Web page? You cannot paste the code where you want to because you will see HTML code instead of the image, text, effect, or other feature that the code is representing. You could paste the code in HTML view, but if you do not know how to read and write HTML, you will be at a disadvantage because you won't know where to paste the code. Copying and pasting the code into FrontPage's Normal view will display the actual HTML code instead of its equivalent object such as text, images, and more.

To make it easier for you to insert HTML code, FrontPage provides a method of inserting HTML code to a Web page by not having to use the HTML view. Follow these instructions to insert HTML code from the Normal view:

1. Open the *html.htm* file in FrontPage.

2. Place your mouse cursor in the line below the text. The mouse cursor should be aligned to the left side of the document.

3. Select Insert | Web Component to launch the Insert Web Component window. Select the Advanced Controls command from the Component type menu box, select the HTML command from the Choose a control menu box, and click the Finish button. The HTML Markup window will appear:

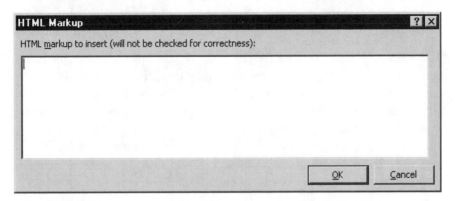

4. Type the following code into the HTML Markup window:

```
<form action="http://www.osborne.com" method="link">
<INPUT TYPE=submit value="Visit Osborne's Web Site">
</form>
```

5. Click OK to close the HTML Markup window. Instead of seeing the HTML code you just pasted, you will see an icon with a question mark instead:

FrontPage, visit kirupa.com.

6. Save the *html.htm* file and preview the page in your browser. You will see a button in the place of the HTML code.

Tip

After inserting some code, if you switch from Normal view to HTML view and back again, you will see that the cursor stays in the same location.

Ask the Expert

Question: When I copy and paste HTML code from a Web site into FrontPage, the HTML code pasted in FrontPage looks nothing like the code on the Web site. There seem to be a lot of extraneous information that is causing errors. What can I do to solve that problem?

Answer: HTML code pasted from a Web site often includes special formatting that the browser uses to display the code on the Web page. The formatting can prevent the HTML code from working. To solve that problem, copy the code from the Web site and paste it onto a text editor like Notepad. Copy the pasted code from Notepad and paste it into FrontPage. Because Notepad does not interpret the extraneous tags used by the browser, the HTML code will be in its original form without any formatting that might cause the HTML code not to work.

1-Minute Drill

● What makes HTML displayed in FrontPage easier to read?

● What window do you use to insert HTML?

Cascading Style Sheets

CSS is a language used to format the styles of a Web page. While HTML enables you to format the styles of a Web site, CSS enables you to predefine a number of styles and apply them consistently throughout a Web site. The breadth of styles and formatting CSS supports such as text sizes, border colors, paragraph formats, and more surpass the simple formatting styles of HTML.

● HTML code in FrontPage is color coded.
● The HTML Markup window

You have used CSS several times in this book from applying themes to formatting border styles to absolutely positioning objects such as text, images, and tables. There are two variations of the CSS language:

- **CSS Level 1 (CSS)**   Used to format text. Elements of text such as font styles, colors, and paragraph formatting are improved.

- **CSS Level 2 (CSS2)**   Used for precise measurement and placement of objects on screen.

Creating a CSS Style

A major benefit of CSS is the ability to create styles and apply them consistently throughout a site, though the CSS styles do not have to be applied to the entire site; they can be applied on one line of text, portions of a table, whole Web pages, and more. Instead of having to format each element individually, CSS enables you to format several elements of a CSS style with a few clicks.

The following instructions will guide you to create a CSS style and apply it to some text:

1. Create a new document in FrontPage.

2. From the Format menu, select the Style command. The Style window will appear:

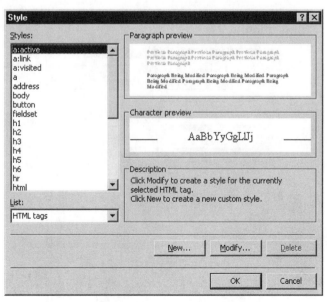

15

3. Click the New button in the Style window. The New Style window will appear. In the Name field, enter **funny**. In the Style type drop-down menu select the command for Character:

4. Click the Format button and select the Font command. The Font window will appear.

5. Select the Comic Sans MS font in the Font menu box and select the Bold Italic command in the Font style menu box. Select 24pt in the Size menu box. Click the Color menu and select the Navy color. Check the box for Overline from the Effects area. Your Font window will look like the following illustration:

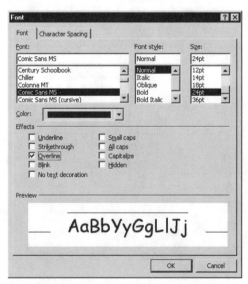

6. Click OK to close the Font window. Click OK again to close both the New Style and the Style windows.

7. In your empty document, type **Clown**.

8. Highlight the word "Clown" and click the Style drop-down menu. From the Style drop-down menu, select the funny style:

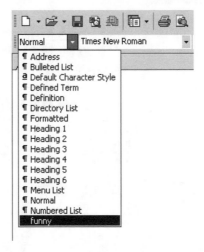

9. After you select the funny style from the Style menu, "Clown" will be formatted with the CSS styles that you created in the Style window. You can type more text and apply the funny style to them as well. The funny style you specified will stay the same throughout the document.

10. Save this file as *styles.htm*.

Keep this file open because we will use it in the next section.

Modifying CSS Styles

An advantage of using CSS is that CSS styles applied to objects can be globally changed throughout the document. Instead of reapplying the CSS styles to each line of text, if you simply modify the CSS style itself, it will change the font style of all text to which it is applied.

The following instructions will guide you to modify a CSS style:

1. In the *styles.htm* file from the last section, select the Style command from the Format menu. You will see the Style window. In the Styles menu box, you will see the style span.funny listed. While our style was simply called "funny" the word "span" is added to signify it is a style that you created. If you do not see other styles displayed in the menu box, select the User-defined styles command List drop-down menu. Select the span.funny style from the list:

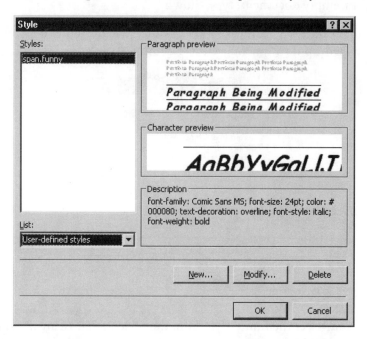

2. After you have made the selection, click the Modify button. The Modify Style window will appear. Click the Format button and select the Font command from the menu that appears. The Font window will appear.

3. While in the Font window, uncheck the Overline box. Click the Color drop-down menu and select the More Colors command. Select an orange color from More Colors window and click OK. You will be taken back to the Font window. In the Font menu box, select the Verdana font. Click OK to close the Font window. Click the OK buttons to close both the Modify Style window and the Style window.

4. Back in your document, you will see that "Clown" has a different font style applied to it. Without you having to highlight the word and change it, the font style automatically updated itself because the CSS style was changed by you.

5. Save the *styles.htm* file. Keep the file open because we will use it in the next section.

Note

When you modify a CSS style, all objects such as text that use the modified style will be updated automatically with the modified style. The reason is because objects that have CSS styles applied do not have the actual font name, font style, and more defined individually. The CSS style you modify from the Style window is applied to a certain portion of HTML code, as opposed to individual objects. The HTML code containing the CSS styles you modify is referred to when applying a style to an object.

Differences in HTML and CSS Styles

From the *styles.htm* file from the previous section, highlight "Clown" and press the HTML command from the bottom of the FrontPage window. Notice the line containing the highlighted word does not contain any of the formatting. To compare the difference between CSS and regular text formatting for this example, please refer to the following HTML codes.

The following HTML code is for text formatted without using CSS:

```
<p><i><b><font size="6" face="Verdana"
color="#FF9933">Clown</font></b></i></p>
```

The following HTML code is for the same text as this, except it is formatted using CSS styles:

```
<p><span class="funny">Clown</span></p>
```

The CSS style has the actual formatting defined elsewhere in the HTML. By choosing the HTML command, you will see grayed-out text with the span.funny style displayed. As you can tell, using the Formatting toolbar for large documents with similar styles is far too impractical as opposed to using CSS. Besides, there is no way of updating the styles of text formatted using the Formatting toolbar without having to select all the text individually and changing the formatting. With CSS, you modify the style once, and the whole document will be updated with the new CSS style.

Creating a CSS Style Sheet

In the previous example, the CSS style was created and displayed in the HTML file containing the object (which was text). For applying styles across several pages, having to copy and paste the CSS code becomes quite inefficient.

15

To overcome that inefficiency, CSS styles can be applied to a Style Sheet file. A Style Sheet file is a page created in FrontPage that contains only CSS styles and ends with the *.css* file extension.

To create a CSS style sheet, follow these instructions:

1. Go to File | New | Page or Web. The Task Pane will appear. In the Task Pane, select the Page Templates command. The Page Templates window will appear. In the Page Templates window, select the Style Sheets tab. In the Style Sheets tab, select the Normal Style Sheet command, as shown in Figure 15-2.

2. After the Normal Style Sheet command has been selected, click OK to close the Page Templates window.

3. FrontPage will create a new style sheet for you to modify. Notice from the filename tab that this file ends in the *.css* extension. The Style toolbar should be displayed automatically. If it is not, select View | Toolbars | Style to display the Style toolbar:

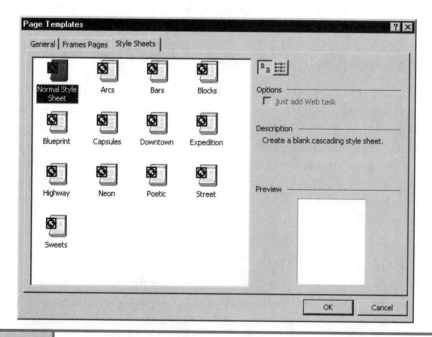

Figure 15-2 Selecting the Normal style sheet

⊣*Note* ⎯⎯⎯⎯⎯⎯⎯⎯⎯⎯⎯⎯⎯⎯⎯⎯⎯⎯⎯

In this file, you will be adding the CSS styles that you wish to apply to a Web page. You should not add any text, images, tables, or regular items normally found in a Web page in a Style Sheet. The Style Sheet should only contain CSS-specific information such as styles.

4. To add CSS styles to the style sheet, press the Style button on the Style toolbar. The Style window will appear.

5. In the Style window, press the New button. In the Name field, type **a:hover**. The hover style will specify the style that a hyperlink will take when a visitor hovers over the hyperlink.

⊣*Note* ⎯⎯⎯⎯⎯⎯⎯⎯⎯⎯⎯⎯⎯⎯⎯⎯⎯⎯⎯

Styles that begin with *a:* are used by FrontPage automatically and cannot be applied by using the Style menu. For example, the style for a hyperlink is *a:* link because when a hyperlink is added, FrontPage automatically knows to underline the hyperlink and change the color. You can modify styles that being with *a:* just as you would any other style.

6. Click the Format button and select Font from the menu that appears. The Font window will appear. Select the Arial font and select 10pt from the Size menu box. Check the Underline box in the Effects area:

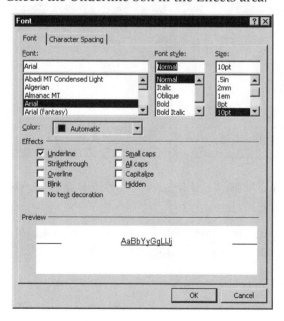

7. Click OK to close the Font window. Click OK to close the New Style window. You will be taken back to the Style window.

8. Select the HTML tags command from the List drop-down menu. Select the a:link command from the Styles menu area and click the Modify button. The Modify Style window will appear. Click the Format button and select the Font command from the menu that appears.

9. The Font window will be displayed. Select the Arial font and select the 10pt command from Size menu box. In the Effects area, check the No text decoration check box:

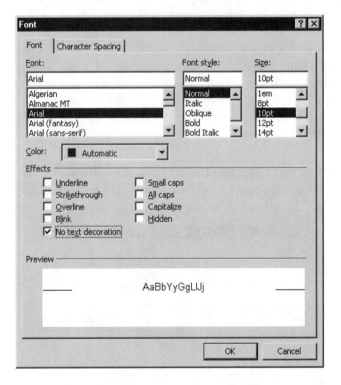

10. Click OK to close the Font window. Click OK to close the Modify Style window.

11. We will add one more style. Click the New button and the New Style window will appear. In the Name field, type **table**.

12. Click the Format button and select the command for Border from the menu that appears. The Borders and Shading window will appear. In the Style menu box, select the ridge command.

13. Click the Color menu and select the More Colors command. The More Colors window will appear. Select the Orange color from the colors listed. Click OK to close the More Colors window. In the Width field, enter **3**. Enter **4** in the Top, Bottom, Left, and Right fields. Your Borders and Shading window should look like the following illustration:

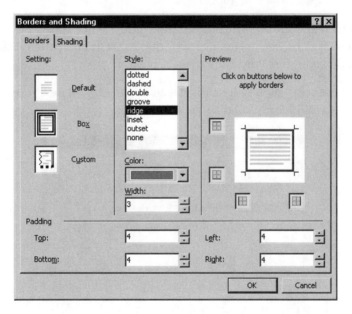

14. Click OK to close the Borders and Shading window. Press OK to close the New Style and Style windows. Your document will have the CSS styles listed.

15. Select File | Save As. Navigate to the folder where the downloaded files for this module are. In the File Name field, enter **newstyle**. Click the Save button to save the style sheet you just created.

Because style sheets only work when applied to an HTML page, you will be unable to preview the page in the browser.

Applying a CSS Style Sheet to a HTML Page

To see how the style sheet you created in the previous section works, you will need to apply it to a HTML page. The following instructions will guide you in applying a style sheet to a HTML page:

1. Open the *apply.htm* file in FrontPage.

2. From the Format menu, select the Style Sheet Links command. The Link Style Sheet window will appear.

3. Click the Add button. The Select File window will appear. From the Select File window, browse to the newstyle style sheet you created. Select the newstyle style sheet and click the OK button.

4. The style sheet's path will be displayed in the Link Style Sheet window. Your path will look similar to the following:

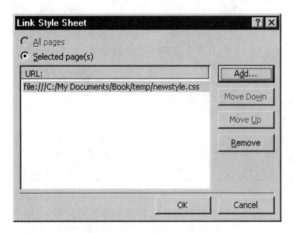

5. Click the OK button to close the Link Style Sheet window. Save the file and preview it in your browser.

Because the style sheet had styles defined for a table and hyperlinks, the hyperlinks and the table in the *apply.htm* file were modified. You can see that you did not have to modify the style for the table and each hyperlink individually. When style sheets are loaded, the styles they define take priority over the styles defined in FrontPage.

1-Minute Drill

- What menu would you use to apply a style to an object such as text?
- Does modifying a CSS style require you to modify each object that the CSS style was applied to?

index.htm
list.htm
contact.htm

Project 15-1: Applying CSS Styles

The following are the goals for this project:

- Apply a CSS style sheet
- Insert HTML code

Step by Step

1. Open the *index.htm*, *list.htm*, and *contact.htm* files found in the project folder that you downloaded for this module. Use the file tab to display the *index.htm* file first.

2. Go to the Format menu and select the Style Sheet Links command. The Link Style Sheet window will appear. Click the Add button and select the *project.css* style sheet.

3. Because we want to have the style sheet applied to all pages currently in the FrontPage Web, select the All Pages option in the Link Style Sheet window. Click the OK button to close the Link Style Sheet window.

4. Click the list.htm tab. Highlight the words "Collection List" and select the large-heading style from the Style drop-down menu:

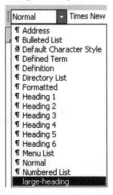

- The Style drop-down menu
- No

5. Select the contact.htm tab. Highlight the words "Contact Us" and select the large-heading style from the Style drop-down menu.

6. Place the mouse cursor after "234SLK3" and click ENTER. Your mouse cursor will be one line directly below the address. Select Insert | Web Component.

7. The Web Component window will appear. Select Advanced Controls from the Component type menu box. From the Choose a Control menu box, select the HTML command and click the Finish button.

8. The HTML Markup window will appear. Type the following HTML code into the HTML Markup window:

```
<form action="mailto:examples@kirupa.com" method="link">
<INPUT TYPE=submit value="E-Mail Us">
</form>
```

9. Click OK to close the HTML Markup window. Go to the File menu and select the Save All command.

10. Select the index.htm tab and preview the page in your browser.

Summary

Without the HTML programming language, there would be no World Wide Web. The flexibility offered by HTML helped spur the World Wide Web's growth. The ability to format styles in a document makes CSS a valuable addition to HTML. Using FrontPage, all the HTML and CSS are automatically taken care of for you.

☑ *Mastery Check*

1. What does the acronym CSS stand for?

_____

_____

2. What does the HTML view enable you to do?

_____

_____

3. How is HTML inserted via the HTML Markup window displayed in FrontPage's normal view?

_____

_____

4. What file extensions do CSS style sheets have?

_____

_____

5. Can one style sheet be used throughout a site?

_____

_____

15

Module 16

Integrating
Microsoft Office
into Your Site

The Goals of This Module

- Copy and paste among Microsoft Office programs
- Insert Microsoft Excel spreadsheets
- Publish Microsoft Office files

Although FrontPage primarily deals with Hypertext Markup Language (HTML) and HTML-based languages, it supports a host of technologies that bear little resemblance to HTML. With an efficient method of using file converters, file formats from popular applications such as Microsoft Word (Word), Microsoft Excel (Excel), Lotus 1-2-3, Corel WordPerfect, and more can be converted to HTML and posted online by using FrontPage.

Because FrontPage belongs in the Microsoft Office (Office) suite of applications, content between the Office applications and FrontPage are shared more easily than with other applications. In this module you will learn how to copy and paste content, insert the content by using a file converter, and import and export Excel spreadsheets.

Incorporating Content from Microsoft Office

One of FrontPage's highlights is its capability to incorporate content from other programs such as Word and Excel while, at the same time, preserving the original formatting. In this section, you will learn how to incorporate content in the following ways:

- Pasting from the Windows Clipboard
- Inserting the content

For the directions in this module, please download the various images and sample source files for Module 16 from http://www.kirupa.com/frontpage or http://www.Osborne.com.

Pasting Content from Word

The easiest method of incorporating Word content into FrontPage is by copying and pasting. The following instructions will guide you in pasting content from Word into FrontPage:

1. Open *example.doc* in Word.

2. Select all the content in the document by pressing CTRL - A. All of the text, image, and table will be highlighted. Press CTRL - C to copy the content.

3. Open FrontPage and create a new page.

4. Click anywhere in the new page.

5. Press CTRL - V to paste the content from Word into FrontPage.

If you compare Figure 16-1 and Figure 16-2 you will see that there are no differences in formatting or style of the content. Because the latest version of Microsoft's Office suite, Office XP, further integrates HTML and Web technologies in its file formats, inconsistencies and differences between the HTML format and the application's native format are minimal.

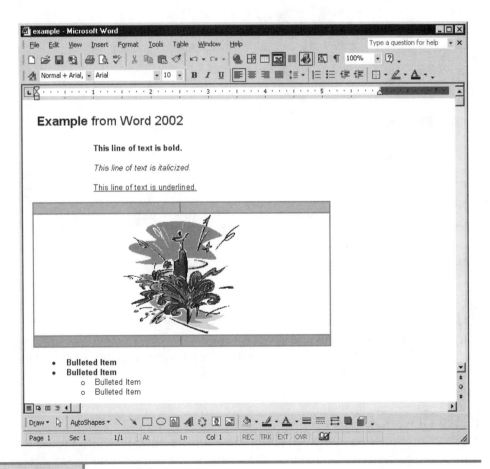

Figure 16-1   Content copied from Word

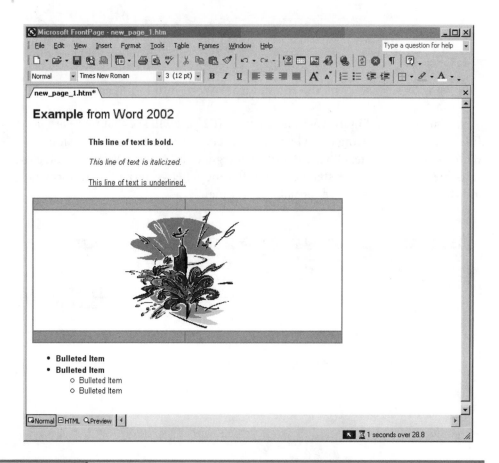

Figure 16-2 Content pasted from Word into FrontPage

Tip

You can use menu commands instead of keyboard shortcuts for selecting all, copying, and pasting content. The Copy, Paste, and Select All commands can be found in the Edit menu in Word and FrontPage menu bars.

Inserting Content

An alternative method of incorporating content from other files into FrontPage is by inserting the actual document. When you insert content into FrontPage, a special program called a *file converter* is used to convert the code from another program to FrontPage-readable HTML code. Unlike copying and pasting contents from another application, content that is inserted often loses its original formatting.

The following instructions will guide you to insert a document from Word:

1. Create a new document in FrontPage.

2. Select Insert | File. The Select File window will appear. Browse for the *example.doc* file and click the Open button.

3. The contents of the *example.doc* Word document will be displayed in FrontPage:

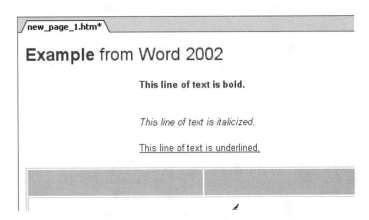

If you look at your FrontPage window, you will see that the style of the contents in the *example.doc* file is not the same as the original version of *example.doc* in Figure 16-1: the colors and text styles vary from the original file.

Note

You may have to insert your Office Installation CD to install the file converter. You will be prompted if you need to do so.

File Formats

Even though FrontPage belongs to the Office family, it can incorporate content from various programs such as WordPerfect, Lotus 1-2-3, and others.

To see the file formats from which FrontPage can incorporate content, display the Select File window by choosing Insert | File. Click the Files of type drop-down menu:

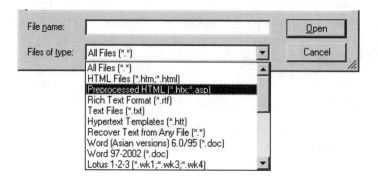

The various file formats FrontPage supports are displayed in the Files of type-drop down menu. Table 16-1 displays the various formats supported by FrontPage.

File Format	Extension
HTML Files	.HTM, .HTML
Preprocessed HTML	.HTX, .ASP
Rich Text Format	.RTF
Text Files	.TXT
Hypertext Templates	.HTT
Any Text (Recover text from Any File)	Any file containing text
Word (Asian Versions)	.DOC
Word 97-2002	.DOC
Lotus 1-2-3	.WK1, .WK3, .WK4
Microsoft Excel Worksheet	.XLS, .XLW
Word 6.0/95 for Windows & Macintosh	.DOC
Word 4.0 - 5.1 for Macintosh	.MCW
Word 2.x for Windows	.DOC
Works 4.0 for Windows	.WPS
WordPerfect 6.x	.WPD, .DOC
WordPerfect 5.x	.DOC
Works 2000	.WPS, .WPT
HTML Document	.HTM, .HTML, .HTX

Table 16-1   File Formats Supported in FrontPage

File Format	Extension
Word 6.0/95 for Windows & Macintosh	.DOC
Windows Write	.WRI
Word 5.x for Macintosh	.MCW

Table 16-1   File Formats Supported in FrontPage *(continued)*

—Note

Most file formats listed in Table 16-1 require a file converter to be installed. Prior to inserting content from a file, FrontPage will automatically prompt you to insert your Office installation CD to install it. If your computer already has the file converter installed, you will not be prompted to install it.

Inserting an Excel Spreadsheet

Incorporating data from an Excel spreadsheet is the same as inserting a Word document. When you inserted content from a Word document in the previous example, only the font styles and some minor cosmetic errors occurred. When inserting Excel files though, the information can become unreadable.

Follow these instructions to insert an Excel spreadsheet in FrontPage:

1. Create a new document in FrontPage.

2. Choose Insert | File. The Select File window will appear. Select the Excel file *chart* and click the Open button.

3. An Excel spreadsheet will be displayed:

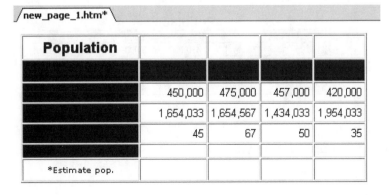

As you can see, the information is not legible. Instead of having a simple cell background color, the text inside the cells is not visible. While you could manually touch up the Excel file in FrontPage by changing the colors, adjusting the font, and so on, there is an easier method: copying and pasting.

Copying and Pasting from Excel

As you have learned from the previous section, inserting Excel files in FrontPage does not always produce the best results. To preserve the original formatting of the Excel spreadsheet, you will have to copy and paste the information from Excel into FrontPage just as you did for copying information from Word and pasting it into FrontPage.

The following instructions tell you how to copy and paste from Excel into FrontPage:

1. Open the *chart.xls* file in Excel.

2. To select all the information that needs to be copied, press CTRL - A.

3. After all the information has been selected, press CTRL - C to copy the selected information.

4. Open FrontPage and create a new document.

5. Place your mouse cursor in the place where you want the information to be pasted. Press CTRL - V.

6. The Excel spreadsheet will be pasted at the spot where your mouse cursor was.

new_page_1.htm*				
Population				
	1999	2000	2001	2002*
People	450,000	475,000	457,000	420,000
Plants	1,654,033	1,654,567	1,434,033	1,954,033
Animals	45	67	50	35
*Estimate pop.				

7. Keep Excel open because you will use it again in the next section.

If you compare the results you achieved from copying and pasting the Excel spreadsheet and inserting the spreadsheet, you will see that copying and pasting is more effective. There is no surefire way of knowing which method of incorporating information into FrontPage works, but copying and pasting is usually the best method because the original formatting is preserved.

Importing Data into the Office Spreadsheet Component

In Module 12 you were introduced to the Office Spreadsheet component. The Office Spreadsheet component enables you to work with Excel documents within a Web browser in a similar way as you would work with Excel documents in Excel itself.

Ask the Expert

Question: If the same information is being copied into FrontPage, why does pasting information and inserting content from the same program produce two completely different results?

Answer: The difference is in the way FrontPage interprets the information. When information is copied and pasted into FrontPage, the original formatting is usually preserved because FrontPage records every single formatting style by using Cascading Style Sheets (CSS) and other related technologies. You learned in Module 15 that CSS is a more efficient language in recording and applying styles. When information is inserted into FrontPage by using the Insert | File command, FrontPage converts the file into standard HTML.

Standard HTML is not capable of interpreting the eXtensible Markup Language (XML) values, data structures, CSS styles, and more that exist in a simple Excel spreadsheet. When a file is inserted, key formatting and content information is omitted because it does not conform to HTML standards. One advantage to using the insert method instead of the copy and paste method is compatibility. Older browsers do not recognize advanced programming languages such as CSS, XML, and more, so they usually won't display content that has been copied and pasted.

The following instructions will guide you in importing data into a spreadsheet in the Office Spreadsheet component:

1. Open the file *import.htm* in FrontPage.

2. Select the spreadsheet with your mouse. After the spreadsheet is selected, click the Commands and Options button (it is the second button from the right).

3. The Commands and Options window will appear. In this window, click the Import tab:

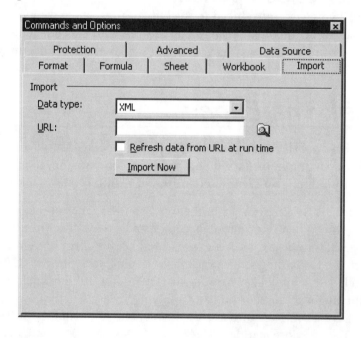

4. In the Import tab, click the Data type drop-down menu and select HTML.

5. In the URL field, type in the following HTML filename: **excel_import.htm**.

6. After you have entered the filename and selected HTML in the Data type drop-down menu, click the Import Now button.

7. An Excel spreadsheet will be displayed in your Office Spreadsheet component:

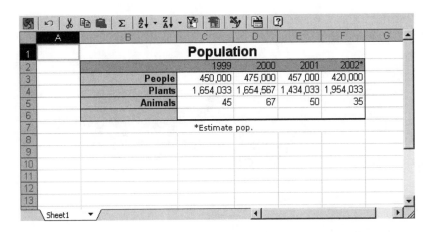

8. Save this HTML file as *spreadsheet.htm* and keep it open because we will be using it in the next section.

Note

The *excel_import.htm* file is simply an Excel spreadsheet saved using the Save As Web Page command in Microsoft Excel.

Exporting Data from the Office Spreadsheet Component

Now that you have data imported into your spreadsheet, we will learn how to export the data. Unlike Excel, you will not be able to save the data contained in the Office Spreadsheet component to an Excel file. What you will be able to do is export the data directly into Excel. After the data is in Excel, you can use the plethora of methods Excel has to save the data in various file formats.

The following instructions will guide you to export data into Excel:

1. Open the file *spreadsheet.htm* that you saved in the previous section.

2. Select the spreadsheet by clicking anywhere on it with the mouse pointer.

3. After the spreadsheet has been selected, click the Export to Microsoft Excel button. The Export to Microsoft Excel button is the button with the Microsoft Excel logo superimposed with a pencil.

4. After the Export to Microsoft Excel button had been clicked, Microsoft Excel will launch with the data from the spreadsheet in FrontPage displayed:

	B	C	D	E	F
1		\multicolumn{4}{c}{**Population**}			
2		1999	2000	2001	2002*
3	**People**	450,000	475,000	457,000	420,000
4	**Plants**	1,654,033	1,654,567	1,434,033	1,954,033
5	**Animals**	45	67	50	35
6					
7		\multicolumn{4}{c}{*Estimate pop.}			
8					

1-Minute Drill

● What are two ways you can incorporate content from other applications?

● Can a spreadsheet in the Office Spreadsheet component window be saved as a file directly to your hard drive?

index.htm
about.htm
statistics.htm

Project 16-1: Using Microsoft Office in FrontPage

The following are the goals for this project:

● Copy and paste content into FrontPage

● Import data into the Office Spreadsheet component.

Step by Step

1. From the project folder you downloaded for this module, open the files *index.htm*, *about.htm*, and *statistics.htm* in FrontPage. Use the file tabs to display the *statistics.htm* file first.

2. In the *statistics.htm* file, select the Office Spreadsheet component. Click the Commands and Options button. The Commands and Options window will appear.

3. Select the Import tab in the Commands and Options window. Click the Data type drop-down menu and select the HTML command.

● By copying and pasting and inserting the file
● No. You have to export to Excel first.

4. In the URL field, type **project.htm**. After the address has been typed, click the Import Now button.

5. Close the Commands and Options window by clicking the X in the upper-right corner of the window.

6. Select the *about.htm* file tab. Launch Microsoft Word and open the *about.doc* file. Press CTRL - A to select all the text and then press CTRL - C to copy the text. Go back to FrontPage and place your mouse cursor in the empty row below the words "About Us."

7. Press CTRL - C to paste the content from Microsoft Word into FrontPage.

8. Select File | Save All to save all the files currently open. Select the *index.htm* tab and preview the page in your browser.

Summary

As you have learned, Microsoft FrontPage is a versatile program that enables input from other applications such as Word and Excel. While the information covered so far does not scratch the surface of Office XP's Web features, this module does help you to combine FrontPage with key applications from the Office suite. FrontPage's capability to incorporate content from other applications makes sharing files easier and, best of all, makes the files accessible to anyone with a Web browser.

☑ *Mastery Check*

1. Which method of incorporating content produces a nearly exact copy?

_____

_____

2. When importing content from files, is FrontPage limited to importing only from Office applications?

_____

_____

3. What is the keyboard shortcut for copy?

_____

_____

4. In what two programs can an Office Spreadsheet component be modified?

_____

_____

5. How can you export the data from a spreadsheet in the Office Spreadsheet component to Excel?

_____

_____

Part V

Appendixes

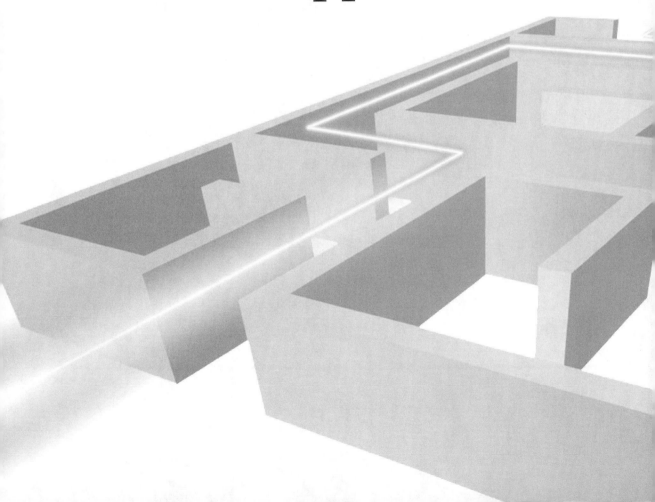

Appendix A

Answers to Mastery Checks

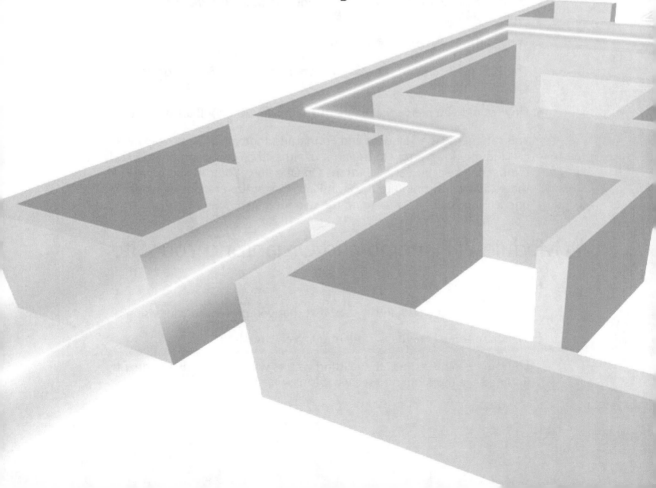

Module 1: The FrontPage Interface

1. How can you tell if a menu has submenus?

Most menus that contain submenus have a small arrow at the right to indicate whether a submenu is available or not. An example of a menu with submenus is the Reports command under the View menu.

2. What would be the easiest way to get help on a given topic?

The easiest way is to use FrontPage Quick Help by simply typing your question in the search box in the upper-right corner of the FrontPage window.

3. What steps are necessary to create a custom toolbar?

Go to any Customize Toolbar option. The Customize menu can be accessed by either right-clicking any menu or toolbar and then choosing Customize. From that window, selecting the button for New will enable you to enter the name of the toolbar. From there, you can drag and drop your custom toolbar options.

4. Why is the Task pane useful for users?

The Task pane helps to show all the common tasks for FrontPage in one central location.

5. How would you merge the Standard and Formatting toolbars into one row?

You can merge the Standard and Formatting toolbars into one row by clicking the down arrow to the right of either the Formatting or Standard toolbar and selecting Show Buttons On One Row. You can also merge these toolbars by going to the FrontPage Customize Options menu and unchecking the box for merging the two toolbars.

Module 2: Planning and Organizing Your Site

1. What is typography?

Typography is the text and style of text that you present to your visitors.

2. What are some benefits to updating a Web site often?

You can fix minor errors, and existing visitors will tend to visit a frequently updated site more often to see what is new.

3. Briefly, what is layout?

Layout is how information is organized on a site.

4. What is a FrontPage Web?

The FrontPage Web is a location either on your hard drive or on a server that has all of your Web site's files and folders.

5. How can templates help you?

Templates can help you create complex or unique pages easily.

6. How can you change the default location for a FrontPage Web?

Go to the FrontPage Web Site templates window and modify the Web location under the options area on the right side.

7. How do you create files or folders in the FrontPage Web?

Right-click an empty part of the main FrontPage contents window, select New, and then select either Folder or Page.

8. What are the steps necessary to import files into a FrontPage Web?

Click File | Import. From the Import window, specify a location for a folder or file, and click OK. The files or folders will be imported into your FrontPage Web.

Module 3: Using FrontPage to Create and Modify Your Site

1. Why are hyperlinks used?

To navigate a Web site, to navigate within a Web page, and to send e-mail.

2. Why are bookmarks important?

Bookmarks enable visitors to use links to move to a specific section of a Web page.

3. What is the difference between the extensions *.html* and *.htm*?

There is no difference.

4. When formatting text, should text be all bold?

No. Too much bold text makes reading more difficult.

5. When clicked, does an e-mail hyperlink launch an e-mail program?

Yes

6. How can you add font styles to text?

By right-clicking the text and choosing Font.

7. How are ScreenTips in a hyperlink helpful?

ScreenTips display additional information or comments from the author on what a hyperlinked page is about.

Module 4: Using Images in Your Pages

1. What file extensions will FrontPage automatically convert your images to?

GIF or JPEG.

2. Will the Pictures toolbar automatically appear when I select an image? If it does not, what steps should I take to display the Pictures toolbar?

It usually appears automatically. If it does not, select View | Toolbars | Pictures.

3. When you crop an image, does the image resize?

No. When you crop an image, the areas that you have cropped are simply discarded.

4. What underlying Web technology/language is fundamental for positioning and stacking elements?

Cascading Style Sheets (CSS)

5. Why would you use the Highlight Hotspots icon?

To more clearly see where the hot spots are located when the images and graphics prevent you from seeing the hot spots clearly.

6. How would you watermark a background image?

You would check the Watermark box in the Background tab of the Page Properties window.

7. Is clip art confined to images such as banners and arrows?

No. There is an infinite number of clip-art images for you to choose from.

Module 5: Drawing and Using Multimedia

1. What language is largely responsible for the use of shapes in FrontPage?

Vector Markup Language (VML)

2. Can text inserted using the Text Box icon be modified and formatted like regular text?

Yes

3. What is the difference between an arrow line and a regular line?

Arrow lines have an arrowhead at one end, while regular lines do not.

4. Can 3-D shapes be modified and rotated like regular shapes?

Yes. Everything you can do to a regular shape you can also do to a 3-D shape.

5. What is WordArt?

WordArt is custom formatting effects that can be applied to text.

6. What are the two most popular file formats for sound on the Web?

WAV and MIDI.

7. What is the default number of times videos will play when inserted in FrontPage?

The default is one time.

Module 6: Using Tables in FrontPage

1. Is table background color independent of cell background color?

Yes. The background colors of both tables and cells are independent of each other.

2. What are the ways you can access table commands in FrontPage?

You may use the Tables toolbar or use the Table menu at the top of the FrontPage window.

3. What is the difference between cell padding and cell spacing?

Cell padding is the distance that contents in a cell are separated from a cell's edge. Cell spacing is the distance separating actual cells in a table.

4. Can cells be split within another cell?

Yes. Cells can be split within another cell.

5. What is the difference between pixel and percent when adjusting the size of a table or cell?

Pixel is an exact value for the width or height of a table, and the width and height of a table will not change. Percent, when regarding the size of a table, is the percentage of the screen the table will take. Tables applied with a percentage width will automatically adjust to display correctly in various browsers.

6. What happens when you merge two cells?

The cells combine to form one cell.

7. Why should you not apply No Wrap to large pieces of text?

Because many users would have to scroll horizontally to read the information.

8. How would you horizontally align content in a table?

You would horizontally apply text as you normally would. You use the Align Left, Center, Align Right, and Justify buttons on the Formatting toolbar.

9. What does the Table AutoFormat icon do?

The Table AutoFormat icon adds custom styles to enhance the look of your table.

10. What are nested tables?

Nested tables are tables contained within a cell of another table.

11. If you set your table's width to 900 pixels, will visitors on resolutions lower than1024x768 have to horizontally scroll to view the entire table?

Yes. Users having screen resolutions less than 900 pixels wide will be unable to view the entire table.

Module 7: Using Frames in FrontPage

1. What is a frameset?

A frameset is a group of frames contained in a Web page and controlled by a single file called the frameset page.

2. In a frameset, are the HTML pages independent of each other?

Yes

3. When saving pages contained in a frameset, how can you tell what page is currently being saved?

The Save As window will highlight the frame of the corresponding file being saved.

4. How can you open a frames page in a separate FrontPage window?

Right-click the frames page and click the Open Page in New Window command.

5. How do you insert an inline frame?

On the menu bar, select Insert | Inline Table.

6. How do you assign a name to an inline frame?

Go to the Inline Frame Properties window and enter a custom name in the Name field.

7. What can you do to make the inline frame blend seamlessly with the surrounding background?

You can remove frame borders for the current inline frame.

Module 8: Creating Lists

1. What is the best way to change the font color for a whole list?

Change the font color of a whole list by right-clicking and navigating to List Properties | Style | Format | Font.

2. What is the difference between a list and a list item?

A list is the whole portion that contains all the list items. List items are the individual bullets and sections that make up the list.

3. Do collapsible lists always have to be initially collapsed when created in FrontPage?

No. You have the option of modifying the initial collapse state from the List Properties window.

4. When using an image as a bullet, what physical dimensions should the image have?

The images should be about the size of a regular bullet. In other words, the images have to be quite small.

5. What will happen when you try to enter a line break to your list by pressing ENTER instead of SHIFT-ENTER?

You will break the line and start another list item.

6. How many times should you click the Increase Indent icon to indent a list item?

Twice

Module 9: Modifying and Publishing Your Site Online

1. What are the two ways the title of a page can be modified?

A title can be modified from the Page Properties window and from the Save As window.

2. What is the difference between changing the page font from the Page Properties window and modifying the Default font in the Page Options window?

Changing the page font from the Page Properties window enables your visitors to see that font style in their browser. Changing the Default font option in the Page Options window modifies the font you see in FrontPage only. The font you select as the default font will not be displayed in a Web browser.

3. What are the FrontPage Server Extensions?

FrontPage Server Extensions is a set of tools that is installed on a Web server to help you publish your site and maintain it using FrontPage 2000.

4. What are some of the benefits of using the Reports View?

The Reports View windows provide you with vital information regarding your site. You can use that information to organize and modify your pages and files.

5. What is the best way to delete files that have been found unused by the FrontPage Reports View?

From the Reports View (View | Reports), delete the file by selecting it and pressing the DELETE key.

6. How do you access the Navigation view?

You access the Navigation view by selecting to View | Toolbars | Navigation.

Module 10: Using Forms

1. Why is it recommended that you assign name values to form objects?

It makes it much easier to identify the form information with the appropriate form object in the form confirmation page.

2. How will you change the order of an item listed in a drop-down box?

You select the item in the Drop-Down Box Properties window. Then you can use the Move Up and Move Down buttons to arrange the order of the items.

3. What can you use to help organize form objects in a form?

Tables can be used to organize form objects in a form.

4. Can custom confirmation pages be created?

Yes

5. What Web component is used to enter form content on a confirmation page?

The Confirmation Field Web component

6. Is it possible to limit the number of characters a person can enter into a text box or text area?

Yes. You can limit the number of characters inputted by the user by adding validation checks.

7. How do you make a folder private so that Web browsers cannot view HTML pages contained within it?

You right-click the folder and select the command for Properties. From the Properties window, uncheck the Allow files to be browsed check box.

Module 11: Animating Your Site

1. What does the acronym DHTML stand for?

Dynamic Hypertext Markup Language or Dynamic HTML

2. When do page transitions play?

Page transitions can play during the following events: page enter, page exit, site enter, and site exit.

3. Hover buttons are what?

Java applets

4. What extension format should the sound added to a hover button be in?

.au

5. What is a marquee?

A marquee is the text that scrolls horizontally on a page.

6. When swapping an image using the Swap Picture command in the DHTML toolbar, how many images are involved?

Two images

Module 12: Using FrontPage Web Components

1. Can you customize the time that an image in a Banner Ad Manager component appears for?

Yes

2. What is the difference between the Page based on schedule component and the Page component?

The Page based on schedule component displays a page automatically during a certain date that you specify. The Page component cannot be made to change automatically on a set date.

3. What does a hit counter do?

It displays the number of visitors who have visited the page that the hit counter is on.

4. Does the slide-show layout of the Photo Gallery component automatically create the necessary links to display the photo?

Yes

5. What is an advantage of using the automatic content components?

The automatic content components update the information automatically without you having to modify the information.

6. What is the easiest way to edit a page that has been inserted using the Page component?

Right-click the information inserted by the Page component and select the command for Open Page in New Window.

Module 13: Using Themes and Templates

1. What do themes do?

Themes automatically modify a document by applying consistent design style comprising colors, graphics, and text.

2. What does the Active Graphics check box in the Themes window perform?

It enables short animations, such as image rollovers for navigation buttons and other page objects, in a theme.

3. What is one key requirement for making a Page Banner component work?

The page that the page banner is being inserted to must be part of a navigation structure.

4. What makes guest books unique compared to e-mail and regular forms?

The comments that your visitors submit can be read by anyone who visits your site.

5. Can themes be applied to a Discussion Web?

Yes. There is an option in the Discussion Web Wizard for selecting a theme.

6. What is a submission form in a Discussion Web?

The submission form is the form that your visitors will use when submitting information to be posted in your Discussion Web.

Module 14: Plug-Ins, Controls, and Applets

1. What is a plug-in?

A plug-in is a piece of software that displays information on a Web page and supports interactive features such as virtual reality, panoramic views, and more.

2. Who developed the Java language?

Sun Microsystems

3. Do ActiveX controls work in all browsers?

No. Most versions of Netscape browsers do not support the use of ActiveX controls.

4. What window will you use to access a plug-in file's properties?

The Plug-In Properties window

5. What are a Java applet's parameters?

Java applet parameters are settings that are used to control various functions of a Java applet.

6. What are files that extend with the CLASS extension?

Java applet files

Module 15: Web Programming Languages

1. What does the acronym CSS stand for?

Cascading Style Sheets

2. What does the HTML view enable you to do?

The HTML view enables you to view, modify, and add the page's HTML.

3. How is HTML inserted via the HTML Markup window displayed in FrontPage's normal view?

FrontPage displays the HTML inserted via the HTML Markup window in the form of an icon with a question mark.

4. What file extension do CSS style sheets have?

.CSS

5. Can one style sheet be used throughout a site?

Yes

Module 16: Integrating Microsoft Office in Your Site

1. Which method of incorporating content produces a near-exact copy?

Copy and Paste

2. When importing content from files, is FrontPage limited to importing only from Microsoft Office applications?

No

3. What is the keyboard shortcut for copy?

CTRL-C

4. In what two programs can an Office Spreadsheet component be modified?

FrontPage and a Web browser such as Internet Explorer.

5. How can you export the data from a spreadsheet in the Office Spreadsheet component to Excel?

By clicking the Export to Microsoft Excel button.

Appendix B

Resources

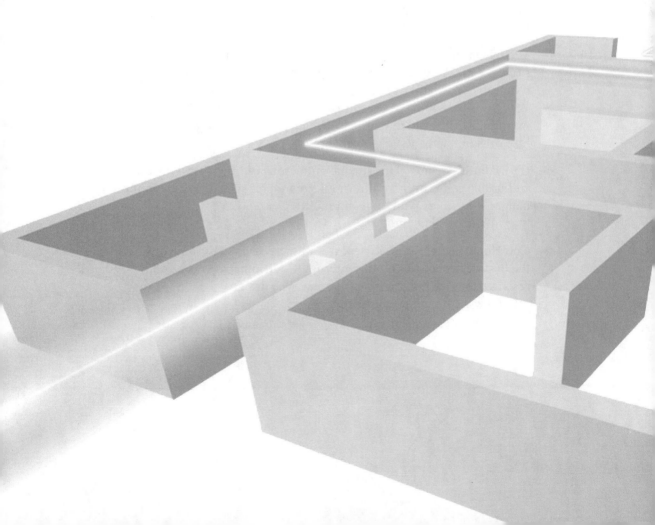

The following is a list of Web sites that are designed to help beginners and experts alike in exploring and learning about Web design and development:

- **kirupa.com—FrontPage**   This is the author's site regarding *FrontPage 2002: A Beginner's Guide.* In this site you will find vital book information, corrections, file downloads, support, and more. http://www.kirupa.com/frontpage

- **FrontpageGuru**   An excellent resource for FrontPage users. Chris Dimaano created a wonderful site with numerous tips, tricks, tutorials, downloads, and more. http://www.frontpageguru.com

- **Webmonkey**   This site features information and tips ranging from color to database programming to HTML. A worthwhile visit to improve your skills in Web design. http://www.webmonkey.com

- **MSDN Online Web Workshop**   Learn about various Web technologies such as Cascading Style Sheets (CSS), Dynamic HTML (DHTML), eXtensible Markup Language (XML), and more in this ever-growing site that is part of the Microsoft Developer Network (MSDN). The free samples provide valuable code to enhance your Web pages. http://msdn.microsoft.com/workshop/

- **CNET builder.com**   This site has numerous tutorials, tips, reviews, and usable code covering almost all Web topics such as Flash, online images, e-business planning, and more. http://builder.cnet.com/

- **CoolHomepages**   This site features numerous links to some of the best-designed sites on the Internet. CoolHomepages is a good resource for viewing examples of great Web design. http://www.coolhomepages.com

Index

I

M

N

T

X

Z

INTERNATIONAL CONTACT INFORMATION

AUSTRALIA
McGraw-Hill Book Company Australia Pty. Ltd.
TEL +61-2-9417-9899
FAX +61-2-9417-5687
http://www.mcgraw-hill.com.au
books-it_sydney@mcgraw-hill.com

CANADA
McGraw-Hill Ryerson Ltd.
TEL +905-430-5000
FAX +905-430-5020
http://www.mcgrawhill.ca

**GREECE, MIDDLE EAST,
NORTHERN AFRICA**
McGraw-Hill Hellas
TEL +30-1-656-0990-3-4
FAX +30-1-654-5525

MEXICO (Also serving Latin America)
McGraw-Hill Interamericana Editores S.A. de C.V.
TEL +525-117-1583
FAX +525-117-1589
http://www.mcgraw-hill.com.mx
fernando_castellanos@mcgraw-hill.com

SINGAPORE (Serving Asia)
McGraw-Hill Book Company
TEL +65-863-1580
FAX +65-862-3354
http://www.mcgraw-hill.com.sg
mghasia@mcgraw-hill.com

SOUTH AFRICA
McGraw-Hill South Africa
TEL +27-11-622-7512
FAX +27-11-622-9045
robyn_swanepoel@mcgraw-hill.com

**UNITED KINGDOM & EUROPE
(Excluding Southern Europe)**
McGraw-Hill Education Europe
TEL +44-1-628-502500
FAX +44-1-628-770224
http://www.mcgraw-hill.co.uk
computing_neurope@mcgraw-hill.com

ALL OTHER INQUIRIES Contact:
Osborne/McGraw-Hill
TEL +1-510-549-6600
FAX +1-510-883-7600
http://www.osborne.com
omg_international@mcgraw-hill.com